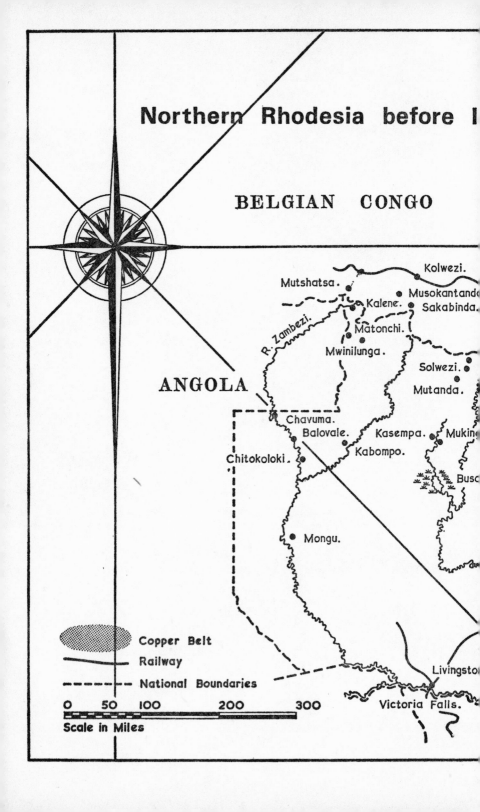

Northern Rhodesia before I

BELGIAN CONGO

Kolwezi.

Mutshatsa.

Musokantanda
Kalene. Sakabinda.

R. Zambezi.

Matonchi.

Mwinilunga.

Solwezi.

ANGOLA

Mutanda.

Chavuma.

Balovale. Kasempa. Mukin

Chitokoloki.

Kabompo.

Busc

Mongu.

Mukin

Copper Belt

Railway

National Boundaries

Livingstor

0   50 100   200   300

Victoria Falls.

Scale in Miles

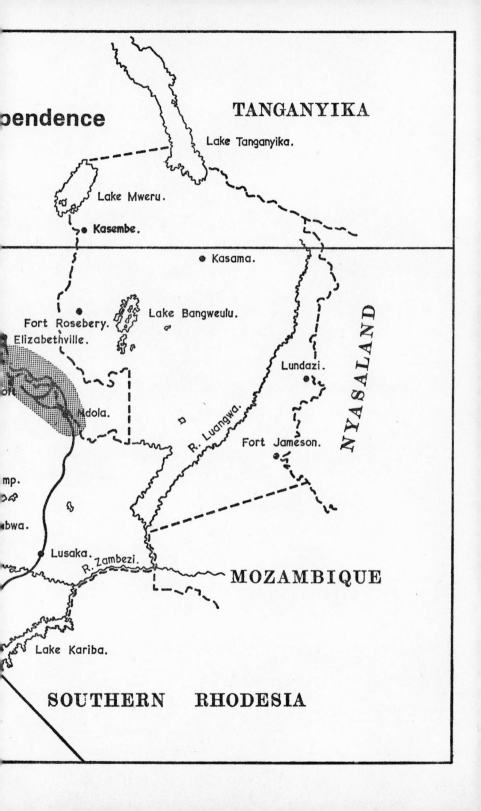

pendence

TANGANYIKA

Lake Tanganyika.

Lake Mweru.

● Kasembe.

● Kasama.

Fort Rosebery.

Elizabethville.

Lake Bangweulu.

Lundazi.

NYASALAND

or

dola.

R. Luangwa.

Fort Jameson.

mp.

bwa.

Lusaka.

R. Zambezi.

MOZAMBIQUE

Lake Kariba.

SOUTHERN   RHODESIA

AFRICAN SUNSET

AFRICAN SUNSET

ROBIN SHORT

JOHNSON

LONDON

ROBIN SHORT ©

First Published 1973
ISBN   0 85307 123 3

MADE AND PRINTED IN GREAT BRITAIN BY
CLARKE DOBLE & BRENDON LTD
FOR JOHNSON PUBLICATIONS LTD
11/14 STANHOPE MEWS WEST, LONDON S.W.7

CONTENTS

LIST OF ILLUSTRATIONS

To the District Messengers of
Northern Rhodesia

ACKNOWLEDGEMENTS

*T*HERE *are many debts which I gladly acknowledge in writ-ing this book. First of all, to the late R. C. Melland, District Commissioner, whose neglected masterpiece of sympathy and observation,* In Witchbound Africa *still awaits discovery and recognition, and his collaborator Mr. J. L. Keith, happily still living and at work. To Dr. V. W. Turner, anthropologist, for his studies of the Lunda-Ndembu people, particularly perhaps for his fascinating work,* The Drums of Affliction. *To Mr. Ivor Graham, Government Archivist in N. Rhodesia and Zambia for permission to explore the old District Notebooks collected for the first time in Lusaka shortly before Independence. To Mr. David Steer for the maps, and drawing of a Lunda rain-making shrine. To the Information Department, Government of Northern Rhodesia, and to certain friends, for some excellent photographs of people, places, and types. To all of them I give my grateful thanks.*

Place names I have retained, as I knew them when I wrote.

My friends, African and European alike, I take the opportunity of greeting through this book. I remember them all, and I wish them well.

AUTHOR'S PREFACE

BY the year 1961 Macmillan was at his height. In the House where he commanded with half-contemptuous ease, his epigrams gave pleasure and a sense of security and control. But unlike Disraeli, he scattered them along his retreat. At the Colonial Office the bluff honesty of Lennox-Boyd gave place to the cunning of Macleod. The best minds agreed that the new policy was right in every particular—no more Hola Camps, no more Nyasalands. These things would all be settled now without this sort of trouble. The resources of information and propaganda at the disposal of the modern state were brought to bear to reassure opinion, or to manufacture it, upon this point. And if opposition, even on questions of timing should arise, it could be muffled or suppressed, ridiculed or misrepresented, as might be. From a retired colonel it could be laughed out of court, from a business man damned as "interested", or a distinguished administrator could simply be labelled "out of date". Thus a whole climate of opinion was artificially created, and the docile men of the middle-rank followed, as they always do in home politics.

In every Government the Treasury commands great influence and power. But unhappily the architecture of that building afflicts the mental climate of its officials. It is a catacomb, surrounded by a cloister, weighted down by a mighty portico. So, when it thinks of colonies, it follows the Manchester School : it remembers and reveres Peel, Cobden, Gladstone. When colonies are ripe, they drop, like fruit from the tree. Their governing classes, duly grateful for the gift of self-government, the control of their own destiny, tend to prefer British economic interests, and tend to be willing suppliers of raw materials for British industry at reasonable prices. But they are misleading, these vague general parallels between Canada and Australia, and the new

11

States of Africa. With their heads full of an inherent inferiority complex and distrust, rationalized in Marxist suspicions of economic exploitation, such governments will nationalize as soon as they think they dare. They did, they have, they will.

It is unpleasant and disturbing for people to change their mind, and even worse to admit that they were wrong, and that they were led like a flock of sheep. And for a civil servant, Mandarin Class, to admit that his judgement was wholly at fault, that is the equivalent to the agony of slow suicide. Yet truth will out, and it broke out of the Continent itself, while Erskine May had hardly been laid on the table alongside the last elaborate silver inkstands. Famine, disease, fire and blood, the desperate remedy of the military coup, they all started out at the comfortable world which had thought to shed its responsibilities. Ghosts walked at noon. A few lucky survivors, who imagined the world would for ever remain as they commanded, were told brusquely to quit the stage. They were no longer worth flattering, for the world had changed. Reality had returned : absent for too long.

A case, a defence even, should be made for Macmillan and Macleod. Munich even, has its defenders. It was not simply a collapse of will, masked by a feeble gesture. There was rational, carefully worked out calculation, but based on completely wrong premises. While it followed the thinking of *The Guardian*, it took its tone of smug infallibility from *The Times*.

In Africa it was simple. Too many young men, literate, politically innocent, boundlessly ambitious, had been turned out by the educational system to be satisfied by the jobs. Hundreds of disenchanted young men, full of spirit and increasing daily, were thrown back either on to primitive villages, or rotted unoccupied in the towns. From the strength of the country they were allowed to become a burden, then a menace. It was a choice, to govern, to hand over, or to shoot. Rhodesia solved that problem, despite all that could be brought against her : no-one was shot there. But the British Government did not. In the surprising words of Duncan Sandys, quoted by Sir Roy Welensky : "We British have lost the will to govern." That was enough. But the failure, and its causes, were to be found in England, not in Africa. As yet we in Africa were unaware of this strange process.

Or, put another way, what is now called the "revolution of rising expectations", the justified and acute hunger for material benefits could not be met from British resources at that time. It is fair to say also that while it retained political control the Federal Government concentrated on developing the South. There was not enough money—there never is—for radical improvement in such vital but mundane fields as housing, agriculture, medicine. The broad flow becomes a trickle by the time that it reaches the end of the furrow in Africa, then it vanishes into the ground. To be accurate there was no imagination or will to find this money : and no plan to spend it.

What were the causes of the sudden shift in England? The professional Left, hating their own country, always true to form. Nearer the centre, the nests of Fabian dons and their influence on the cleverer young men of the 1930's who would arrive as senior civil servants of the 1960's, and who had always despised and derided imperialism. Their antecedents, if still of interest, may be traced back to the late Victorian philosophers, to Shaw and Wells, and to such pioneers of the new sociology as Seebohm Rowntree. They filled a need in England, not so appropriate in Africa.*

Besides this, Macmillan was sick. The staff will hold up a wounded general in the field and his presence may turn the battle. While this loyal instinct holds good in civil affairs, conditions are perfectly different, and the battle can only be lost. A sick man has no right judgement, only instinct in the intervals of pain, an instinct that can be guided down almost any path by skilled reason, skilled flattery, or a blend of both. The instinct of the sick man is to avoid conflict : a sick man in himself only desires retreat to quiet.

So the will sagged and failed. Unknown to those on the perimeter the mainspring at the centre had run down. And no Government can be carried on without will, the best and the

---

* One of the minor ironies of history. A submarine purchased by the South Africans from the French, since they were forbidden to buy from Britain, was named the "Emily Hobhouse". Emily Hobhouse, an early liberal and virulent feminist, took up the cause of the Boer women in the re-settlement camps in 1901, and was summarily deported from South Africa by Lord Kitchener.

worst, from the admired ancient Greeks of Edwardian Eton, to Papa Doc in his Haiti.

Africa swallows men. But it cleanses them. Now in 1962-3 the British Government began to give off the same odour of corruption as the old Third Republic of France. All the names, Burgess and Maclean, then Vassall, and others were the hallmarks of decay. In a word it was decadent.

Thus it was a calculated decision to grant independence, but at the expense of the ordinary people—to beat the drum to drown confusion, to usher in the new era with a burst of fireworks and to raid the reserves of colonial government prudence. All the playthings of a new "nation"—national dress (with slogan and picture of the Leader), the international airport, the bright new University complete with bright new dons to applaud a Leader's philosophy, the great hall for resounding Parliamentary debate and grandiloquent conference. It was silly, it was pathetic, and above all it was tragic. Henri Quatre had settled for a chicken in the pot for France : Africa may well have to settle for less until good sense returns.

Macmillan, Macleod, the senior officials, they could all see this. There was no lack of information : there is indeed usually too much for those responsible to absorb, to do more than to decide essentials. Yet these essentials are always there, and it is at that moment, whether in London surrounded by official deference, or in Africa, alone, that a man's character is shown. Does he stand : or does he side-slip, postpone, or take the easy way with an air of determination? At that moment the man is judged. He is judged, not from the documentaries of the moment nor from the weighty Apologia in old age, but by comparison with other men in other times. How did they comport themselves? That decisive moment in a man's life passes for ever, and by that moment he stands or falls in the eye of history. History alone is just : and while it may be charitable to a sick man who had done good service but who stayed too long in his high office, it will never forgive the ghastly damage that he did. Nor I believe, in the years to come, will the Africans themselves excuse or even mitigate his failure, as it is duly borne in upon them.

For in the absence of decisive action, of which the West has made itself incapable, the African tribes and peoples north of the Zambesi are doomed to the eventual choice between chaos and communist rule. Whether the communists attack the schools and universities, the rural villages, the urban proletariat, the Trade Unions or the armed services, or play permutations of groups and classes, they must succeed somewhere. Pathetically weak, the successor states of the African Balkans are in no condition to resist. In the new Russian roulette one backs both colours and takes the Bank if either comes up.

Our own new ambassadors, the youths, teachers and experts, full of goodwill but all on contract only, can hardly command an equal influence. Some are half-converted themselves, others think themselves too intelligent to be dedicated to anything. Communism is dedicated to advance and to rule. In Africa that will succeed, for it is that which is needed.

Africa is not democratic in the sense we understand it. Africans' thoughts and desires run on a more basic, simpler scale. Their shaky governments cannot identify themselves with the West because there is always a majority of the disenchanted ready to coalesce against them if they do. It is much easier to embrace, safely and happily, a system which will promise above all quick material wealth to the people with the parade of national pride on a world stage; and one which will, in the last resort, gun down anything in its way. If anything is sure in Africa, that easy way will be taken.

This book describes the road down the hill in Africa in the 1960's, and how both Africans and Europeans, who did all they could to stop this descent—to stand against this foolish and evil tide—were brushed aside and overthrown. Overthrown, not by superior force—for they were never beaten in the field—but by the very institutions into which they had put all their heart and faith. Above all this was a tragedy for the Africans who had no other home. They had to live with what was done in their name, but for their doom.

CHAPTER I

KASEMPA—THE ENCLOSED KINGDOM

Geographers, in Africa maps
With savage pictures fill their gaps,
And o'er unhabitable downs
Place elephants for want of towns.
(Jonathan Swift).

KASEMPA, a point on the map of Africa, marked like a middle-sized town because it was once the headquarters of the Kaonde-Lunda Province of Northern Rhodesia, had in fact five European inhabitants, the District Commissioner and his family and the Cadet. I was the Cadet. The view fell away to the eastward over miles of green tufted trees to a range of low hills over which the rain advanced in a solid line, first with a whisper, then with a roar over the leaves. Behind the white thatched cottage the red earth road curved gently into the distance to Solwezi, to the Copperbelt, to the Cape and civilization. A road down which I could gaze on a hot empty afternoon, and long for escape.

Kasempa, a quiet place, has its memories. The last public hanging, of three Africans who shot a labour contractor, in 1912; or the District Commissioner who drove his Morris Cowley in an excess of rage to the top of an ant-hill, and left it there to rot and moulder, and others, but of work mainly, hard, dull routine work over the years. And of loneliness, unrecorded but deadly, which drove some to grimness, or despair, or folly. Kasempa, like a shell, was a world of its own, with its own people and hierarchy, its own "characters". Into this world I entered, two hundred miles from a town, and so it closed in about me, until I became totally absorbed in it. For better or for worse I had my own place and

17

my own part. What happened in the other, outer world became of little interest or concern. Wars, disasters, the rise and fall of kings, dictators or ministers, or the absurd mass amusements of the uninitiated, became dwarfed in size before a bridge that had fallen, the death of a Headman of traditional importance, or the defalcation of a Chief's clerk. A world once experienced that I remember. I cannot forget, for it was a world of the Middle Ages, enjoying a brief time of peace under a good King.

At the same time a hard world. For an African only justice, order, and the minimum of necessities such as roads, schools and hospitals were provided. A man might go hungry, he and his children might die of any number of strange diseases, or wild beasts take him by night, and the world would continue just as before. His name would indeed be crossed off the Tax Register at the Boma but unless his death has been remarkable or mysterious there would be the end of the matter. And, lurking in the background would be fear, fear of witchcraft in its many forms, and equally, the fear of being accused of it, for in that case unless he moved rapidly away to a far distance, he would be killed.

The Kaonde people, to the number of about 30,000, live in an area roughly square, a hundred and fifty miles long and broad, around Kasempa. A further 20,000 are to the north-east, about Solwezi, and another 10,000 to the south near Mumbwa, cut off by the Kafue River and a thick belt of sleeping sickness country, inhabited only by game and Tse-Tse fly. To the north are their cousins the Lunda, stretching into the Congo and Angola, to the west the Lovale and other miscellaneous immigrant tribes; to the east the Lamba, and tucked away to the south-west towards Barotseland, the gentle, primitive Mbwela people, content with wild honey and fishing, and sought after for their skill in ancient medicines and herbs.

The country is shown on the maps as "Savannah", which gives the impression of wide high grass-lands where one rides alone into the sunset. But this romantic idea is not accurate. Savannah means woodlands, unending stretches of trees about twenty feet high, very few beautiful or straight; the long grass and bushes beneath are green in the rain, dark brown in the dry season, prickly, inconvenient, but never impassable. So the land is covered with trees, and clear streams flow through it all the year round. Far to the south are the great open plains of Busanga, the fishing grounds and the sanctuary of game.

It is in the clearings in the forest that the people live, people whose villages are connected to each other and to the roads by narrow winding paths wide enough only for a bicycle, people in villages numbering fifty strong. They build huts of strong poles, plastered inside and out with mud, and thatched with grass, golden brown the first year, turning to grey with age. The huts are in two lines, with smaller kitchens behind, sometimes ornamented with fantastic drawings of the crocodile and lion, or with little gardens of flowers: one, with brilliant caricatures worthy of Low, of a District Commissioner, face uplifted to receive a glass, while a District Messenger stood ready at the salute.

The Headman of the village wears a thick ivory bracelet on his left wrist, and he is personally responsible to the Chief, and so to the Boma, for the state of his village and for all those living in it. Sometimes—often—an ungrateful task.

It was Senior Chief Kasempa, the tenth of his line, who ruled Kasempa. He was an autocrat, which was expected of him, and he was afraid of no-one, African or European: not even of the Boma, where the District Commissioners wielded their sway. Kasempa was of medium height, with great charm; his long narrow hands would gesture gently. When he spoke it was in a low melodious voice. His temper was quick with his own people: opposition was intolerable. On tour, he reproved a Headman for his untidy village and fined him 10s. on the spot. The Headman at once began to expostulate: it was all bad luck, it was the confounded laziness of the women.

"Doubled," said Chief Kasempa. That was the end of the matter.

Under the Senior Chief in the Kaonde hierarchy, each with about 60 or fewer villages, were Chiefs Mushima, Chizera, Ingwe, Kalasa, Chinsengwe, Kasonso, Nyoka and Munyambala. The last five chiefdoms had been abolished officially in 1948 by the central government and incorporated into Kasempa; later they had been resurrected and given their own courts of justice again, except for Munyambala. An example of ill-judged economy a few years previous prompted by a circular from the Secretary of State about local government. This caused much confusion and ill-feeling, the attempt to impose a county borough system on a population of one per square mile, and in due course it was quietly abandoned.

To get to know these people was the first and prime duty of the Cadet.

Of the survivors Mushima was sluggish but amiable enough, Chizera, a man of character and courage with two ambitious heirs and over thirty children, and Ingwe old, failing and drunken. Each of them was assisted by a staff of two court assessors, two *kapasus* or rural policemen, and a clerk to record their cases and to collect and enter tax from each male, which stood then at 6s. or 7s. 6d. per year.* A Chief of any energy and competence could look after his area of 2,000 or 3,000 people without difficulty, helping the old and ill, watching for hunger or epidemics of disease, improving the villages and bringing the minor offender to justice in his court.

Cases were not many, there was peace in the land, while the Government officials did what they could for development, a bridge, a school, a road, and appealed for money to do more. But above all a man could go about his business without fear of open violence, whatever his secret fears of witchcraft might be. If he suffered an injury unjustly he knew that in due course it would be righted, if not by the Chief, then by the Boma, whose officers were all the King's men sent there for that very purpose, and with a special brief for the African, particularly the African of the village.

As with many of the tribes of Northern Rhodesia the Kaonde start their history with Mwatiamvu,† the Great Chief or Great King of the early Portuguese travellers' tales. He ruled on a tributary of the Kasai River in the Congo, as his descendants do to this day. At some time in the seventeenth century a woman called Luezi Manga'anda lived in her village in the Kazhilezhi stream with her sister Kasanzhi. Luezi was a Chieftainess, and

* In 1951.
† See Appendix I for the list of Mwatiamvu.

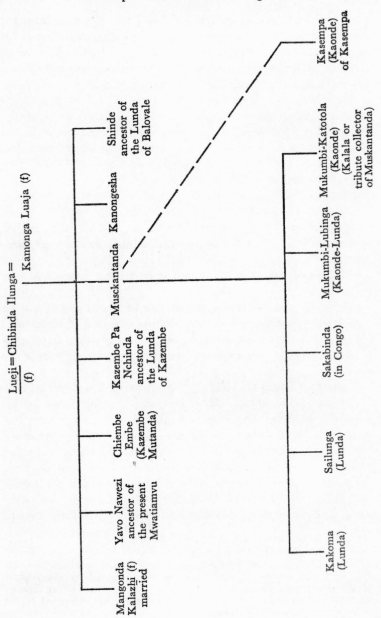

married a certain Chibinda Wa Katele. And when she married him she gave him a *lukano* insignia or bracelet, as a sign of his chieftainship, and called him Mwatiamvu. There were at least seven children, all by Chibinda Wa Katele's second wife Kamonga Luaza, Luezi being barren, but not jealous.

There have now been 17 bearers of the Musokantanda Chieftainship and a similar number of Kazembe's of the Luanda. When Chief Shinde of Balovale visited Chief Kazembe in the 1950's he found himself able to understand the language of that court, after a separation of probably two centuries, and over some 700 miles.

Kasempa and all the Kaonde Chiefs acknowledge the overlordship and paramountcy of Musokantanda and ultimately of Mwatiamvu. But though the first Kasempa, Chiboko, received his *lukano* from Musokantanda his control is remote and theoretical.

Tributes of tusks, of slaves and guns are no longer taken to his court.

About 1800, so far as chronology can be traced among a tribe with good memories, but with no written records of their history, Chiboko Kasempa was given the *lukano* by the then Musokantanda, and so far as the succession can be traced it is given in the notes.*

Jipumpu Kasempa VII "The Great", ruled when the Europeans came (*circa* 1882–1911) and was succeeded by his nephew, Kalusha Kasempa VIII (1911–1926). Thereafter nephew succeeded nephew, as the British carefully preserved the traditional selection patterns. Kibunda Kasempa IX ruled from 1926 to 1947, and he too was succeeded by his nephew, Samusi Kawande Kasempa X, who became chief in 1947, and was my friend. Melland, in his forgotten masterpiece of sympathy and observation, *Witchbound Africa*, gives three groups

---

* Chiboko Kasempa I succeeded by his nephew (sister's son in all cases), Nkumba Kasempa II succeeded by his nephew Nkonde Kasempa III, succeeded by his nephew Miyamba Kasempa IV (who died approximately 1858 and was known as the GOOD CHIEF), succeeded by his nephew Mudongo Kasempa V deposed and succeeded by his younger brother Kambambala Kasempa VI (circa 1851–1880) killed and succeeded by his younger brother Jipumpu Kasempa VII.

of Kaonde people who came down from the north, probably a northern section, with Chiefs Kasongo and Mushima; the Kasempa Chiboko sections; and the Ntambu section, now in the southern corner of Mwinilunga District.

These Kaonde groups wandered to the south, pushing the more peaceful A-Mbwela before them. The Chief of the A-Mbwela, called Mwene Kahale, once had his village near Kasempa Boma. The Kaonde met with resistance, to the south from the Ba-Ila, to the south-west from the Lozi and to the east from the Lamba.

The Kaonde then returned to the lands that they now occupy, and led a precarious existence, harried by civil war, raided from the west by Mbundu slave traders, and from the east by half-caste Arabs by then coming to the end of their slaving days. Their villages were large and strongly stockaded; their leaders had to be strong men. If they were lucky and in power with the coming of the Europeans, they were to be recognized as Chiefs. Cultivation was precarious, and life was a harassed affair as one village, and one Chief, would not hesitate to raid another of the same tribe if he thought he was stronger. The final resort of these unfortunate people was to hide in the bush or in caves from rival war-parties. The life of the Kaonde, without any central organization or authority, was indeed precarious, and might at any time be cut off by war, witchcraft or disease. Those of us who like to look back on pre-medieval England as a golden age when man communed with nature and with God are too apt to forget the reality of a hunted existence in hunger and disease and misery. It takes years to banish them from the land. A single month may be enough to bring them back, as though the years of security had never been.

In 1882, Jipumpu having killed his elder brother Kambambala and a rival claimant named Chilungulungu, took his chieftaincy of Kasempa. He is described in appearance as a short, stout man with an undershot jaw:

"He had thick lips and wore two long tusks like the warthog on his upper jaw," Simon Chibanza, the Chronicler of the Kaonde, puts it succinctly.

Like Caesar, Jipumpu preferred stout well-filled men, and would laugh at anyone taller than himself, saying that their parents would have done better to cut them in half to make two of them. It it very clear from accounts that he ruled by fear, not by love, nor even by good-nature.

It was in 1891 that Jipumpu first clashed with the Lozi. A representative of King Lewanika named Matale was living at the Chief's village, sending leopard skins to Mongu. His boys drawing water quarrelled with those of Kasempa when neither would give way on the path to the river. Matale, when he heard of this, unwisely fell to cursing the Kaonde and their Chief. They were instantly shot and killed by the Chief, and Ingwe his son, and his people. Only one man is reported to have escaped into Barotseland. King Lewanika, when he heard the tale, had other concerns, and so refrained from sending a punitive expedition.

After two years Jipumpu moved his village to the Kamusongolwe hill at Kasempa : with a single path and steep precipitous sides, it formed a sure refuge. At the top were caves and a spring. There he prospered, and kept ten wives. However, he suffered the same fate as many medieval despots, his sons became restless, and two of them were found to be co-habiting with his junior wives. Characteristically, and without hesitation, he had them killed.

In about 1897, in consequence of a complaint made to him by Chief Mushima of the abduction of two of his wives by Ingwe, and remembering Matale, Lewanika decided to send an expedition to punish Jipumpu. It is recorded that two or three thousand men left Lealui, but it is doubtful if they numbered as many hundred, as the country could not support more men than that gathered together for long.

Jipumpu had word of their coming. He abandoned his village at the foot of the hill and took up a position near the summit together with Ingwe and Mumba Kasempa, his nephew. The Lozi had in their armament several muzzle-loading guns, and were led by Matale, the younger brother of him whom Jipumpu had killed. After several hours of firing and shouting insults Matale led his assault on the hill at about ten o'clock in the morning. There was only one narrow path. Matale was in front, carrying before him a thick shield which covered the whole length of his body. On the top of the hill, behind the fighting men, sat Mukokomi, the Chief's first wife, and three others, on earthen pots containing medicines and charms. From time to time they would make water into the pots and onto the medicines, while making derogatory remarks about the enemy.

These powerful war-engines succeeded in their purpose, for when Matale appeared at the head of the file he was shot dead by Ingwe at point-blank range. The Lozi army, seeing their leader fall, turned and fled headlong down the hill, pursued by the Kaonde with rocks and poisoned arrows. Matale's head was cut from his body and added to Jipumpu's collection on his stockade.

After this, however, Jipumpu thought it politic to conciliate King Lewanika. He went to Lealui taking with him an ivory tusk, two big calabashes of cooked honey, and many skins. He was received honourably by the King and given a woman, Shibamba, whom he married, in exchange. Thereafter they lived on terms of honourable friendship; Jipumpu had paid tribute for about four years when the Europeans came and the tribute gradually ceased.

The battle of the Kamusongolwe Hill has passed into Kaonde heroic legend as a famous victory. Certainly Jipumpu showed courage in defying the great Lewanika, and a sure tactical sense in his choice of ground on which to fight. The Kaonde could retreat no further : and it is to their credit that they stood, fought, and triumphed.

So far as the Kaonde were concerned in attack, they fought only among themselves once the A-Mbwela had fled. Before setting forth they would gather at an ancestral shrine in the village, and dig a small hole. A large quantity of beer would be poured in; first the warrors, then the youths would drink, to the accompaniment of drumming. After prayers to the family spirits the war-party would set out, armed with spears, bows and arrows and perhaps one or two muzzle-loading muskets.

They would rely on surprise. Spies would go ahead in the guise of visitors, to assess the enemy strength. If they brought favourable reports the attack would be at dawn. If successful the men would be killed and the women, children and loot seized. Occasionally the upper portion of the skull of a dead enemy would be cut off and used as a drinking cup. Such petty wars as these were fought for loot and for slaves, often between men of the same tribe.

Dr. Livingstone appears to have skirted Kasempa by the west and north, but in 1898 George Grey, the brother of Sir Edward Grey of Falloden, pegged out the claim to Kansanshi Mine, some ten miles north of what is now Solwezi Boma. With him began the age of the European, and all the good, as well as the evil, that he has brought to Africa.

Official administration soon followed from Kalomo, then the capital, through Barotseland. In October or November, 1901, Sergeant Major Mobbs and Trooper Lucas, with a small party of Barotse Native Police pitched camp on what is now the football pitch at Kasempa. In 1902 Captain Stennett arrived and a police camp was built, later to be enlarged with earth-works still dimly visible : and F. B. Macauley came to start the civil administration. Like so very many of the early administrators he met his death in the 1914–1918 War. One, Mr. E. A. Copeman, who arrived in 1905, survived to be decorated by Sir Arthur Benson, Governor, at the age of over ninety.

Civil administration began. Houses were put up, a census was taken, and a small tax instituted and information gathered about the District. A force of District Messengers was recruited, whose first uniform was a leather belt only. They were at first what their name implied, Messengers only, but as will be seen, they soon became the eyes and ears, and the arms also, of the administration.

Early in 1909 a Trader, Richardson by name, was murdered by his *capitao*, or foreman, on the Shambila stream; he had had a bad reputation in the country, and had flogged people for demanding their rightful wages which he refused to pay. The murderers all escaped, and were never brought to justice.

It is hard to imagine today the difficulties of the early administrators. All their provisions must be brought with them : they lived, until they could build, in nothing more solid than a tent.

It is surprising what they achieved. Even their clothes must have been a burden—the long trousers, tightly buttoned coats and high collars and heavy boots, crowned by the solar topee or peaked cap. True, as was once remarked, that the topee was more than a hat, it was a symbol, but at the same time it is likely that the early administrators would have been equally efficient in some less cumbersome headgear. Even more arduous was the constant recurrent malaria which most of them had. Quinine protected to a certain extent, but seldom completely. Taken in excessive doses it brought on blackwater fever, usually fatal. An old-fashioned remedy for malaria was to "drink it down"; and it is no surprise to hear that some of the early administrators were men of impatient, not to say fiery, temper. No real cure was known in those days for sleeping sickness, and the first administrator of Mwinilunga District, Mr. Bellis died tragically of it. The treatment was then massive doses of arsenic injected into the system : I have known two only of the older generation who had it and recovered. The majority died, a slow and painful death.

Soon after the beginnings of civil administration came the Labour Recruiter and trader, Frykberg, an ex-Sergeant Major of the Matabele War, who is described as a "difficult character to deal with". By birth a Swede, he is buried at Kasempa Cemetery. He had various trading and recruiting ventures in the District.

In 1910 some four hundred Kaonde recruits were sent down to Southern Rhodesia. Unfortunately, during a smallpox epidemic some one hundred were stricken and died. Compensation was demanded from Frykberg, in accordance with what was the native custom, a payment of money to the relations. None was forthcoming.

A further batch of recruits were ready to be sent down, among them Tumila, Topeka and Kungwana of Makabula village. They ran away, were caught, imprisoned for a brief period for breaking their indenture, and then allowed to go to their village to visit their relatives before they went south.

They determined never to go back. At first they decided to kill Frykberg himself, but he was away. Then their choice fell upon Severts, an aged relative of Frykberg who eked out a scanty existence some thirty miles to the north of the Kaimbwe salt-pan. But "why should we kill him?" they said, "he is like one of ourselves, and all he has is a little salt".

So they determined to kill Ohlund, another Swede, who had been associated with Frykberg and was working a small gold property at Shudanvwa, thirteen miles from Kasempa.

They watched him through the window of his small house as he ate his supper: then, as he began to work at his typewriter they each shot him in the back, and fired another single shot to frighten away any of the villagers who might come. Then they fled together into the bush. It was eleven months before they were caught, as they clearly had the passive sympathy, if not the open support, of most of the local people. Both Chief Ingwe and Sub-Chief Kapeshi suffered a long sentence of imprisonment for not coming forward with information. Some forty people from their own village and their neighbours gathered round them in the forest, and the first attempt to capture them miscarried.

The Police, with Lieutenant de Satge,* left Kasempa by night and made a dawn attack. But there was no surprise: only five or six men and fifteen women and children were captured, and the murderers escaped. They fled north-east towards Solwezi, then doubled back into the country of Kapeshi near the Busanga swamp, then northwards, across the Kabompo River. There they began to quarrel among themselves, a quarrel which resulted in the deaths of two or three people. Later, crossing the West Lunga, one man and some women and children were drowned.

The remainder of the party, including Tumila, Topeka and Kungwana, crossed into what is now Portuguese territory and settled at the village of Katetandimbo, tired of wandering and, as they hoped, far enough from their crime. But word reached Kasempa, and Katetandimbo was offered £20 reward, enormous wealth in those days when wages were 5s. or 10s. a month, to help in their capture. He agreed, and arranged on a certain day to hold a dance so that the approach of the Government forces would be unheard.

* Ex-Sub-Lieutenant R.N. Died of wounds, 1916, as a Lieutenant in the K.R.R.C.

1. An Ngoni chief with his *kapasu* and staff of office : Chief Pikamalaza, Lundazi.

2. In Their Days of Power : Chief Mphamba, Senior Chief Magodi, Chief Pikamalaza at Emusa.

Meanwhile, at Kasempa, the Asst. Magistrate and the Lieutenant in charge of police made their plan of campaign. It was clear that no white man could go, for they would be far too conspicuous. So the Head Messenger, Kanyakula, commanded the party, consisting of himself and eight other Messengers, among them Ngwanjila, Watumabulo and Kaseya. Katetandimbo did his part, and the Messengers captured the criminals without resistance, Sakutenuka* Tumila, the leader, was carried back to Kasempa in a strange but effective fashion. Head Messenger Kanyakula cut off the bark of a tree, encased him in it, and lashed it round with bark rope, after making small holes through which he could be fed and breathe. Tumila reached Kasempa safely, though as the bark shrank and stiffened on a journey which must have taken at least ten days he must have become less and less comfortable. Katetandimbo received his reward, and today his descendants live in the Kabompo District.

During his examination before his trial Tumila confessed to another killing; while serving as a District Messenger a few years before he had killed an African hawker near Kasempa, and taken his goods.

After due trial all three murderers, Tumila, Topeka and Kungwana were publicly hanged outside Kasempa Prison on 11 November, 1912, in the presence of all the Chiefs of the District and a large number of Headmen who were called in to watch the ceremony. On the scaffold Tumila greeted his people and the Messengers; and to the Europeans said: "Although I am being killed like this I hope you also will bite the earth and follow me underneath." The tree stands to this day.

This affair did of course mark the end of labour recruiting in Kasempa District. It never revived.

Kasempa in 1950 was no longer the headquarters of the Kaonde Lunda Province, which had been abolished. Administrative officers looked upon Kasempa as something of a punishment station. "Coming men", even then the bane of a Service whose ideal was a "band of brothers", did their best to avoid such a posting. It put character before cleverness.

* Sakutenuka, a nick-name from Lovale, meaning "a cruel man".

B

Yet apart from malaria the climate was ideal. The Boma, or government headquarters, was well laid out, with a rose-garden and a swimming pool to refresh ourselves. We shared it with the frogs. The people of Kasempa seemed to me the most friendly, courteous and good-natured in the world. They had their own hard, mostly hidden life, of custom and village, which they carried on as they had always done. In their dealings with the official, alien, outer world, they were direct, and as one looks back, remarkably forebearing. The Mission, elementary schools, roads, houses of brick for the Government African staff, two post offices and four dispensaries had appeared since 1912. D.C. had succeeded D.C., some going thankfully without trace, others leaving their memory behind them for years, as hunters, or as builders, dreamers, or men of violent and ungovernable temper. These became part of the history of the place, and of the tribe : they were a law to themselves and any little eccentricities that they had flourished in an encouraging climate two days by motor from any town.

The District Commissioner was the captain of the ship : responsibility rested on him alone. Within the District he was supreme and enjoyed very great power and patronage; he had the means to make life uncomfortable for the dissenter or malcontent. Men from the town, even then, returned to the village with new and disturbing ideas. The necessity of living, the pressure of Headman and of Chief, and the very presence of the Boma, partially re-absorbed them within the framework of village life, and their ideas were heard no more. Dissent, from what seemed then to be the established order of things—the King— the remote, sometimes muddled British Government—His Excellency the Governor—the District Commissioner as his personal and effective representative—was unknown, unimaginable and unimagined.

True, there was a dissenting religious movement called "Watchtower", but its members were quiescent and lived in a remote and unhealthy part of the District. With ample funds at its back from America, from whence it sprang, and armed with apocalyptic doctrines which had a strong superficial attraction, the Jehovah's Witnesses or Watchtower Movement gained many adherents in parts of Northern Rhodesia in the 1920's. Their doctrines were taken up with disastrous results by an independent prophet, Mwana-Lesa (the son of God), who proclaimed the end of the world as imminent, and who was responsible for the deaths of some hundreds of people, before he was finally captured and hanged for murder.

The Watchtower Movement was always banned in the Congo, as a result of Roman Catholic missionary influence, and suffered the same fate in Northern Rhodesia in about 1940, for general sabotage of the war effort. Their American superintendents were expelled from the Territory, and their literature placed on the small private Index kept by the Government, along with the works of the Communist, R. Palme Dutt, and an Indian herbalist selling harmful patent medicines. The ban was lifted after the war.

Every independent non-conformist religious sect had overtones of African nationalism in that it was independent and run by and for Africans themselves, with all their faults and virtues. For this reason too, they attracted the odd-man-out and eccentric type of individual, and their attitude to the Government Bomas was seldom more than luke-warm. The British Empire was far too large an institution to descend to petty acts of persecution. The sects were left alone to work out their strange destinies. By following this course we often found that, deprived of persecution, the sect either fell to pieces, or set an example to others in good conduct, village building and agriculture.

Independent African Governments have not had the same solidity, real or apparent, and there have been many reports of persecution of Watchtower followers, both in Zambia and from Malawi.

In 1951 police were unnecessary. The eighteen District Messengers sufficed: and after a little while, when one knew them, one could play upon them like a piano. Some were hunters, others road and bridge makers, one or two were detectives. They could turn their hand to everything. The seniors had all served for fifteen to twenty years. They had memories which were worth books of records and files. If I asked: "Where does this man come from, and what does he want?" the Messenger replied: "He is Kalusha, from Kalulu's village: he will ask about compensation for his wife."

D.O.: "Has he gone to the Chief?"

Messenger: "No, the Chief has already heard his case and dismissed it."

D.O.: "When was that?"

Messenger: "In Bwana Face's (Facey's) time, about 1943."

D.O.: "Why is the case brought back now?"

Messenger: "He brings it to each new D.O. who comes to the Boma. Furthermore, he is a troublesome man, and was suspected of killing his cousin in the Congo."

D.O.: "Very well, bring him in, please."

To the east of the District, in ex-Chief Nyoka's area, a new group of Africans had sought refuge from tribal sanctions in a sort of thieves' kitchen. They were men who had left their own villages because of "some trouble", or who had drifted there. Among these odder refugees was an acrobat and tumbler from a travelling circus in Johannesburg. It was no surprise to receive from Nyoka's enclave the report of the murder of a woman and child by poison. District Messengers were sent to the scene, but the man had already fled. The Chief's *kapasus* came up with him and made the arrest: but they could not hold him and he escaped. Kasumbalesa, a Messenger of fifteen years' service, went after him alone and arrested him again, and they appeared handcuffed together at the Boma about a week later. On questioning Kasumbalesa appeared tired. No wonder, he had not slept for two nights on the journey back, but had sat up watching his prisoner. That was the spirit of the District Messengers, until the end.

Lukwakwa was the man's name: an educated clerk from Barotseland, who had served at Kasempa Boma, smooth, smiling, perfectly at ease and apologetic for the trouble he had caused by running away. Everyone at Kasempa was convinced that he was a murderer and he was detained in custody. The cooking pot and its contents were sent away for analysis. The analyst's report said that the fish had been bad, and that the cooking had merely made it more poisonous. Lukwakwa, released, decided to return by the quickest route to Barotseland: the Africans at Kasempa had no time for forensic science, and Lukwakwa lived in their collective memory as "the Lozi who poisoned the woman and her child near Nyoka".

*   *   *

I arrived and set up house alone at Kasempa, with a few plates, bags of sugar and flour and other necessities; it was a wonderful stimulus to learning the language, quickly, fluently and thoroughly. One must eat. Even as a bachelor one must set up rudimentary machinery and routine to get household tasks done. No one knew English, except the African clerk. If I wanted roast chicken for dinner, I had to first find and buy the chicken. It cost about 2s. 6d.; then I had to give instructions for its despatch and appearance, well stuffed, on the table. I had to master the basis of the dialect. Once I could converse I was able to enter, even a little, the world around me.

Without that, one might have gone mad. The rule, rigidly enforced, was that Cadets could not marry for their first two or three years. It had a purpose, though it was a hard one. It was to force Cadets to bury themselves in wherever they found themselves, and if they were lucky, come to love the people where they lived.

Even so, it was hard to live alone. Holidays were worse than days at work. The illustrated papers from England, the pictures of slim girlish figures, tulip-shaped, at Ascot or at a dance, bittersweet. Who was there to talk to at Kasempa? Sometimes, what was there left but brandy, and to stare at the full moon, the blank reflection of one's own loneliness? The ugly hours, the hours of despair—yet always the cheerful face to the Africans! At weekends, hearing a car miles away with ears unnaturally attuned, then to find it was a trader's lorry, or it did not stop.

Starvation of company: it was only by pretending that food did not exist that one could live at all. I acknowledge the excellent principle behind the rule of isolation and celibacy; yet I would not wish it upon my worst enemy.

On the outside of the door of the cottage looking onto the garden and out over all Africa lived a spider—my spider. Every day she would repair her web, and every day dash out in the evening with ferocity to entangle, with professional skill, insects far larger than herself. For months she bore a charmed life and solaced my loneliness : she became a kind of talisman. For as long as she lived, all would end well. But at last her luck ran out : a gaping hole in the web was unrepaired and she vanished. She reappeared briefly, but thin and listless, and soon after she died.

I felt that the Kaonde were watching me, not maliciously, but just from interest, to see how long I would last myself. But after all, "one must not give way". Was I not the second man in authority in the District after the District Commissioner, and in charge of the station when he went on tour? I thought of the Indian civilians in the early days who served twenty-five years without leave, or of the White Fathers who were reputed to go home once after ten years, and never again. No, I was here to stay.

The rainy season at Kasempa lasts from October until the end of March. Then the cold winds begin to blow, the low clouds clear and are swept along high in the sky, and the grass and trees go brown. Malaria, with its remarkable hallucinations and aftermaths of depression, had been and gone. It was the African autumn, but it felt more like spring. There was even dew on the grass.

It was April when Ndaliya, a Lovale by tribe, and his assistant Nkonde were brought in from a village on the edge of the Busanga swamp. They were witchdoctors and had been caught with their equipment by a zealous policeman on patrol. The policeman produced a small calabash of castor oil, two old tin mugs full of unpleasant black medicine—"for rheumatism", and one bottle filled with long sticks like asparagus.

Finally, the prize item, *Kahaya*, an idol or doll made of wood, about two feet high. This *Kahaya* was a famous figure in the District, and ensured her owners a comfortable income. So, appropriately, she was well dressed in a blue shift with numerous beads round her neck and waist. Her charges were 10s. for each consultation : she could cure illness, banish evil spirits, point out adulterers, and most important, protect against witchcraft by indicating the person who was practising it against one.

It was *Kahaya's* business to know all about everybody, and about everybody's private affairs. So when the patient crept into the dark mud hut having paid his 10s. in advance, the witch-doctor would amaze him, like a circus fortune teller, by telling him that he had had a quarrel with his wife, or a case of debt unpaid, bad luck hunting, or pains in his back and legs caused by witchcraft.

To do this *Kahaya* had a small horn stuck into a hollow in the top of her head. This horn, filled with congealed blood, human remains and other disgusting substances, would fly out over the countryside, down the paths and into the villages, busy gathering gossip. As the horn travelled, like a small satellite, it would make a slight whizzing noise and had even been known to tell innocent travellers to get out of its way. After a long journey, say five miles, the horn would tire and *Kahaya* would complain of exhaustion. Ndaliya, the owner, made a good living from people's gullibility and fear. Was the witchcraft more than the darkened hut and his skill in ventriloquism?

Two of the court assessors had heard her speak, and no one, not even Chief Kasempa's *Ngambela*,* nor Makyona Kanyakula the headmaster of the local school, both balanced, educated men, would touch *Kahaya*. I took her to my house where her baleful expression and evil reputation gave me an uneasy night. But only one. For the witchdoctors always have the last word. As *Kahaya* did not speak or visit me with retribution what I had in my house (and have to this day) is merely her facsimile : the real *Kahaya*, having seen the police approaching, went away on a visit leaving this absurd dummy behind to deceive the poor silly Europeans. The District Commissioner was an understanding man; no evidence was offered against Ndaliya, so he and his assistant departed leaving only their equipment, which was of no value.

In case it should be thought that Kasempa changed greatly between 1951 and 1960 with the advent of modern technology and more advanced political thought, I give the following list

* Head Councillor or 'Prime Minister'. (A Lozi word).

of objects brought in to the Boma by a "prophet" from Mankoya from August to November, 1960.

He was called Jack Motocar Simbunda and he went through the villages urging the people to give up their charms over an area containing some 1,650 males and 2,000 females. This is the official list of what he surrendered.

Item : 738 small packages of medicine
„ 5 dolls (similar to *Kahaya*)
„ 9 rattles
„ 1 comb
„ 31 shells
„ 9 amulets
„ 6 claws—of chickens or other birds
„ 2 rabbits' feet
„ 5 bones
„ 10 tortoise shells
„ 48 horns
„ 8 beads
„ 15 bottles of medicine
„ 11 gourds
„ 49 bits of wood
„ 1 human knee cap
„ 1 hippo tooth
„ 2 turtle claws
„ 1 eland tail, and some scales of a sea fish

One or two of these, the District Notebook drily observed, were worn for protective purposes only.

Soon after *Kahaya*, the leopard came to the Boma. As he preferred chicken to ordinary game, he would visit the hen houses in turn, and if a single chicken escaped she was lucky. At five o'clock in the morning my cook, Swanampanga, the Headman of a village nearby, shook me by the shoulder to tell me that he was in my neighbour's run, a high wood stockade about 100 yards away. There was a gun in the hall, left by my predecessor, a .303 which appeared to have a slight bend in the barrel. I loaded with five rounds and put one up the breech, and advanced with Swanampanga close at hand. The leopard crouched growling within the stockade and I thought it better to fire first between the small tree trunks that made it up. There was no real danger and it was all over in three shots. He lay panting and heaving with magnificent rope-like tail lashing to-and-fro. After a little I turned to go back to the house : I found my legs were soaked. I had forgotten to put on my shoes.

It was the custom among the Kaonde to wear a red feather or a red flower when a man had killed a lion or a leopard. There were some fine red flowers in my garden and I was tempted to wear one to the Boma that morning. I did not. All the same I regarded the gun with the barrel designed to shoot round corners with affection. I felt proud—it was impossible not to. The older Messengers asked respectfully about the leopard : two of the juniors were sent up to skin it for me. I felt that I had arrived. I had done what Kasempa had expected of a new D.O. : I had begun to be one of the Boma family.

Chapter II

THE SUNLIT WEST

The tumult and the shouting dies,
The captains and the kings depart . . .
Lord God of hosts, be with us yet,
Lest we forget—lest we forget!

(R. Kipling—Recessional).

IN 1901 Sergeant Major Mobbs and Trooper Lucas with the Police of Barotseland pitched their tents at Kasempa. My District Commissioner, Mr. Clark, who had a sense of history, decided to mark the fiftieth anniversary.

The last Governor to visit Kasempa and hold an *indaba* of Chiefs and Headman had done so in 1936, fifteen years before. After weeks of correspondence it was announced that Sir Gilbert Rennie, K.C.M.G., M.C., Governor of Northern Rhodesia, would come in person. The whole Boma plunged into a fever of preparation. The offices were re-painted, the grass-cutters were doubled, with their grass slashers like toy golf-clubs, the roads were made up, and the Boma carpenters were pressed into service to make a new round dining-table for the D.C. His Excellency was a fellow-Scot. Even so, Mr. Clark was disinclined to yield the head of his own table to Sir Gilbert as etiquette demanded; he hit upon this admirable compromise. If the table was round it followed that no-one could sit at its head : no doubt Sir Gilbert imagined that where he sat was the place of honour, and that was enough. Mr. Clark silently kept his own supremacy.

On the day appointed the D.C. proceeded to the border of the District some 70 miles distant. All had been prepared. It was a dry hot day, with a brisk wind blowing across the Boma. Attired in trilby hats and tropical suits we stood in a line, the

Clerks, the Post-master, the Game Scout, the Well-Digger, with the two African Traders, all looking fit to be presented.

Then, a whiff of smoke, then stronger smells, and soon billows of smoke in our faces. The dry grass of the Boma had taken fire and was carrying swiftly towards the thatched roof of the Postmaster's and other houses. Should we stand solemnly and watch them consumed? The Postmaster at least had no doubts. He left the line, followed by us all, with the District Messengers. Branches were seized, a rough line formed, and we began to beat the blaze. Some of us brought buckets of water and threw them on the thatch, while others again brought hoes and began to clear a fire break. Men, women and children, all joined in. In a quarter of an hour the blaze was under control and began to sputter out. Gasping, we returned to the Boma, blackened, sweating and well-satisfied. A car drew up, and out of it climbed a large portly man wearing a solar topee. Could this be the Governor? No, just the Provincial Commissioner. I raised my trilby hat to this senior official. I had put it on for this purpose; and attempted to explain that there had been a fire. This was unfavourably received: the topee remained in its place.

"Get these people into some sort of order," said the P.C. "H.E. will be here in five minutes."

So he was, and he regarded the dishevelled band with disfavour. No doubt he thought that that was how we customarily received Governors—*en déshabille*—at Kasempa.

Next morning was the day of the Indaba. Since dawn the Headman and people had been pouring into the Boma. Senior Chief Kanongesha had come in from Mwinilunga; Kapijimpanga, Mumena and Shilenda from Solwezi; Indunas Matavu and Kasuku from across the Mankoya Border in Barotseland, and the Mumbwa Chiefs, Mumba and Kaindu. The longest trek in was Kanongesha's, some two hundred and fifty miles. It was an occasion such as Kasempa had never seen before. The P.C. was in full uniform and fussed about, giving anxious instructions. The Chiefs and ex-Chiefs jostled for precedence on the front benches, and an ancient drummer, Chief Kasempa's own, supported round the waist by two young men, hammered the *Kin-*

kumbi, the drum of ceremony hollowed out of a tree trunk. His drum-sticks were topped with a fat blob of native rubber at the end. In the centre of the front row, his head circled by white *mpande** shells, in a long red skirt, with his feet on a lion skin, Chief Kasempa sat impassive.

His Excellency arrived, with quick short steps, and mounted the dais, followed by P.C. and D.C. The crowd rose, and in dead silence, led by Chief Kasempa, went down on one knee to give the ceremonial greeting of the Kaonde people, a triple series of hand-claps. The Governor sat unmoving. Addresses of welcome—the African civil servants pressing for more opportunities and promotion, the Traders asking for better roads, and then, the Chief himself stepped forward, stiff in his ceremonial clothes like a figure in a Jacobean masque. He asked for more schools, more hospitals, and for the restoration of ex-Chief Nyoka. This upset the ceremonial. Nyoka, a small wiry figure with a pointed imperial, and a remarkable record of loyalty and good service, had been deprived of his chieftaincy as a result of a misguided circular from the Colonial Office on the benefits of local government councils in 1948. No wonder that Nyoka listened intently.

At length Sir Gilbert Rennie rose to reply, a small impressive figure with his plumes, his orders and his medals from the 1914–1918 War. But alas, the speech! a dry, formal accountant's inventory of the Territory, abounding with figures but not of the slightest concern to the Chiefs or the people. It would have done excellently as the opening to a conference of Chambers of Commerce, or even at an annual banquet of Chartered Accountants.

But it did not answer for the Ba-Kaonde. There was a dryness, an inhumanity and detachment about it, which repelled them. We watched them as they shrivelled, and turned to each other in dismay, as though to ask, "What is this great man talking about? Whatever it is, he is not talking to us." What had Rennie to say to a people, with their Chiefs before them, who had twenty different dances, music and a hundred songs? Behind the plumes, they sensed the rolled umbrella. Here was the Government, personified, in ceremonial dress but—*la France s'ennuie.* It was a tragedy, and mercifully it soon ended.

* Large white circular shells with a hole in the middle. Emblem of traditional eminence.

There was an inspection of the station in the afternoon. This Governor would go to the brickfield and pick up a brick at random from the pile that had been baked. He would examine one and then drop it across another on the ground. If the brick broke, the D.C. responsible was a broken man : if it stood, he was made. On this occasion Rennie contented himself with chipping with a penknife at some new cement plaster. When he had broken his piece off, he stared at it in silence. The D.C. remained in suspense for nine years, until he was appointed a Provincial Commissioner.*

Mr. Clark was a brisk, colourful—and thoroughly nonconformist—Scot. He taught me the most important thing in Africa . . . that all Africans are people.

At dinner that night, once the toast to the King had been drunk, the party unbent a little. In unaccustomed dinner jacket I did my best to infuse a little warmth into the stiffness of Colonial society. Sir Gilbert would give vent to an occasional dry chuckle as he recounted his early experiences in Ceylon. I thought that the evening had been a modest success : one had been witty, perhaps, without being bumptious, humorous but not pert. I regarded myself complacently in the mirror before bed; unfortunately my tie had come undone and was hanging down as far as my waistcoat.

So much then for the Empire, at what should have been its most splendid : for everything that we had been taught to regard as the course of nature. The supremacy of Great Britain, the Union Jack over remote outposts, impossible to be too generous, too glorious, too grand! In its place only Rennie's Samuel Smiles exhortation to self-improvement; the direct and colourful approach of the early days had gone.

Without the human contact there was nothing but empty state and ceremony : if we went on like this, we should lose these people for ever. If we did not speak to them, they would soon cease to speak to us. So in the end, it fell out.

When the dust of His Excellency's departure had died down it was strangely quiet. The vegetable garden under the shadow of Kamsongolwe, where the battle was fought, was cool and sheltered, with a little stream running through it. And on the path

* See Appendix III for the official hierarchy.

leading down the butterflies would gather, big swallow-tails, cabbage whites and tiny frittilleries, around the pools of mud. Their long tongues would shoot in and out and they would fly up and settle on one's hand. To what purpose this gathering? To protest against black-birds, or more simply for a cool drink? The social life of butterflies has remained unexplored by the men with their nets; and even by the great Fabre himself.

As the weather grew hotter, the flying-ants would launch their queens and consorts on the single flight of the year. Upwards in slow circles they would fly, meet in mid-air and drop to earth shedding their wings. At the entrance to each hole would squat three or four toads, enormously swollen by their banquet, whose tongues would flash in and out, drawing in a queen. These distended monsters would not stir even if prodded with a stick, but would sink down where they were, replete, or lumber off to their lairs. Returning to the house the spider would still be there, weaving her web ready for the evening flight.

Provincial Commissioners of the old school considered "tours" the summit of felicity. An aura surrounded Touring, and older officers would nod approvingly if one had accomplished a large number of days "under canvas". A cadet who had declined to tour without his wife had been packed off the station in a lorry within twenty-four hours of joining by a D.C. with traditional ideas. Carriers were gathered together at a selected point by the District Messengers, and Cadets rode out on a lorry with a bicycle, bedding and provisions for a week or ten days. Often the Chief would come, or his councillors and assessors with their separate and subordinate establishment. With us were the tax books of the area, divided into villages, with a space for each taxpayer and for remarks about the villages at the beginning. Comments varied from year to year. "Much sickness", or "good crops", or "idle Headman". Sometimes a matter of greater interest, "witchcraft case involving Headman", or "suspicious death of Kalanda reported 1949".

It was the custom of the women to sing the District Officer and Chief into the village, a custom which endured even to the end of 1962. They would gather on the path in their blue print dresses and knitted woollen bonnets, with their babies slung over their backs and glaring sideways with pouched cheeks. One dismounted and walked in in the middle of them. The old Headman, with his few men behind him, would await one under a tall tree, or if it was wet in the little open-sided thatched hut which was the meeting-place and centre of the village. Seats, usually a primitive deckchair, on which one sat with caution, were provided. The Headman would lead the traditional greeting, three series of slow hand-claps, to which one might reply by gently patting over one's heart with the right hand.

"*Mutende, Ba-Chiboko, mwa kosa-tu bulongo.*" (Greetings to Chiboko, are you strong?)

"*Eee, mwane, Twa-kosa-tu bulongo.*" (Yes indeed, we are strong.)

And then would come a quick roll-call of the names in the register, each man answering his name by a hand-clap. It was not customary to linger over the roll unless there was a point of interest; it was merely a check to see that all were present. The more important part was to see how the people lived. A quick glance, after a little, would reveal the general state of the village, whether well-kept or slovenly; this invariably depended on the energy and ability of the Headman, most often a solid man in early middle age, but sometimes a bent patriarch who could remember the days "before the coming of the Europeans". The houses were revealing, unlit by windows, smelling of wood-smoke and with unsuspected corners and crannies where one did not peer. Sometimes, too, a spotless interior with a single book, the Bible, lying on a white cloth on a table knocked together out of sticks. And always the gun, the muzzle-loader, often beautifully decorated in the butt with brass studs or bound with copper-wire. Tower Muskets with their Crown, and Springfields with the American Eagle, with a few Prussian and Danish models, some looking just out of the armoury, well-oiled and cared for, others a danger to their owner. One would slap the butt sharply and if it rattled one would mention it. An unsound gun was a poor investment: they were habitually overcharged with gunpowder and they could blow up in their owner's face, with horrible results.

But of course it was only the surface that was visible in the village. For one day in the year, the occasion of the official visit, the village appeared "on parade" in a posture designed to please the remote and mysterious Government. For the others it carried on its normal life under a supervision neither close nor oppressive. There was hunger, privation and struggle to live. The laziness of the African was much censured by the Europeans at the time, and by implication also, by the Government. Why did not the Africans develop themselves, help themselves more?

I wonder what we would have done ourself in a village, equipped with axe, hoe, a few pots, a gun and some chickens. The house was not there—it had to be built, from trees, and mud, and grass. All must be gathered and put together with one's own hands. Water, often a distance away, must be brought. There was no light, no bath, no cooking stove. If one cut one's foot on a tree stump—no shoes—there were African poultices made of leaves. One might recover, or one's leg might gangrene and one might die. There was a blanket or two and some skins: the mattress was a sleeping mat. For meat, one must hunt. No, the people of the village had plenty to do to keep alive, and they listened to exhortations to self-improvement with a sceptical expression. "It's all right for you", they seemed to say, when urged to new and exciting forms of agriculture, or to attend night-school. "It's all right for you, but what about our next meal?"

But after work they had beer, and music, and dances: sometimes perhaps they would drink too much and dance too long, but they were human. *Mbote*, the honey-beer, made from wild combs, was the Tokay of Kasempa, fermented honey, like Anglo-Saxon mead. The honey bird had led the honey hunters to the hives of wild bees in the forest. Honey in Kasempa was used for sugar as well as for beer. When the honey bird had led a hunter to the tree, he would climb up with a burning brand and smoke the bees out, throwing the comb down to his friends on the ground and putting into a calabash any loose honey. Unfortunately this wrecked the hive, for, although it was etiquette to leave a tiny bit of honey for the honey-bird guide, the combs were all shattered and wrecked. Hence perhaps the small size and savage nature of the African bee, and the potency of the brew. Pieces of comb and bee would float on the surface of the cup: and one cup was enough.

But *mbote* was a luxury for a festival and the staple was *malwa wa mebele*, beer made from Kaffir-corn. Three cups of this could be drunk in safety. For teetotallers there was also *munkoyo*, a white milky substance from maize which so far as one could see had no taste, and no alcoholic content. Lime juice was preferable to this. The Chief Councillor of Kasempa, David Mukimwa, a round, charming and shrewd man with brown berry eyes, slowly approached with a calabash full of the "right stuff" and we drank our fill together by the great fire in the camp, each growing steadily more fluent in the other's language.

In the villages there was dancing, to a shrill cacophony of whistles and shrieks, to the beat of the drum. *Kawelila* was the women's dance, when one was circumcised. *Jimbalakata* took place when an elephant had been killed and was a dance of rejoicing, for there would be meat for all for a month. But *Mutomboko* was danced in triumph when a lion or leopard was killed. The Chief, or the Headman, if permitted, sat on the skin. The head of the animal was cut off and skinned. The Chief danced holding the skull, then the Headman took it up, and then those who had previously killed a lion. The mature fighting men drank beer from the skull to give them strength in war : and after it was kept as a trophy in the *Chipande* or hunting shrine. To kill a lion was to be remembered, and respected, even when old, as an elderly French officer wears the Legion of Honour in his buttonhole.

Or other dances, held in private rather than in public—*Bakaseba*—the dance which takes away sickness in women. When a witchdoctor cured a woman by taking away the evil spirit which was upon her she became a dancer and might cure other women. She wore a kirtle of reeds which made a susurrating noise, and little round calabashes that rattled were tied to her calves. As she danced she broke into different dialects not known to her before. So long as she did not eat the meat of the bush-buck or the zebra or the guinea-fowl, she retained her power. If she broke the taboo, it was gone.

The *Buyembe*, certainly not held in public, at least not anywhere near a Government official, was the dance of the witchdoctors. Possibly it was held from time to time to attract custom when the elders felt that things were growing slack, or that there was a hint of scepticism in the air. The chief witchdoctor would go to a grave and dig up a corpse: he would strip the flesh and burn it. He would give the bones to his fellow doctors who would all run to the village carrying them in a basket. Dressed in skins of monkeys and wild-cats they would dance from noon to sunset and on into the night gnawing their human bones. Presents would be offered by the congregation, and not refused. A *Buyembe* dancer, as they would say, was a man to be respected.

The *Bwilandi* was another dance held in secret. The dancers took a drug of the same name, which produced a kind of ecstasy and gave super-human endurance. The dancer became "as a lion", and was "able to travel a hundred miles in a night", all the time "as a lion", far swifter than a human being. But little was known of this dance; it was a secret jealously kept. If one inquired about it one was told it was *Kala-Kene*, old-fashioned and had quite died out; only laughing, ashamed references were made to these "obsolete old customs". How obsolete were they?

When night came the official restraints of the day would be put off. The Kaonde were not self-conscious, and their Chiefs not hedged about with too much etiquette. By the light of the fire and the moon the two lines of sweating glistening bodies, men and women, would advance and recoil time and again to the time of the drums and shrieking whistles, or be joined together by the arms in one great circle. Could one, ought one even, to join in the fun? I felt the rhythms drawing me in—to be part of them— at one with humanity—on equal terms with my fellow human beings. Would that I could have! Chief Mushima, who had a pawky humour under his stolid exterior remarked with double-meaning:

"Does the Bwana then, wish to stay all night?"

Then sadly to the tent, to a bed which felt too lonely to be possible.

Everyday life among such people is hedged about with as much unconscious ritual and ceremonial as is our own. Births, marriages and death always continue whatever the head-lines in the newspapers. Change is gradual and slow: and brought about not by them but by people living in the country, by their example and by their memory. Suppose a young man finds himself in a position to marry in Chief Mushima's area, where elderly men still thought it no disgrace to wear skins. The man has picked out his girl at a dance. He approaches the parents, or her maternal uncle, and suggests the match. Should they think him suitable and agree, he returns home and sends his mother or sister with a gift to her parents. It may be a gun, or cloth, or a blanket. The man's parents then ask the girl's parents if she is a good girl—not necessarily a virgin—but not flighty, and sufficiently skilled in her household tasks.

Should the answer be "yes" then the marriage is agreed upon. The parents return, and tell the young man the good news, and name the day. He proceeds to the girl's village, with his brothers, sisters and brothers-in-law. The girl's parents provide a spare hut, or it may be that the widowed grandmother or aunt has to move out of hers. That night the girl is fetched and taken to the hut where the man is waiting. No connection is said to take place, but the word *Kulajika* (to break) is used, which carries unmistakable connotations. At dawn the next day the girl's mother cooks a big bowl of porridge, *Chipununa wukala*, the husband can possess his wife, and takes it to their hut. The bridegroom's brothers go to the hut and eat it hot. Meanwhile the bride has departed elsewhere: the bridegroom stays in the hut and does not eat. Next night his marriage is officially consummated, and after appropriate rejoicing the relatives return to their own village.

But that is not all: there are well-defined obligations on both sides. First, the "present" given to the bride's parents or to her uncle. This has grown into an institution, and cash is often substituted for goods. This is, as it were, a security for good behaviour in the marriage on both sides. If a man so ill-treats his wife that she leaves him, he may lose cash or goods on the merits of the case. But if the parents should interfere and by poking their noses in cause family dissent, and a divorce results, then they are liable to pay back what they have received. As there are no banks in remote villages they will most probably either have spent the money or used the goods: it will be a real effort to pay them back. Hence prudence and restraint by ordinary parents-in-law in marital life. At the same time the man treats his mother-in-law with the greatest respect and does not even look her in the face. There is a multitude of petty sanctions on all sides in village life, but it is the interest of all to rub along as best they can. A good Headman is one that keeps peace within the village.

Now, as for the ordinary man in marriage, he takes on wide obligations to his wife's family, which can only be averted by cash payment too large for the ordinary man in the village to encompass unless he is particularly fortunate. First, he must take up permanent residence in his wife's village, and become part of her family. The husband may stay for a year if he is lucky, for ten years, or maybe for life. In the olden days, if the wife had borne four children, then he had licence to return to his own people, provided that:

(a) the mother-in-law did not refuse (which she could do for almost any reason);
(b) the wife agreed;
(c) his wife's relations in general agreed;
(d) she did not mind leaving his children with the wife's mother. The children belong to the wife's family, who can and do claim the right to bring them up.

Should the wife die, then the wife's mother, brothers and sisters have a prior claim upon them over the children's father.

But if, after a reasonable time, a man insisted upon returning home, he could insist by claiming a divorce and the restitution of his marriage gifts. But on nothing else: he would go alone, without his wife or his children. In this society it is apparent that it is the female child who is considered the asset: and as the marriage gift is so small, the child, now married, is still considered an asset. The real price (or dowry) that the parents get for her is represented by their children, and all the help and work done by the man in his long enforced residence in his wife's village.

It is sometimes thought that this system, payment, dowry, or whatever it may be called, is a crude cash sale of a girl: "£5 for my daughter": it is in fact no such thing, but a highly developed system of checks and balances between the contracting parties to a marriage, extending deep into their families, and offering great scope for reconciling the inter-play, the variety, and the frailty of human behaviour in its many aspects.

The cash sale is a crude view indeed. But in the days of slavery there was a similar slave system of marriage. A "slave" wife cost far more than a proper wife, and the following might be given for her by the man :

7 pieces of cloth
5 blankets
1 gun
1 packet of gunpowder
1 tin of caps
3 strings of beads;

an outlay say of about £30 today, and about eight times the price of an ordinary wife. A slave wife became the man's absolute property. She had no rights, and was no longer a part of her own family. She could not divorce her husband : her children were his and his family's, and she lived wherever her husband chose. A useful escape from the full rigour of Kaonde custom, which has in its turn crumbled. I saw no sign of a tribe of harassed males ruled by Matriarchs, and I doubt if it was ever so. In a social system where ordinary men had two or three wives the male had plentiful opportunities both to assert his pre-eminence, and by a little dexterity, hold the balance of power.

If a man married a girl before puberty, as he could, he did no more than "book" her, and shut out possible rivals. They did not co-habit. Now, unfortunately, it is different, and there is sometimes marriage of immature girls. A truck was leaving Kasempa with some Game Guards, and in the middle of them a tiny frightened girl of about ten years old.

"Stop that truck !" Mr. Clark ordered, and the girl and her husband were taken off. The man was somewhat indignant : after all the parents had agreed and he had paid the dowry almost in full. The girl was taken over to the hospital to be examined by the doctor to see if intercourse had taken place. Outside the little brick hut a young man passing by picked out a melancholy tune on his little *Kajimba* or hand-xylophone. The sun was hot : it was a sad contrast to the Song of Solomon, or to marriage as one thought of it. There was no sign of intercourse, and so the Game Guard went on his way free, and the little girl, still frightened and bemused, was sent back to her parents. But for this one case there must have been twenty undiscovered, and the result too often was a premature birth by a girl of fourteen, the baby too large to get out, no doctor near to perform a Caesarean, and death in agony in the dark, from exhaustion and native medicine. There lay—and lies—the tragedy of many short and hapless little lives, betrayed by the greed of unworthy parents for the price of a new bicycle or a gun.

When a Kaonde bride conceived a child her husband went to find a small piece of cloth and made a belt of it. On this belt he rubbed wet clay, and gave it to his mother-in-law with a few beads wrapped up in it. That evening the bride's sisters bring a calabash of water which they place outside the hut and call the bride. They fill their mouths with the water and spit it over her, saying, "You have conceived". Then they tie the cloth round the bride's waist and return to the village to dance. The next morning she is put on a mat in front of her brother's house, and she and her husband are anointed with castor-oil.

The child is born, and is examined by the mother and her family to see that it is "all right". Cripples or malformed children seldom survive. It is simply that village life can afford few or no passengers. And if the child should cut its upper incisor teeth before its lower, the mother will simply go to the river and drop it off her back into the water, without looking back. The child is *lutala* or bewitched. Every time one of its milk teeth drops out a person dies: and if a nail comes off, someone dies. Suppose a woman allowed her *lutala* child to live and kept it secret. She would be responsible for the death of a great number of people, she would doubtless be found out in due course, and it was a risk that she could not dare to take. In very rare cases it is possible for the mother to obtain a reprieve. All teeth are kept, and nails and parings, and all hair cut, and put in a calabash. After the last tooth is out the calabash may be carried like a baby on the mother's back, and dropped into the water in place of the baby. As the calabash drops into the water she calls "here is the *lutala*", and if all goes well and there are no deaths round and about till the matter is almost forgotten, the people are satisfied.

I have used the present tense advisedly. Little has changed. I received a letter at Fort Jameson from a Chief of the Kunda in 1963 asking advice about a *lutala* child. Whether it was allowed to live I do not know : but there are many letters which are never written, or received.

If a child does not walk when it should it is known as *chisheta* and killed by drowning. The mother again cannot, dare not, refuse, because the child is believed to be waiting till all its relatives are dead before it will walk. No such risk can be taken.

Until the end District Officers granted tax exemption for a year for twins. Some tribes killed them too for reasons of superstition, but not the Kaonde, where their birth was a cause of rejoicing. Each had to receive identical presents, and when the new moon came the mother and another woman carried them round the village singing and dancing. They carried a flat basket to receive more small presents, tobacco, or beads, or a little piece of cloth. After a while as many relatives and friends as could be collected went to visit the Chief, and gave him expensive presents, as much as they could afford. The Chief dressed up in clothes of ceremony, with his *mpande* shells round his head. Food and beer was brought. He then gave a present to the twins and said: "Now the twins will be able to visit me, and I shall be able to eat food cooked by their mother." And all rejoiced. It was always a pleasure to give tax exemption for twins, often dressed in little bonnets and tiny bootees: though all too often the mother only had enough milk for one, which flourished, while the other pined.

Chief Kasempa had the grand manner. He would go through his country like a crowned king of many subjects. His people knew his failings, but they knelt before him in the dust. He fell ill, miles from a road or a hospital, on tour. It was clear, after two days, that he had pneumonia, and he looked as though he were dying. There was no medicine but iodine, aspirin, quinine, kaolin. There was only some penicillin ointment, which was boiled up in a saucepan of water. A good doctor tries his medicine upon himself before his patients, and so I swallowed a good spoonful : no ill effects followed, so it was administered to the Chief. It seemed to revive him and he was well enough to be carried in a chair to the road, whence he was taken to hospital and recovered. He had great courage : and sat in his chair jolting for miles over rough paths. He was supported only by his will-power; his courage was rewarded and he recovered to govern his people again.

Death comes too often to a village for the relatives to grieve long. A brief, almost formalized wailing, the funeral, and the struggle to live must go on—the water drawn, the field cultivated or the meat hunted. There can be no long indulgence in grief, but it is felt. Particularly over children : there are so many of them, and so many die. Fat little dictators with round eyes, crawling and tottering about. But once they have left their mother there is no more milk, and they are a prey to all the diseases of Africa— and those of Europe—particularly colds, bronchitis and pneumonia. Many, weakened by poor diet and then by illness neglected until too late, do not survive early childhood. The parents are left as desolate as any parents can be.

Kabowo, the Chief's head assessor, a fine man of great character and presence, came upon his own village on tour. The houses all had little flower gardens and bushes in front of them, but there was an air of lassitude and decay. The roll was called but there were few to answer, and almost all the children had gone : there had been an epidemic of whooping-cough. Suddenly, in the middle of the court, poor Kabowo burst into uncontrollable tears. Almost all his family had been wiped out, and as he then lived far away, at Chief Kasempa's own village, his relations had not dared to tell him the worst. What could I do to try to comfort him then? Only resolve that as far as lay in my power, every group of villages should have its own dispensary with proper modern facilities and medicines to save these people.

Leprosy was in some villages where we passed. A victim, as the disease got worse, would be set a little apart in a grass hut nearby. The relations would bring food, but there was little else that they could do. The sores would irritate, grow worse, then toes and fingers begin to fall off, until at last the body became little more than a suppurating mass and death would come as a relief. When officialdom visited the village the unfortunate people would crawl away if they could into the forest, where if they were lucky, or unlucky, they would be found by a District Messenger or *Kapasu*, and brought back to the Mission hospital by reluctant carriers on a stretcher. Even there they were miserable enough. The cure, Chaulmugra oil, was useless, and as it was injected into or near the sore, very painful. Better treatment, better diet, arrested the progress of the disease, but the end was the same. But within the last few years medical science has made wonderful advances, and men and women and children, whom I had mourned as doomed, are alive and recovered in their villages today.

Others were not so lucky. The sight of a youth lying in a grass shelter, too weak to move and covered with huge open sores. He was the grandson of old ex-Chief Kalasa, and must have had some kind of cancer. The women fed him on honey-beer, which was all that he could take : he was near the end. I only hope that they had enough beer to deaden his pain.

Nor were our own medical facilities so advanced. Recovering from the glorious hallucinations brought on by malaria and quinine I was involved in the delivery of the child of the wife of the Building Foreman. He, poor man, was lying ill in the same room with pneumonia, while the District Commissioner had gone to escort the Secretary of Native Affairs to a film of Charlie Chaplin being shown to the African Welfare Society. The course given to cadets at Cambridge, though replete with information on law, anthropology and practical bridge building under tropical conditions, had unaccountably omitted gynaecology. As usual it was to the D.C.'s wife that I turned; as I remarked, she had had three children. She hastened to point out that she had not delivered them herself, but had been unconscious under an anaesthetic. However, armed with a Medical Dictionary, we decided to tackle the case. Mrs. Clark, with considerable resource, went in and began operations, while I remained outside the door in charge of the hot water and the Dictionary. Mercifully the doctor arrived before we had got far : a fine son was born by the time Charlie Chaplin had ended.

It was one of our routine duties to review the run of court

cases sent in by the Chiefs. Usually a brief account in Kaonde of a quarrel, or an adultery, or some such petty dispute. One particular case caught my eye, an account of a dog who had been had up for talking, indeed of using obscene language, and expelled from the village called Chiembe. It happened like this. A woman was alone, cooking her porridge in her kitchen, and she went outside to gather more wood. When she returned she found the dog with its head in the pot, eating the porridge. Enraged, she picked up a stick to beat the dog, at which instead of running away, it turned upon her, and appearing to laugh, distinctly said, *Kongwe*, which translated meant a reference to the woman's private parts. The dog was driven out of the village forthwith by a hail of sticks and stones: but the woman was so disturbed by the experience that she went straight to the Chief and related it in Court. After due inquiry the expulsion order was confirmed by myself. What became of the dog? Nobody knows: but may one hope that he is still at large in the forest and at a ripe old age teaching the other animals a proper irreverence for the human race?

Chapter III

THE FOREST PEOPLES

A servant with this clause
Makes drudgery divine,
Who sweeps a room as for Thy laws
Makes that and the action fine.

(George Herbert).

NOT a ruffle disturbed the calm assurance of the Government at Kasempa in the long silent days. We thought that the British Empire would continue for ever on its way, slow, ponderous and honest—blinkered, but intent on doing good. A politician, a small round man with spectacles, did indeed announce his arrival by telegram. His ideas, throughout a long and tedious evening, made remarkably little impact even on the "intelligentsia" of about twenty-five clerks from the Boma and the stores. He went next day, and was forgotten. He was not even an omen or a portent, and the people were not concerned with him. He went as he had come, a small round man, wearing spectacles.

What interested the Kaonde in the early 1950's was meat and beer, and at a higher level, tribal politics, and the clash of rival Chiefs, even though founded upon very recent tradition.

When a Kaonde grew angry, he gave due notice of the fact: there was a proper ritual of rage, which he would go through. He would smear his face with red earth, or put a red feather in his hair, and then shout and stamp round the village, threatening his enemy. Women and children would fly with cries of fear: and in extreme cases the man would even fire off his muzzle-loading gun. The news would spread quickly through the villages, and his enemy would either return defiance or a suitable present and an apology. That was *Kipingo.*

The Ntondo family was honoured in Kasempa, although the

clan was one which was falling into decay. In Chief Kalasa's country the first headman of that name had driven all the people away from his village by his practice of ceaselessly examining the footprints around his huts, and making heated accusations of adultery to all who had passed by. At Ingwe the headman had constructed an enormous wooden palace, which he had abandoned in disgust before finishing. He lived in a small mud-hut alongside his folly. At Kasonso, in a fit of sudden dissatisfaction with his village site, Ntondo the third had set fire not only to his own house, but to everyone else's as well. Fortunately nobody was killed, but this Ntondo spent many years paying for the damage.

A young man unwisely gave a lift to a married woman on the handlebars of his bicycle and was taken up for adultery with her. A clear case and proved, said the Court. If it was not consummated it was for lack of opportunity, the guilty thought was there. Besides, as the Kaonde proverb went, "How can a woman refuse a man?" Pomposity and self-importance could grow with tropical speed.

As the tall Kaffir-corn swayed and ripened in the fields the birds would descend on it. Every available tin and noise-making instrument was banged or clashed and the children shouted out the names of the birds, *Kiawala, Kiawala*—"parrot, parrot"—at the most voracious of all.

Kasempa was real, the outer world but a shadow, and letters from it, from ghosts. It made many Europeans terribly assertive. One acted one's part upon an enormous empty stage: the "compleat man" was untrammelled if unseen. Grey of Falloden feeding pigeons, Gladstone hewing at the trees, even Dr. Watson with a brisk manner and a bottle of iodine. One could play out such fantasies in real life, with real people. Any European at Kasempa was a "character". That certainly developed their characteristics.

In 1951 the more intelligent of the Councillors around Chief Kasempa began to apprehend that the Kaonde tribe was scattered widely and dis-united under a number of small Chiefs. Hence, when they approached the Government for more money to build schools, roads and hospitals, they spoke with a feeble voice and were ignored. Kasempa was young and strong-willed, and his Councillors decided that the moment had come to put him forward as Paramount Chief over all the Kaonde.

Historically Chief Kasempa's claim was not a strong one. True, for the space of one night in 1926 a meeting of chiefs had accepted his predecessor as their superior, only to change their minds the next morning in the light of tribal and family jealousies. But there was the shadow of a tradition that he had once held sway to the borders of the Lamba to the east and the Lozi to the west. He was the only Senior Chief among the Kaonde, and Government knew him, with careful ambiguity, as "primus inter pares".

The meeting held at Kankolonkolo in the cold weather of 1951 aroused far more interest than any purely political question. It was tribal, and concerned the powers of the Chiefs. The District Commissioners of Solwezi and Kabompo came to the meeting as well, each determined to see that no Paramount Chief was recommended by the Council. Difficulties were inherent in the presence of a Paramount in a neighbouring District. It would have given the Paramount Chief countless opportunities for influence and appeal to outside the Kingdom of Kasempa.

Senior Chief Kasempa sat with the other Chiefs on a raised platform. There was Mujimansofu, round and jovial from Solwezi —not yet struck down by cancer, and carried, a living skeleton, back to his village on a lorry. Kapijimpanga, that white-haired old fox, the son of the usurper; Musele, the Lamba, nephew of Musokantanda, and Mushili, the Senior Chief of the Ba-Lamba. Kasempa's only supporter, Mumena, wearing in his lapel a brooch in the shape of a jewelled spider. Mushima from Kasempa, embarrassed and afraid to voice his jealousy of the Senior Chief in public, Nyoka, the fierce little ex-Chief from the east, and Ingwe, old and sodden. From Kabompo only Chizera, a tall man of splendid courage who would shoot elephant with his muzzle-loader, was unalterably averse.

The Councillors, in the front rank below, and behind a mixed collection of whiskered important Headmen, evangelists and local characters who thought they had the right to attend. And behind all, the D.C.'s and the interpreter. For a day the argument went

back and forth without result, and at the evening it was clear that
Chief Kasempa was beaten. He was too much of a prince to
quibble with opposition, too calm, too measured, too self-con-
tained. Opinion must be unanimous, or almost so, or he would
withdraw. In the event only Nyoka and Mumena spoke for him.
Mujimansofu, Kapijimpanga, Chizera, and Mushili were solid
against. The Kasempa Councillors had had their idea, and it was
a good one: but the Kaonde were not yet prepared to be united
as a tribe, and they are not united to this day.

Chief Kasempa remained Senior Chief, remained "primus inter
pares", but lost his appeal court from the Kaonde of Solwezi
District, a relic of the time when that Boma was closed. This unsuccessful venture in local imperialism caused our District Commissioner deep chagrin and for a little time relations with our
neighbours were cool. Each District was like a separate state, four
hours distant or more by road. It had a self-consciousness of its
own and its own personality. Solwezi at that time was full of new
theories of local government reform, with a huge card index
system containing cross-relationships of families. It had a female
Treasurer at the Native Authority who, unmarried, produced two
children. The old Adam remained. Kabompo was for community
development, sewing classes and the like. A distraction for a while
from the endemic tribal underground war, but a distraction and
no more. Kasempa remained gloriously Kasempa, without frills,
without theories, and with its Chiefs, Headmen and villagers all
knowing where they stood, and many trying, as best they may, to
grow new crops or build new roads and generally to improve their
society.

To the west, in Mushima and on the Musondwedzi river, the
Luchazi under Samuzhimu were a dissident group and a thorn
in the side of the Kaonde. A group of about 25 villagers had
crossed together from Angola after the war. They had gone to
Mankoya, but trouble followed, then to Kabompo, and added to
its unsettled state. From there they had arrived in Kasempa, a
troublesome minority, unamenable to laws, taxes, sanitary rules
or to the authority of the Senior Chief. They were supposed, by
people who knew nothing about them, to have great poten-

tial as agriculturalists, who would have a wholesome effect upon the "lazy Ba-Kaonde". Nothing could have been more absurd. The Kaonde despised them from the first as dirty, undisciplined, immoral and avaricious, and treated them accordingly. As for their agriculture, it consisted of huge fields of cassava, of little nutritive value, and in keeping large herds of pigs which wallowed in their already filthy villages. By no means an attractive people.

It was the custom of those days to give a brief description of the people in the Tour Report sent to headquarters. This description of the progressive Luchazi met with little favour from authority, and my transfer to Kabompo, the centre and nucleus of the tribe, followed within weeks.

Gone was the Kamusongolwe Hill where the battle was fought, the thatched cottage with the view over the trees. Far worse, all my friends, the Chiefs, the Messengers, the Medical Orderlies (some of the best and most intelligent of Africans), and old Nkundwe the gardener in his sack-cloth apron. The place where I had shot the leopard, and the window where I had cut my initials on the glass. Nor did I see Kasempa again for another thirteen years.

Kabompo, a hundred and sixty miles to the west, was another, separate world.

It was my introduction to the political duties of a District Officer, and a lesson that I did not forget, that people who live quite near on the map may be fundamentally different in character, background and in almost every other respect. It was a lesson also in how easy it was in Africa to make serious mistakes through lack of considered thought, and one's own immaturity.

As far as the Kabompo River, the District had formed part of the old Empire of Lewanika of Barotseland, and to the north, the Lukwakwa, touching Mwinilunga, the home of exiles and of those who had fallen into disgrace at court in Mongu. An Induna who had grown troublesome at court was sent into honourable exile to govern the sandy wastes and miserable people. "Go out—and govern New South Wales."

In 1941 the Lunda and Lovale people of Balovale had revolted against Lozi rule, and they and the people of Kabompo had been excised and joined to the Kaonde-Lunda, then to the Western Province. An old Lozi Induna, Imasiku, the last relic of the ancien régime, had been left with his Court at Manyinga : a turbulent mob of immigrant tribes had been allowed, a few years after, to invade his headquarters, slit his royal drums, and drive him ignominiously back to Barotseland, where he soon died.

An Mbunda* Chief, Sikufele, previously exiled from Mongu to Angola, had been allowed to return, and placed in the uneasy position of Senior Chief over the eight tribes, Luchazi, Chokwe, Lovale, Lunda, Nkoya, Kaonde, Mbundu, and his own Mbunda, with a mixed Council drawn from each of them. It is round this amiable and harassed man, shaped like a Bourbon, and his Ngambela or Prime Minister, Ikanjilwa Kabwasa, that the story of the District revolved for the next few years.

Strict Lozi etiquette prevailed in the capital. A stockade surrounded the royal house, which commoners entered at a crouch and clapping gently. In Council the Councillors sat on the floor and clapped before and after they had given their advice. These relics of a bye-gone age in Lealui annoyed the immigrant tribes, who had a strong sense of independence and held that one man was as good as another. They were individualists who had no headmen as such, and governed their villages in a kind of Soviet. To them the hallmark of success was to become rich, and they were keen traders—to the extent that they would on occasion put out their wives to hire—or interchange them if they felt inclined. These men took very unkindly to antiquated custom, and indeed, to authority in any form at all from any quarter.

The immigrant tribes who had started to infiltrate after the Chokwe rebellion against the Portuguese in the 1920's, were in the great majority, some 23,000 against 8,000 of the Lunda, Mbunda, Nkoya and Kaonde. They took every occasion to assert their power, although the Councillors from those tribes at Sikufele's court were loyal to him, and appalled at the possibility of the whole District falling into chaos if there was no-one and nothing at its centre.

Very soon after my arrival there Chief Sikufele wished to

* A subject tribe to the Lozi: and the hereditary witch-finders at King Lewanika's Court.

3. The Boma Drum at Mwinilunga (the drum is hollowed out of a tree and is called 'Chinkuvu').

4. A Chief on Tour: Chief Sikufele with his 'Ngambela' (Prime Minister) Ikanjilna Kabwasa.

appoint his nephew Joseph Sikufele as an assessor to the Pontoon Court, an area inhabited by the immigrants some eighteen miles from the Boma. This unwise appointment led to serious trouble. To begin with, Joseph, while a man of good character, lacked personality and stature. His only asset was his uncle, and that was not enough. The Luchazi and Chokwe who lived there thought that he was being appointed as a sort of Induna over them, which indeed he was. By his birth he would dominate the court there, and the people saw a Lozi enclave in their midst. Let Sikufele reign on sufferance at Manyinga with his Lozi habits, but let him not send his nephew to trouble them in their own place.

The appointment was impolitic to the point of folly. It was a challenge to the Luchazi and Chokwe at a time when there was no force to meet it. Four policemen and eighteen Messengers were no match for a furious and determined crowd.

I judged by Kasempa standards: hints of "trouble" there meant no more than a few Headmen coming in to complain, with the greatest possible respect, to the D.C. or the Senior Chief. The idea of any more action than that was unthinkable and absurd. But in Kabompo I was new; I demurred, and asked for confirmation from the Senior Chief and his Council. This was quick to arrive, and I had either to offend the Senior Chief, at the very beginning of my tenure, by turning away his nephew, or deal with "trouble" only known by vague hints and reported grumbles.

Unfortunately at this time I was alone. Three other Europeans on the station were concerned with Agriculture, Roads, and Building. The Officer in Charge of the Province, who might have advised by telegraph, was away at a conference. In any event the wireless had broken down. So, for that matter, had the ancient vehicle. Moreover, some four of the best District Messengers were away giving evidence in a murder trial. Altogether we were much reduced.

The decision was taken. Joseph Sikufele was duly appointed Assessor to try cases at the Pontoon Court. It did not take very long for things to happen. The leading Chokwe and Luchazi Headman from the Pontoon and other areas converged upon the Chief's headquarters at Manyinga with their followers, and

c

hoped, by a show of strength, to over-awe the Chief into revoking the appointment. Their names were Samalaho, Chaminuka, Kuzwa, Katende, Mutekenya, Sachikatu, Ngoshi, and Zakeyu Zendu, and they were all, except Mutekenya, men of substantial following.

Had the Headmen approached the Chief with a little wisdom instead of with a large following at their back, they would have made a better impression. But rebuke by the Chief led to heated remonstrance and disrespect, and before, I suspect, either party had had time to think calmly, the eight Headmen had been peremptorily sentenced to various terms of imprisonment. So they all arrived with a case record, followed closely by 200 irate supporters, at Kabompo Boma on a February morning in 1952.

On such occasions one is very much alone. In the Army one has orders, in the Navy, the rules of navigation and experience when the sea is high. When there is trouble abroad in a District the nearest parallel for the D.C. is to a new doctor, wondering whether or not to operate on a desperate case. The doctor is quite alone, and he is responsible not only to the patient, but to God, for whatever may happen. I was the District's political doctor: and I was very new.

A mob is the most stupid thing in the world. Once it is formed and has cohesion it will invariably choose the worst course for itself and for everyone else. It is so stupid that it does not know what it is doing until it has done it. It is the lowest common factor of the intelligence of the people who make it up. It is invariably as much of a menace to itself as to others: it is, in fact, a headless monster. *Crowds* can be faced, and good humour will send them away happy and safe to their homes. But once an invisible dividing line has been crossed, and *crowds* have cohered into *mobs* bent on mischief, then it is necessary that they be faced, and out-faced with superior force or the pretence of it.

Very early that morning a crowd had gathered on the grass outside the Boma and sat down, two hundred strong. It was a lonely walk from my house to the office. I had heard stories of how these people had rioted before: and, unwisely as I now think, I ordered the three policemen on duty to fix their bayonets and stand on guard on the verandah. Of course I issued no ammunition, and to have fired upon the people would have been unthinkable. Still, the rifles and bayonets were there, and must have had an exciting effect upon the members of the crowd. With a little more wisdom I should never have produced the prisoners that day, and should have spent it in the middle of the people, talking to them. But an upbringing in the Army, followed by Kasempa, gave me the idea that opposition of this sort—persons engaged in disputing the authority of the Chief—should be out-faced and over-borne. It turned out not to be so simple.

The eight Headmen were brought in and sat on a bench in front of me. The case record was read out. There was one hope left now, and only one. The whole affair had been a series of unfortunate misunderstandings between the Senior Chief and themselves. I was not angry with them : but the Senior Chief and his Council had of course the right to appoint any man of good character whom they wished to a position such as Assessor. I trusted that they would see the point, and go peacefully back to their villages, while Joseph Sikufele would follow as soon as an interval of calm had elapsed. The prison sentences would remain in abeyance. This highly irregular suggestion had the advantage of being practical, if illegal, and for a moment I thought that they would accept. What I should have done was to have sent them back to the prison for the day to think it over.

Instead, starting with their leader, Samalaho, I put the question at once. With a glance at his followers outside he returned his answer "No", and the others followed him.

He could not withdraw, in the face of his people : neither could I, as the representative of the Government. We were all caught in an impasse, and must go forward together, in a sense, as fellow victims. So I proceeded quickly to ask the prisoners if they had more to say, and to confirm their sentences. They were then removed under escort.

If I had hoped for quiet to return, I was mistaken. As the prisoners, between a file of Messengers and Police, moved through the Boma towards the prison, an angry clamour broke out. I thought it well to go outside and address the crowd, but as I raised my hands for silence, it broke away, and began to follow the prisoners at a run.

I was astounded: at Kasempa my arrival would have been the signal for a respectful silence. To run after the people would not have been dignified for a Magistrate—all D.C.s were also Magistrates—a few minutes after sitting in his Court, but I walked, and at a pace which became very brisk.

I soon came up with the procession, with the prisoners in the middle, between the Messengers. Angry shouts, and fists were shaken in my face: they were not good-humoured, and not susceptible to good humour. In a little while, unless we took the initiative, they would cease to be content with shouting curses, and do something silly. What to do next?

As we passed through a defile between some houses, we had our chance. The prisoners and their escort passed through, and the other Messengers formed a line so that the crowd did the same.

Before they could think of the next move the prisoners had gone, and I addressed them in tones loud and indignant. I berated them for their disrespect, for their disloyalty to their Chiefs (whom they hated) and for their bad conduct. Who were they to set themselves up against lawfully constituted authority, against the Chief—against the Boma—yes, the Queen herself! For two hours I addressed them, slowly calming and reducing the tempo, until to me at least, the whole matter was an unfortunate misunderstanding which men of goodwill could resolve.

So they left peacefully, I hoped for home. But we were not so lucky. They had decided to remain encamped at the Boma and to await developments: and their talk and behaviour became more menacing as the days passed. No word came from Provincial headquarters, where I had sent a Messenger to ride day and night: the Jeep remained immobile, the wireless silent.

While the Headmen remained in prison, which was no more than a long hut made of grass, sticks and mud, the crowds increased. At any time they chose they could have regained their prisoners and swept us aside. Strategy was all that remained.

Eighteen miles to the north-east was Chief Sikufele's headquarters: and it was fair that he should share in some of the stress and strain. If I were to go there, with a force of Messengers, I would draw the malcontents after me. The Pontoon section would be twice the distance from their own area : some would follow, others might return home. Others might be over-awed at the thought of appearing before the Chief in a state of semi-rebellion, and in any event the large body daily growing in menace at the Boma, would begin to break up into individuals. And reinforcements could be expected from Chief Sikufele's Kapasu force. So it was with all possible parade and publicity that I set out the next day.

All was in vain : as I proceeded along the road I was met by further crowds of angry villagers asking why "their leaders" had been put into prison. The Chief, when I arrived, gave little help. Some troublesome characters had been dealt with by his Court. What more was there to be said or done? Justice must go forward. The jaws of the trap set for the malcontent party had failed to close, even to move, and far from drawing them off and breaking them up away from their own country, I had brought out further opposition which hastened in to join the bands at the Boma. These had failed to stir, and grew in number and menace as the days went by. I returned to the Boma, inwardly a desperate man.

At last, after ten days of silence the P.C. had returned to Solwezi to find my messages on his desk, and had acted at once. More Messengers arrived, and offers of help from every man on the next station if need be.

The eight Headmen were removed discreetly to Balovale, a hundred miles away. The greater part of the band followed them at speed on their bicycles, while others began to return home. The immediate crisis was over : but it was apparent that Kabompo was very different to Kasempa.

A new District Commissioner relieved me of my temporary tenure. Secretly I was grateful to be free of a responsibility that had become overwhelming. For the first time in Africa I had been afraid. Afraid to a certain extent for myself, though I did not lock my doors at night : but more afraid of the hatred that I seemed to have aroused in such a short time, and of the forces of unreason which could gather and explode so quickly—of the thinness of the fabric of Government and of the ease with which it could be torn down—given a cause and only a little organization.

The new District Commissioner, Herbert Horatio Stewart, was

a man of great determination and stern kindliness. He remained at this inhospitable station for five years, at the end of which all that could be done for Kabompo had been done. The authority of the Chief had been restored, with the consent of all the tribes, the station had been rebuilt, and money poured in for agriculture, roads, dams, hospitals and all the benefits of modern civilization. No one man could have done more, and have done it better. He was the architect of Kabompo.

As for the eight Headmen, they were brought back after an interval and put before the Native Authority. Five, Samalaho among them, who had been ringleaders in previous attempts, were sentenced to be deported to Angola from where they had come.

This the Provincial Commissioner confirmed and I escorted them, with their goods and families, from the last village in Northern Rhodesia out into the sandy wastes. It was not a friendly parting, and we separated with relief.

Two years later Mutekenya returned and was recognized by a District Messenger on the Copperbelt at Chingola. It was necessary to enforce the order of deportation and he was arrested and brought before me. We looked at each other in the small office. I pitied him—I wished I could have let him return if he wanted to so much. Suddenly he flung himself full length on the floor and gripped my left ankle with his hand. Pity mingled with an impulse of revenge as I looked at this abject man stretched out. I gently removed his hand, and I am ashamed to say, sent him away again across the border.

I had revenged my lonely nights of fear at Kabompo, but I am ashamed still, to this day.

Ten years passed, and it was 1964 when I visited Kabompo again. As one does I fell into conversation with an African: he had heard of me, dimly, in some connection or other.

"Short?" "Was I the man, might he ask, who had exiled Samalaho and the others after the trouble?"

I was. Samalaho himself was dead, and so was Kuzwa. "Did the others wish to return?" "No, they were all settled happily now." "Tell them, if they wish to return, it will make no difference now. Things have changed, let them come if they will."

We were caught up together, Headman, Chief, and I, in forces which we could not control. It was I who lacked wisdom, as well as they. Regrettably it was the Headman who suffered for us all.

*   *   *

John Derecksen was the Water Supply Foreman at Kasempa, and Ted Hough, the Game Ranger, was his friend. The first was a South African miner from the Rand who had had silicosis. He would do anything for you, from mending a motor-car, or cutting your hair, to cheering you up if you were ill. He had great fists like pile-drivers, and he was the gentlest and happiest of men. Ted Hough was ex-R.A.F. with a moustache like a pair of wings. He was my companion and relief after months of solitary gloom. The General Election of 1951 and the return of Winston Churchill to power were celebrated by a *feu de joie* of all arms round the Boma, which was deplored by the other inhabitants. He kept a peregrine falcon, and his house was full of his apparatus of the air.

Our recreations were of the most peaceful kind. On the brown dusty grass in front of the house African bows and arrows were pressed into service for archery practice, enthusiastic but not very accurate. On wet days the long verandah made an excellent .22 firing range. Then there were always the donkeys. In the Transvaal their ancestors had pulled wagons in a long train as they still do today. But somewhere along the line these arrangements had broken down. No Kasempa donkey had worked since it was born, and they were now half wild. They were excellent sport for rodeos as they had a remarkably strong buck, and there was not too far to fall. The herd was only kept in some sort of order by an old man with a jackal skin tied onto the end of a long thin stick. This they dreaded and would obey. In the end a new District Commissioner arrived who believed that all resources should be utilized, and that these idle drones should work. So work they did for five years or so, on a permanent "go-slow" basis. His successor abandoned the struggle. The donkeys, as we all expected, won in the end. It was thus that Ted and I passed our leisure, and in trying to make pieces of strange looking equipment for the hawk which sat silent and menacing in the corner of the room.

Johnny Derecksen had been invalided from the Johannesburg mines with silicosis, and he lived with his wife in a thatched mud-plastered cottage by the great salt pan at Kaimbe.

So much has been written, so much anger wasted on the subject of the "brutal Afrikaner" that I think it a pity that these writers never met Johnny. He had been born in Africa and was a part of it. He believed, not that Africans were of a lower order, but that they were different. He worked with them and they accepted him. What surprised me was his extremely gentle manner in a man so physically tough. He never raised his voice, because he never needed to. Underneath the big tree outside his house he used to cut our hair while we looked out to a horizon without end.

He and Ted Hough had gone fishing in the East Lunga River, which rushes in a torrent between a narrow defile of rock and falls into deep whirlpools. Johnny, a heavy man of nearly fifty, slipped and fell in : Ted caught his shirt, which tore away. As he was swept down and under, Ted followed him into the water. All was in vain. Ted appeared for a moment in one of the whirlpools, and then both went under for ever. For his gallant attempt he was awarded a Queen's Commendation for Courage, posthumously.

Ted Hough lies at Kasempa in company with twelve others, policemen, prospectors, hunters, and a bronze plate riveted to the rock on the banks of the Lunga commemorates them both. The road to the place has already been closed down, and if one day the memorial should be rediscovered by an explorer, here is its story; it is the story of two friends who died together, one giving up his life for the other.

*   *   *

It was in that same year, 1952, that the curious case of the bewitched coffin came to light, in Ndola Rural District, next to the Kaonde country. A woman was killed by a coffin which became possessed at a funeral, by being battered to death in full view of the other mourners. Not a man or woman stirred to save her.

A prominent man in Mbunda Chikapula village, Chichibanda, died in August, 1951. A coffin was made for him of bark, not planks, and the grave got ready. Four young men were the bearers, Lupiya and Nkoshya in front and Lefai and Luka in the rear, and the procession started off, followed by the mourners.

A voice called out from the crowd : "If anyone has caused your death—point him out." The bearers continued towards the grave, then stopped, turned, and retraced their steps to the garden shelter where Chichibanda had died. The coffin dipped in front, and touched the shelter. Slowly the procession returned, and weaved in and out of the people, who stood in complete silence. They were, literally, paralysed with terror. The coffin approached an old woman called Mayamba Lusika, and dipped again, and struck her on the chest. She fell down on her back, for the blow was a hard one.

The two men in front, Lupiya and Nkoshya, pulled her to her feet and said, "Let us go". So the poor woman walked in front of the coffin, towards the grave, like an automaton.

Again she was struck by the coffin, in the back this time, and half-turned to ward off the blow. A third blow, and she went down again. Desperately she tried to break away, but her efforts were warded off by the coffin, and she was penned in by the crowd. When the grave was reached the unfortunate woman lay on her side, began to froth at the mouth, and soon afterwards she died. Her body was taken back to the village by the bearers after the funeral.

At one point an intelligent young man, an agricultural *kapasu* or messenger called Morrison Shilling had taken over in front from one of the pall-bearers. He sincerely believed that Mayamba had been pointed out by supernatural means : he felt pressure exerted upon him by the coffin itself, and seemed to become an automaton. He believed that it was the coffin that caused the woman's death.

In the old days, in the custom of "pointing out" among the Lamba, the coffin would knock the victim gently, and he or she would go to the grave. After the funeral the boiling water test or the fowl test would be administered. The Councillor giving this evidence of native custom omitted to say that this would be followed almost invariably by the death of the accused, already found guilty by the coffin. That, however, was the case.

G*

The four bearers were accused of murder, and pleaded in defence that they were not responsible and that the coffin had become possessed. This was rejected by the trial Judge, who held that they were responsible, but that the actual evidence had failed to show that the prisoners intended to kill or to inflict grievous bodily harm on the deceased, or that they knew that the bumps of the coffin would probably result in her death.

This judicial reasoning is hard enough to follow, when one considers that the woman had screamed after each blow, and that as she had lain on her side by the grave in extremity, no-one, and certainly not the bearers, had moved to help her. And whose was the voice in the crowd which called out? Who indeed? And the coffin was of bark, tough no doubt, but not of the same solidity as planks. Mayamba died of shock resulting from multiple fractures of the chest wall : and partly also, no doubt, of sheer terror.

But "the evidence failed to show that the prisoners intended to kill or inflict grievous bodily harm to the deceased, or that they knew that the bumps from the coffin would probably result in her death"—surely?

Unless one believes in supernatural possession of inanimate objects (which I do not), what is the explanation? Either two of the men, in front or rear, or all four of them, were in league together, with the man in the crowd who shouted, and had combined to make an end of this unfortunate woman.

No-one did anything about Mayamba's death for some time : understandably it was a thing that was not broadcast. The Headman and his people said nothing. In the end it was reported almost casually to a Police Constable who happened to be on patrol in the area. One may well wonder how many similar cases occur which are not reported to anybody. Probably a considerable number.

The four men were lucky. The charge was reduced to manslaughter, three receiving eighteen months' and one, one year's imprisonment. The final remark of the Judge from the Bench deserved preserving in the treasury of judicial *dicta*.

"It was a pity," he said, "that after fifty years of administration the Government had not yet succeeded in abolishing witchcraft."—Not yet succeeded in abolishing witchcraft!

CHAPTER IV

FEDERATION—THE SHADOW
OVER THE SUN

A S late as 1951 we were still imperialists and we believed in the
benevolence and necessity of the British Empire, and in its in-
evitability. There seemed nothing to be ashamed of about it,
and no reason why it should not last for a hundred years. Too
young to have fought in the war, our generation had listened to
Churchill, and sought in peace the opportunity to justify our
generation. England was great, and she and Europe must unite!
Unite not only there; but in Africa also. With one gigantic heave
of the shoulders, and aided by the United States, Europe could
drag Africa to her feet, and bring her peoples to a rich and
honoured place in the modern world. Another new world to
redress the balance of the old, that was the vision, glimpsed far off,
and which we hoped might come to pass.

Instead Europe was too late, and lost the chance. The whole
Continent, even the French Community, was handled in terms
of petty national boundaries, minor accidents of history, and at
length abandoned to chance and fate by men too tired and timid
to do more than fumble and gesture at a fast vanishing audience.
Not a man, European or African, had the vision to see Africa
south of the Sahara as a gigantic entity, to be planned and
run, politically, economically and scientifically, as a gigantic
whole.

The Federation of Rhodesia and Nyasaland was proposed,
perhaps, as a tentative start in this direction. But through a life
of ten years it was still-born; first, because its true objects were
never allowed to be stated, and second, because it was built
upon a lie. It never lived, except as a dummy which highly respectable people said could walk and talk.

How intense African opposition was to it in 1951 was never

realized until too late. Even Kasempa and its council of vener-
able Headmen and greybeards living in the age of Queen Victoria; even Chief Sikufele, with his Lozi pride and background,
would have nothing to do with the thing from the first. We—
and I speak for the bulk of the Administration—felt contaminated
as, under orders, we put forward the official brief, or its advan-
tages. But it was as dishonest economically as it was politically.
It was often said that the reason why the idea of Federation did
not win support among the Africans was because the Provincial
Administration was, in the first instance, ordered to remain
neutral on the Scheme for Closer Association until the matter
had been debated and decided finally in England.

Opportunity was thus given to agitators to exploit this apparent
coldness, and to frighten away the Chiefs, Councillors and people,
from this all-benevolent scheme. Nothing could be more fallaci-
ous. Well before the instructions came to support the idea all
concerned were thoroughly frightened already. There was no
need for agitators to agitate or for malcontents to burrow underground : their work was already done for them, and by the
Scheme itself.

At tribal councils we would watch the sorrowful, bewildered
faces of the Chiefs, as they recalled treaties which they thought
their grandfathers had made with Queen Victoria—we would
watch their bewilderment as they saw men whom they respected
and revered advocating a course which went clean against the
instincts of them and their whole people—Clerk, Messenger,
Teacher and Villager alike. We felt unclean while this operation
was going forward, as though one had been telling a lie, and
what is more, caught out!

Finally in 1952 came the most foolish instruction of them all.
A circular advised D.C.s to tell Chiefs and their Councillors that
as Her Majesty the Queen thought it right for Federation to be
imposed, imposed it would be, despite the opposition or distrust
of all concerned. What happens, we asked each other in despera-
tion, if the Africans will not accept this circular in Her Majesty's
name? If written by an honest but antedeluvian die-hard such
things might be forgiven : but in fact in Northern Rhodesia some
of the most ardent protagonists of Federation became, when

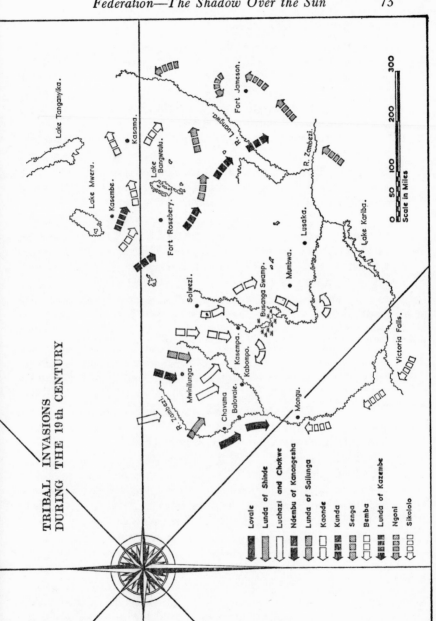

TRIBAL INVASIONS
DURING THE 19th CENTURY

Lovale
Lunda of Shinde
Luchazi and Chokwe
Ndembu of Kanongesha
Lunda of Sailunga
Kaonde
Kunda
Senga
Bemba
Lunda of Kazembe
Ngoni
Sikololo

the wind had changed, the most fulsome and infatuated supporters of Dr. Kaunda and U.N.I.P. So much for them.

In effect matters sank into an uneasy compromise between the Provincial Administration and the Chiefs and their people. Like members of a family, which they were, they agreed not to mention a subject which had become painful. After all, they had to live together and do their work together.

The Secretary of Native Affairs, Mr. Bush, a man of transparent honesty, in 1952 and 1953 went round Native Authorities to say that the Federation would be imposed, as being in the best interests of all the inhabitants of the territory, with an air, it seemed, of acute embarrassment. Equally embarrassed the Chiefs replied that they would never accept it, and that it was a betrayal of the protection that they desired under the Queen's Government, until, after many years, they would be fit to govern themselves. After a long hot day, and dinner, Mr. Bush would nod off in his armchair, as indeed he was entitled to do after nearly thirty years' service. Only to be awoken by a persistent cadet who must ask him : "Why—why—must we have Federation, and ruin the present happy friendship?" Instead of squashing the cadet by a curt answer, as he would have been fully entitled to do, this good man replied that if we did not federate with Southern Rhodesia, that colony would go bankrupt and amalgamate with South Africa. I have not the slightest doubt that Mr. Bush believed every word that he said, and that that was the guiding reason for Federation with officials at his level at that time : that if we did not do it, then even worse would befall.

The imposition of Federation, against the united opposition of the Chiefs and their people, marked the end of true partnership as an official policy, the end of honest trusteeship, and the beginning of distrust, suspicion, and double-talk. In 1953 the shadow of the Leader of the Un-officials, Mr. Welensky, hung over us all. Had he not wielded very great power as Director of Manpower during the war, and increased it ever since? The Chief Secretary would meet him at the airport when he returned to the country. Why? What good had he done to the Africans, what interest, even, did he take in them? His followers, "the settlers", or the non-Government Europeans, and the press, would often mention the idea of a Boston Tea Party. There were some who, if that ever came, were determineed to show that the idea was over one hundred and fifty years out of date.

The business of Government where two races are living together, is to govern without fear or favour to either of them. At that time it governed in fear of the European : but the Africans were very many. Where would it all end?

What began as a dispute within a family, the District Officers and the Chiefs and people, grew and grew. At the end of it both the Boma and the Chiefs were shorn of all power, and of all influence on events, while the representatives of the very worst elements of the people, more aggressive and without any principles except to attain power, clambered on their fellows' backs and proceeded to trample them underfoot. I repeat, the worst elements among the people.

Their leaders in the rural areas were court clerks and store capitaos convicted of fraud—school-teachers who had violated children—policemen convicted of corruption or brutality, and who had been discharged. And always the lunatic fringe, the psychopaths and chronic misfits in society, not actually certifiable, but on the boundary.

The first split was between the Chiefs and their people, mainly the younger generation of unemployed school leavers. There would in any case have been friction between them, but now the young men had a cause, an intolerable injustice had been inflicted. The young felt their future compromised. The unfortunate Chiefs knew that resistance to Government was useless. Two or three of the weaker Chiefs in Fort Rosebery, Senior Chief Milambo among them, had joined their people in a campaign of protest and violence.

Within a very short time the campaign was put down and the Chiefs deposed. Every Chief in the territory knew this, and now they bided their time. And meanwhile, despite the sense of betrayal that one and all must have felt, they clung to the loyalties that they knew, to the District Commissioners whom they trusted as the representatives of the British Government, the Queen's Government. The Federation, despite its Governors-General and its beating the Imperial drum, never commanded any loyalty of that sort. From the first it was to them a foreign imposition, the Government of Welensky.

The closer together in the hinterland that the two services worked, the better on the whole were their relations, though the Federal service was kept far tighter in hand by its political masters. They were instruments of Government policy and they knew it, while we, rightly or not, manufactured our own. Whitehall was distant, Salisbury quite near.

Federal political intentions were not always tactfully expressed, but the matter went much deeper than that. In essence it was the clash between the old patriotism and the new—between that of the Empire, and the Dominion making ready to replace it.

Europe in Africa, that was the romantic's dream, glimpsed afar off. Europe, benevolent, civilized, organized, spreading civilization in the frame of her gigantic plan—raising the people to the material standards of the twentieth century, instead of dying in their villages for lack of drugs, or their children from malnutrition. Retaining control, and an Empire more just, benevolent, liberal and splendid than anything seen since Rome—United Europe and the Federation of Africa—Africa fertilized by European genius, culture and technique. It was to Africa that we owed whatever was good in the traditions of Europe. Our tiny example, fallible as it was, scattered over thousands of people, was never enough. And besides, who "knew the African" after twenty years in the country? Already after thirteen years, we had lost touch with the younger generation. Africa is no remote intellectual abstraction, or a piece of machinery that can be taken to bits, but like ourselves, a vast collection of individuals with a few things in common. Dehumanizing our relations was the fatal thing. To regard fellow human beings as objects or counters—from there springs the fall of Empires!

Nor will the hat-raising, forelock-touching relationship between squire and tenant answer. One will die for one's tenant but will not have him to dinner. That equality is indefinitely postponed. It is a pastiche : personally it works, politically never. Real power must be shared, shared at the dinner-table, and even at breakfast if necessary. But at breakfast as we know it.

In Rhodesia the "settlers" and the "Fabians" were equally

perverse. Apart from the farmers the mass of the Europeans looked on the Africans as counters; useful, essential, but not human. But they would make a point of maudlin exceptions in individual cases. "My boss-boy"—"my old cook", and so on.

The Fabians, not often resident, looked on from afar with high condescension. They assuaged their guilt-complexes and aggression-complexes by proxy on the unfortunate inhabitants of the country. They gloated over bloodshed in print, as they still gloat today. Very often they pursued all unwittingly, but inflated with a vast intellectual conceit, the courses most likely to lead to it. Unfortunately the world has grown smaller, and it is a futile optimism that gives a continent freedom to misgovern itself, slaughter its own people, and spread its confusion in ever-widening circles. There is too much gunpowder lying about. Only the administrator can be judge, with his appreciation of the unchanging fallibility as well as the essential goodness of human nature. And the administrator is at a discount: for the expert in "local government" has ousted him.

For a little time it seemed that the Belgian Congo had begun to build upon the right foundations. The smell of the boulevards in Elizabethville, coffee and spices, and the sight of its many African citizens, well-dressed, happy and wealthy, gave one hope. It was in the Katanga that the prosperous middle-class had made the most progress. M. Moise Tshombe was one of them. Though he married the daughter of the Grand Chef, Mwatiamvwa, he was the son of a prosperous trader. Labour had long been stabilized: there were no humiliating and beastly racial restrictions. There were African doctors, technicians, bank-clerks, and the settlers, with their politics, were under strict control. There was strong official Catholic missionary activity—Christianity and colour in life—on a strong foundation of material well-being: all that was missing in the great godless city barracks further south. All seemed set fair for the future. Alas, the whole fabric, which appeared far stronger than our own, more assured, and with a much greater hold on the African's imagination, crumbled and broke down with terrifying speed into chaos, murder and rapine. It was no consolation that the Africans along the border were asking, years afterwards—"When are we going to finish with this independence—when is it going to end?"

What, during the years that Federation was in being, could possibly have led the British Civil Service, the fine flower of Winchester and New College, Oxford, into so gigantic a miscalculation, that it could begin to work against the unanimous opposition of the complete African population? One thing at least was clear; what we wrote in our reports had not the slightest effect on the policy of the British Government. But what were their motives, what false lights and wildly misleading beacons could have led them to the rocks? Why? Largely because they thought in terms of abstract concepts, not in terms of human beings.

First, the reason that good, honest Mr. Bush went about telling worried officers in the field: "If there was no Federation, Southern Rhodesia would go bankrupt and join South Africa." Dr. Malan on the Zambezi. Bad enough, but there were other means of preventing his arrival.

The second motive, "partnership", was an entirely worthy one. Most unfortunately, under Federation, it was never put into practice. If it had been, the story would have been different. Anyone who had seen at first hand the countless indignities and insults inflicted on the Africans in the Copperbelt in the Federation's heyday could never see it as other than a hollow sham in practice. The historic phrase coined by Sir Godfrey Huggins of the partnership of "the rider and the horse", typified the relationship.

The third reason was to build up a solid, loyal Dominion in the middle of Africa, as an example and a counter-balance to both South Africa and the West Coast. Had "partnership" ever been translated into fact and good-will, even after Federation had been imposed, that might with luck and will-power have been accomplished.

"Partnership" under Federation was a fraud. We had something different for our guide, the "paramountcy of native interests". This meant, not forcing the African into conflict with the European, and then over-riding him with a feeling of smug self-righteousness, but of avoiding conflict wherever possible. If interests clashed, then other things being equal, the interests of the African must prevail. They were, after all, there first. Yet there is a qualification here : the African was not thought to be the best judge of his own interests. The best judges were, let us be frank about it, the administrators on the spot, and ultimately, but very remotely, the Colonial Office. That, at the time and place, was logical and fair. It gave local District Officers a fierce sense of protection towards the Africans; "their people", who were not to be subjected to injustice or indignity.

Mr. Harry Franklin puts it well. He was a District Commissioner, Resident Magistrate and Director of Information, and the author of *Unholy Wedlock*, the story of the Federation's collapse : the inventor of the "saucepan-radio", a transistor wireless-set at a price—for the first time—within reach of the African's income.

"In the years following the war, the African began to feel that the power was passing from their friends and trusted leaders, the officers of the Colonial Service, to the European politicians led by Mr. Roy Welensky, who represented in the main the newer immigrants. The Africans regarded the new European political leaders and those whom they represented as people whose interests were inimical to their own. The Africans still did not lose trust in the good will of the Colonial Service official, but they began to lose faith in his power to retain political control, and with it the policy of the paramountcy of native interests. In the struggle of the new Europeans [Ed. 1946–1955] for power, the two leading politicians, Mr. Welensky said Sir Stewart Gore-Browne, who desired a rapid approach to self-government, conducted in pursuance of their political aims a policy of discrediting the Colonial administration. This increased African fears and quickened the growth of African nationalism."

Unfortunately Mr. Welensky never came within measurable distance of explaining himself, or Federation, to the African people. By the time he attempted to, it was far too late. But from beginning to end he remained an ogre, the Bad Fairy of the Africans' imagination. The policy of discrediting the Colonial Administration rebounded back on him. There was no officious rush to defend him, or Federation, when the subject came up in discussion. Why should there have been? It was a pity that many of us took his political rhetoric literally; but the Africans certainly did so. The price that he paid for reassuring his European voters was to frighten every African in the country.

The war of nerves to get the British Government to agree to Federation had begun in late 1947. It was followed in January 1948 by a threat by the Elected (European) members of the Legislative Council, to "paralyse the Government". This was a pronouncement of quite extraordinary foolishness, and the example was learnt, and followed, many times by Kaunda and U.N.I.P. in the years 1960–62. The difference lay in that Welensky's threat was ignored while Kaunda's was listened to. No Government run by determined men, and the field officers of the Colonial Service were such, permits itself to be "paralysed" by politicians.

The articulate sections of the African population, and more important at that time, the Chiefs with their people behind them, had for years opposed the amalgamation of Northern with Southern Rhodesia. The Bledisloe Commission had investigated as long ago as 1938, and found it even then too strong to be waved aside.

Now Federation was proposed, first by Welensky and the settlers, then by the British Government, as something quite different. It would be unfair to say that it was the same thing under a different name : but the ultimate object was indeed the same, the welding together of the two territories under "responsible" European Government, and the relief of Britain of her responsibility for the area. One would guess that at that time the hope was that such an arrangement would endure for fifty years. At all events, in explaining the Federal Scheme to the Africans, they did not, or would not, understand the distinction, and it is clear now that in essentials they were correct. And as they would say—even in remote Kabompo—if economic association and liaison is so very important, what was wrong with the Central African Council? A Common Services Union, on roughly the lines of the East African High Commission, could do all that was necessary.

It was no use Mr. Welensky saying in 1949 that the Africans' suspicion of Federation had been planted in their minds by the

Press, or by the Colonial officials, or by missionaries. But when, later that year, the Official Members (Government) of Legislative Council walked out of a debate on the subject, rather than vote, as Mr. Franklin puts it: "they shook the very foundation of African trust in them. . . ." "The Colonial officials, the Africans thought, either had not the strength to stand against the settler politicians or might even be in sympathy with them." "Defensive African politics were on the way, not to remain defensive for long."

About that time, we assisted in preparing "Defence Schemes", which even in that peaceful country, were brought up to date every ten years or so. The first question I asked then was naturally, "where is the enemy?" Were we to prepare for a Native Rebellion or a Settler Revolt? Would we be relieved in Kasempa (6 x .303's, 5 x Lee Metfords) by the Kaonde Levies, or the Chingola Rifles? In the event we prepared for both eventualities, but the emphasis was still much on the Native Rebellion, and we were considered too advanced in our thinking. In view of the seditious chatter about the Boston Tea Party in the press and on political platforms, all European, at the time, I doubt that we were.

In March, 1951 the officials' Report, a comparison of Native policy in Nyasaland, Northern and Southern Rhodesia was published. The officials were the three Secretaries of Native Affairs concerned, plus Mr. Arthur Benson, who later as Sir Arthur Benson became Governor of Northern Rhodesia, and did more than any other man before or since, for its peoples.

The officials were, and rightly, cautious and careful, and pointed out, in official phrases, the fundamental difference in the approach of Nyasaland and Northern Rhodesia to Southern Rhodesia. "Policy in the northern territories holds that in order to fit the African to take his place in the community as a full partner with citizens of a more ancient civilization he must be induced to play a full part in the politics and administration of his own area, and must play a direct part in the politics and administration of the whole territory. This is in the belief that without such political education there can be no assurance that the African would be able to play his full part in material and economic development."

"Policy in Southern Rhodesia holds that in order to fit the African to take his place in the community as a full partner with citizens of a more ancient civilization it is first necessary to make him the equal of his future partner in health, material well-being and education. This is in the belief that without such advancement there can be no assurance that he will be fit to play a full part in the politics and administration of the whole territory."

This was true enough : there had been Africans in the Legislative Council of Northern Rhodesia since 1948, Sir Godfrey Huggins expected to see them in Parliament in twenty-five years' time. Urban Native Courts had been hearing the vast bulk of the cases concerning Africans, according to Native Customary Law, since 1938. A delegation of high Southern Rhodesian officials, visiting Kitwe in 1956, were amazed to see this. They were astonished to see the courts functioning efficiently, without corruption or brutality, with proper records and the minimum of supervision, and commanding the complete acceptance of the thousands of Africans in the towns. I can still recall the look of wondering disbelief on their faces. Such cases in Southern Rhodesia were still heard before European magistrates or before unofficial compound elders. That was what the difference in approach meant at ground level. The African was not to be entrusted with responsibility until he had been brought up to European standards of living : and the economic obstacles to this for more than a few were insurmountable.

It is difficult now to recapture anything more than the memory of the indignation and dismay that we felt as Federation advanced from a politician's idea to an accomplished fact, with a capital, a Government, an army and a flag.

After the "Comparative Survey" had been published, a meeting of twenty-seven officials was held in March, 1951. Among them were the three Secretaries of Native Affairs and Mr. Benson. In turn their findings were called "The Report on Closer Association". Some stronger links than those formed by the Central Africa Council were thought essential. The shadow of South Africa hung over them. But African opposition to amalgamation was so strong that it was evident even in London. Finally they decided that such opposition might be overcome if a scheme could be designed containing adequate protection for African interests and providing the services affecting the daily life of the Africans were left outside the scope of a Federal Government.

Unfortunately it was not possible to give the Federal Government any additional powers to those already held by the Central Africa Council, and at the same time not to impinge upon their daily lives. Posts? Hospitals? Higher Education? Customs? What this meant on the ground at the time was not so much that the health and postal services degenerated, though the morale of Government servants received a shock, but that they marked time for several years. Development that might and should have taken place never did so. Gigantic sums were spent and impressive statistics broadcast, but what happened if a new Dispensary was needed in a remote rural District? The question was referred, after months of delay, to the Federal Ministry in Salisbury, where it took its place on a long list from all the three territories. It never seemed to reach the top. The Medical Assistants, one of the finest bodies of men in the Colonial Service, had their pay raised in terms of cash, but their conditions of service as a whole steadily worsened. Their *esprit de corps* was lost: they no longer had the feeling that they were part of a team with doctors that they had known for years. Those doctors had gone with the Colonial government and a cold alien organization, run remotely from afar, had taken its place. It is to their credit that they contrived to work on as they did—often fifty, sixty miles or more, not from a town—but even from a Boma. Unfortunately any Federal Government could not but affect the daily lives of the Africans: and as it did not produce results, and quickly, it served only to add fuel to their opposition.

After the Officials' Report had come out so strongly in favour of Closer Association only African opposition could stop it. At that time African opinion was unorganized, and basically it put its faith in the British Government to protect its interests. There was no thought of "non-violence", sabotage and the like because the authority of the British Government and its officials on the spot was unquestioned and seemingly inevitable as part of nature.

As the sun rose and set each day, so "Government" continued, all pervading.

At the Victoria Falls Conference in September, 1951 the British Government insisted upon three points. First, and most important, that Partnership should be defined. Then that African land rights, enshrined in Orders in Council and setting aside about 95 per cent of land for their use, should be protected, and that African political advance should be kept out of the hands of the Federal Government. This Conference achieved nothing. Partnership was never defined. Because of the fundamental difference in approach between the Colonial Office and the Southern Rhodesia Governments it could not be.

To the Colonial Office it meant that African political control was ultimately inevitable: to Sir Godfrey Huggins it meant the idea of equality in the remote future, but with control remaining in European hands. At the time Africans comprised but 2 per cent of the voters on the Roll in Southern Rhodesia: but it is fair to say that the voters in Northern Rhodesia numbered exactly eleven, and in Nyasaland, nil. Perhaps it is fair to say also that almost every paternalist official who cared for the Africans thought that they would be ready to take over and run their own affairs at the end of his own career.

The one safeguard proposed in the Officials' scheme which gave any confidence or hope to the officer in the field who saw, at first hand, how strong the African opposition had become, was the African Affairs Board. The Chairman of this Board would be a Minister in the Federal Cabinet appointed from among the members representing African interests in the Legislature. With him on this Board would sit three Secretaries for Native Affairs from the territories, with one elected member from each legislature and one African from each country. This strong Board would examine all legislation proposed and give its view of it to the Government, which in turn would pass it on to the Legislature. Should the Board formally object to legislation it could still be passed, but must be reserved for Her Majesty's pleasure, that is, referred to the Secretary of State for his approval. And unless he did approve it could not become law. That gave confidence.

A Board with our own Secretary of Native Affairs upon it

could never approve of anything dishonest or dishonourable, or anything against the true interests of the Africans. There would be no politics about it: if it was not right, it would not be approved. It was argued, and argued correctly, that if Federation came about, with this Board as part of it, the Africans in Southern Rhodesia would enjoy almost the same degree of protection as their fellows in the North.

In the event the African Affairs Board was emasculated at the next Conference in London, at Lancaster House, in 1953: it survived as a thing of no account. It had no power of direct reference to the Secretary of State: the Minister and the three Secretaries for Native Affairs were removed. In its final form it ceased to inspire any confidence and became part of a mere façade. On the one occasion that it was moved to protest later, in 1958, when the number of seats in the Federal Parliament was increased to the Africans' disadvantage, its representations were dismissed with a polite mumble.

In the end only one safeguard remained against, eventually, a complete "take-over" by the Federal Government of the whole machinery in the two Northern territories. It was a passage in the preamble to the Federation Constitution and it was of vital importance. It ran as follows:

"Northern Rhodesia and Nyasaland should continue, under the special protection of Her Majesty, to enjoy separate Governments for as long as their respective peoples so desire, the said Governments remaining responsible (subject to the ultimate authority of Her Majesty's Government in the United Kingdom) for, in particular, the control of land in those territories, and for the local and territorial political advancement of the peoples thereof.

"The association of the three territories in a Federation . . . would enable the Federation, when the inhabitants of the territories so desire, to go forward with confidence towards the attainment of full membership of the Commonwealth."

Those paragraphs were the key. They were insurmountable obstacles to the Federation attaining Dominion status without the agreement of the Africans, which would never be given.

At the height of the Federation's power, in 1957–58, the Federal lawyers dared to advance the argument that by "inhabitants" was meant only the representatives in the territorial and Federal Legislatures.

So Chief Kasempa, who ruled over 30,000 people, was not an "inhabitant"—nor old Chikulukumbwe who had been 2nd Messenger when Kasempa Boma began in 1901—nor Kasosa, the most loyal Messenger who ever served, nor Makyona Kanyakula, the young school-teacher with ideas (good, most of them), nor old Mpanga the cook, whose only reading, very slowly in his glasses, was the Bible, from beginning to end. These were not "inhabitants" in that view. Nor, I am glad to say, was I.

It is said that it was the "Imperialists" within the British Cabinet of 1953, Lords Salisbury and Swinton, Mr. Lyttelton (Lord Chandos) and Mr. Hopkinson (Lord Colyton), who "pushed through Federation".

Did these great men act as they did, with open eyes? I suggest that they were misled because their thinking was thirty years out of date, and in the press of great affairs overlooked that Africans, in any territory, were no longer as they were in their own youth, entirely composed of faithful Headmen, gunbearers, servants, with no contact with the outer world. There were many such— but there were many others, who looked forward, perfectly legitimately and peacefully, to a greater say in the conduct of their own affairs. They looked also to the Queen's protection to ensure in time that they obtained it. At that period they looked no further forward than that.

I am, and always have been, an Imperialist. And so I believe that the form of Government in Northern Rhodesia which prevailed before Federation, provided the best, the most painstaking and benevolent in the world, for all its lack of colour and imagination. Also the most honest. When the British Cabinet approved the Federal Scheme on 24 March, 1953 it was as though a great tree had fallen. True imperialism had crashed to the ground, to give place to something different. What it was time would tell, but it was not what we had known and served. Economics had been preferred to human beings.

Only the Paramount Chief of Barotseland was induced to consent to the Federation. The Governor, Sir Gilbert Rennie, is said to have flown to Mongu, and pressed the argument that as the Queen had agreed to Federation, the Chief should in loyalty agree also. To this intolerable argument the Paramount Chief gave way: there was no more loyal subject of the Queen in Northern Rhodesia.

It is certain that a Circular to this effect was sent to District Commissioners in rural Districts. I believe that the great majority had the tact and decency in the circumstances to refrain from publishing or even mentioning those offending documents. Besides it was the greatest gift to the really disloyal agitator that could be imagined. It could only have saddened the great majority of loyal Chiefs and Councillors, District Messengers and ex-askari, and last but not least, villagers.

The Crown still lived as a powerful force: after all, the Colonial Service were the "Queen's men", something very seldom mentioned but never forgotten. One of the first suggestions put to the Liberal Party when it was formed years later, on the suggestion of a District Officer, was an affirmation of loyalty to the Crown in its Constitution. I am glad to say that this suggestion was adopted. No other party, to my knowledge, thought it worthwhile to do so.

Resistance to Federation was at first ill-organized and futile. Mr. Nkumbula held a rally in Lusaka and ceremonially burned copies of the Federal White Paper. A handful of clerks and office boys sat down outside the Secretariat and refused to go to their work. They were disciplined, and properly so. These foolish antics gave little idea of the real strength of the opposition, which stayed in the hearts of the mass of law-abiding people. There is a school of thought, held by men of the highest standing, which sees the subsequent disorder, violence and murder in the territory as a struggle to be free of a dreadful yoke, unfortunately discredited by the acts of "scum which came bubbling to the surface", but which would be swept away by "good leaders" so soon as the yoke was removed. Unfortunately this theory ignores the time scale, and the six years of comparative tranquillity from 1953 to 1958. Opposition was always there, but it was latent and passive. It did not impinge on everyday life. It was the "froth" that saw the grievances of Federation (and there were many) as a road to power, and seized their opportunity, while the "good leaders" were, and still remain, submerged.

The imposition of the Federation gave a body-blow to the trust between the Colonial Service and the Chiefs and people. It was the task of all men of good will of both races to try to repair the damage. The communion, so tragically broken off between European and African, must be resumed.

Fortunately there were at hand two men of the highest imagination and ability. Mr. John Moffat, descended from Dr. Livingstone, and Mr. Harry Franklin, the leaders of the Liberal Party, and then representing African Interests in Legislative Council. They were both ex-District Commissioners and entirely honest. The result of their efforts was the Moffat Resolutions, passed unanimously by the Council, only Mr. John Gaunt dissenting. They were :

(1) The objective of policy in Northern Rhodesia must be to remove from each race the fear that the other might dominate for its own racial benefit and to move forward from the present system of racial representation in the territorial legislatures towards a franchise with no separate representation for the races.

(2) Until that objective can be fully achieved a period of transition will remain during which special arrangements in the Legislative and Executive Councils must continue to be made so as to ensure that no race can use either the preponderance of its numbers or its more advanced stage of development to dominate the other for its own racial benefit.

(3) During this period of transition, special legislation must be in force to protect, to the extent that it may be necessary, the interests of either race. Meanwhile this Council notes and agrees with the statement of the Secretary of State that it is the duty of Her Majesty's Government to ensure that on contentious issues the balance is fairly held.

(4) Every lawful inhabitant of Northern Rhodesia has the right to progress according to his character, qualifications, train-

ing, ability and industry, without distinction of race, colour
or creed.

These Resolutions were a hope, a beacon-light for the future,
by which the two races might have been guided towards living
together without fear, despite the Federation. Unfortunately they
became embalmed, and they remained only Resolutions. All the
same, how far would they get in the Legislative Assembly of the
new Zambia?

With Federation vanished the whole apparatus of the Federal
Government. In a few weeks it was swept into oblivion and forgotten. With it fell Sir Roy Welensky, a more attractive figure
in defeat than when he rode upon the crest.

Later, it was surprising to find in Southern Rhodesia people
who had believed in the Federation as a means of liberal advance
there; or at any rate as a means of preserving a just balance in
their own lifetime. Sir Roy was one of these.

Thus his fall had an element of pathos, like an old elephant
under the shots of an unskilled hunter. Central Africa was a
smaller place without him, with its politics carried on in a more
narrow way, and by smaller men.

Why did the Federation eventually collapse, almost it seemed
within a month? Briefly, because whatever the motives of those
who founded it, "partnership" was not honestly or decently
carried out in the interests of all the people. No-one would fight
for it; and no-one would die for it. Few, I believe, mourned it
when the end came.

CHAPTER V

KABOMPO—THE BAD RIVER

K ABOMPO was built in the centre of tribes that hated each other, and themselves. There was a peculiar atmosphere of violence that infected the place, born of the hatreds all around it. All were united only in their dislike of the ruling dynasty of Siku-fele. The lives and deaths of the aggressive immigrant tribes were horrid and brutish. Their social life was conducted on a cut-throat business basis even among members of the same family or clan. They were adepts at the illegal distilling of *Lituku* or *Kachi-pembe*, a fierce spirit which frequently drove them mad or killed them. One unfortunate creature nearly beat his way through the concrete floor of the gaol before he died in a delirium. Frightful murders would occur in the villages, seldom, if ever, brought to light. Women would commit suicide in hideous circumstances by the use of poisonous herbs upon themselves. It was a sinister place, and even the house had a ghost or spirit which would rattle door handles and windows with frantic energy, then vanish. It was said that the Boma was built over a graveyard, and always the dull ceaseless boom of the water over the rapids beat in upon one, even in sleep.

The bad atmosphere continued down the years. The old Chief Sikufele died, worn out, in 1958. His successor decided to in-augurate his reign by a visit to the Paramount Chief of Barotse-land. He was very quickly expelled by the immigrant tribes who came like hornets about his ears. His successor was a nephew of the old Chief, a gentleman, who—unknown in Kabompo Dis-trict—had once refused compensation when bitten in the leg by a dog belonging to a commoner, but of little force or fire, or intellect, or even cunning.

It was a typical hot afternoon near the end of the day's work in Kabompo. The D.C. and the D.O. had remained in the office as was the usual practice after the Clerks and District Messengers had gone off duty. Only one remained, the Duty Messenger for the night.

A routine case was brought in by a Chief's *kapasu* or Messenger: the man had been fined for refusing to send his son to school, where the teaching was in Lovale, not Lunda (the teaching language was always that of the majority of the people living round the school). Having refused to pay the fine he had been committed to prison.

He was a man of some stature, called Fumbello, who having served in the war in Burma, had returned to become a District Messenger and Driver. He was energetic but unstable, and he drank. Later, after his discharge, he had distinguished himself in saving the life of a Game Ranger who was being mauled by a lion in Mwinilunga, at the cost of injury to himself. At this time, however, he was unemployed.

At all events, he was not going to pay the fine: and so the D.C., who reviews all such cases, committed him to prison. Instead of proceeding there with the *kapasu*, Fumbello turned and walked out of the office. The Kabompo Messengers at that time were an undistinguished body, having been selected on a tribal basis and not on merit, and the man on duty did nothing. Having just committed a man to prison one looks remarkably foolish if one allows him to wander off to freedom, and in any event the D.C. was a believer in direct action.

He transferred himself from his judicial to his executive capacity and caught Fumbello by the arm. At this Fumbello pulled out a knife from beneath his shirt and stabbed the D.C. in an artery in his neck. He fell: and the D.O., coming up at a run to help, was stabbed also. The 2nd Messenger, Saini Chiyuka, who had lately been transferred from Mwinilunga, hearing the disturbance, came up from his house at the double. He was in time to receive a charge from a shot-gun at long range which stopped him; a pellet lodged at the top of his spine, and he died in hospital a few weeks later. He was a fellow Lunda with Fumbello, and a small, active, gallant man.

With the D.C. and D.O. lying bleeding, people began to run up, and Fumbello plunged down the steep bank of the river and swam across to the dense, uninhabited forest on the other bank. From there he made his escape, and for a while at least Kabompo was too preoccupied in helping the wounded for a search to be made.

After several weeks Fumbello was found by a patrol of Messengers just over the border in Portuguese territory. He must, it is apparent, have had help from the villagers to reach there : but few people in Kabompo would assist in arresting any fugitive from justice. They would be far more likely to aid him. The Messengers, led by another Lunda from Mwinilunga, Joseph Litwayi, stalked Fumbello, came up with him, and shot him while resisting arrest. His body was taken to Balovale Hospital, where great crowds of Lunda came to pay their respects. For a short time he became a kind of folk-hero, and a monument was erected in his honour. The D.C. and the D.O. both recovered, and continued their work.

This kind of purposeless tragedy illustrates the hatreds and feuds which torment the peoples of Kabompo District. Besides Fumbello it cost the life of one of the best of the Messengers in the North-Western Province; it could have cost two more. There can be little doubt that with the general loosening of all bonds of restraint and authority it will be repeated on a greater and more sinister scale.

No view was more welcome than the last of Kabompo Boma between the trees : and the blessed silence as one drew out of earshot of its dark and turbid river.

To return after nearly two years to a country where the Chiefs were respected, where the Headmen and people would greet one with decorous clapping, and the women run out to sing one into their villages, was indeed welcome. I felt that I had come home. Solwezi, though not Kasempa, was indeed Kaonde-land. The character of the people was more solid, more straightforward, more accessible : for a little while one was among friends.

The Kaonde there and at Kasempa are divided into family groups, or what might be called Totems (Mukoka). At first sight, they may not be taken to mean very much, especially now, in the days of aeroplanes, political parties and Youth Camps.

5. A Lunda Hunter, showing his gun, trophies and shrine.

6. *Le Grand Chef*: Paramount Chief Mwatiamvwa XIII.

The origin of the groups is uncertain, and it is likely that they began very simply as groups of people living together, a furtive, harried existence, often on the move, sometimes hiding in the caves and forests from Mbundu and Arab slave raiders.* Then, as life became more settled and people began to travel about, timidly at first, then undertaking longer journeys to visit relatives or to find work, it was found useful to have fellow-members of the group on whom one could call for assistance, for food, water, a fire and a hut on a cold night.

There are said to be over eighty different totems among the Kaonde but the more important are the:

BENA (TOTEM)

MUTEMBUSHI	...	LION
KYOWA	...	MUSHROOM
NGE	...	LEOPARD
BALONGA	...	RIVER-BED
MBUZHI	...	GOAT
MBWA	...	HUNTING-DOGS
MULEMBU	...	BEES
NGONI	...	BIRDS
LUWO	...	BABOONS
CHULU	...	ANT-HILLS
NZOVU	...	ELEPHANT

The Lunda Chiefs, Sailunga and Kanyama, who also are Bena-Ngoni (Birds), though they took little account of totems; while the Kunda ruling house of the Chiefs Nsefu are Bena Chulu (Anthills).

In olden times and to a lesser extent in the 1950's a traveller passing through a village could demand hospitality as a matter of right after making his totem known, and he would be treated as a friend. Food, a mat and a place to sleep were his after a long day, and it happened, a wife as well. But if he should abuse it by

---

* Modern research reveals that a proportion of the slaves sold at Charleston in the XVIIIth. century were from the N.W. Province in Tribal origin. The area was therefore the approximate meeting-place of the caravans from east and west, as I long suspected.

D

taking what was not his, the ordinary laws applied, and it was theft or adultery notwithstanding.

Harmless jokes would be exchanged between members of different totems in the right joking relationship, or *Bunungwe*. The Leopards joked with the Goats, for instance, and the Honey Birds with the Bees. The Leopard catches the goat, and the honey bird leads the hunter on to where the bees have their honey.

The Lunda had much the same custom, called *Muzenze* between themselves and the Ndembu, who live to the west of the Lunga River, while the Lunda are in the east. An Ndembu travelling among the Lunda could say all sorts of outrageous things, things that would have meant a certain "case" in his own village or area, without retribution of any kind.

However, this licence had in fact definite limits, limits which grew narrower. In 1959 a man from Sailunga crossed the river into Chief Chibwika's country, and reviled the Chief himself who was passing on his bicycle. He was arrested by a Kapasu and when he came to himself he pleaded *"Muzenze"*. His plea availed him nothing and he was sentenced to three months' imprisonment. With the increase in travel and politics it is probable that this custom will entirely die out. Politics are not funny.

The Kaonde have no inhibitions about eating the animal of their own totem, though they will refuse as a matter of ordinary custom the flesh of crocodiles, snakes and sometimes leopards. The totem is inherited always through the mother: and a man may not marry a girl of his own totem. This would be looked upon by right-thinking people as incest (*Kimalwa-malwa*) and punished accordingly in the courts. It is likely too that this will fall into dissuetude as the tribe both increases and grows more scattered. After all the relationship could well be so remote as not to matter, and when custom ceases to serve a sensible purpose it fades away.

Tucked away to the north-west of Solwezi District near the Mwinilunga/Congo Border and around the Jiundu swamp were the small sub-tribe of the Ba-Lubangu. Their Chief or Headman was a tall man with traces of the Arab, or it may be Wa-Tutsi, features that are seen also in the east of Mwinilunga. His people were the descendants of the outlaws, or tax-defaulters; anyone who had differences with the British or Congo Governments, and could manage to reach the refuge of the Jiundu Swamp was safe in the early days of the administration.

There they remained in their remote and forgotten corner until 1923. In September of that year the D.C., with Captain Graham and Mr. Ockenden of the Northern Rhodesia Police, "invaded" the Swamp successfully and made several arrests. The villagers' guns were seized and taken to Solwezi, only to be returned at the discretion of the D.C. From that time the villagers began to leave the middle of the swamp and live on its periphery. They were so slow-spoken as to be a joke with their neighbouring Ba-Kaonde and Lunda: talking with them was as though one were lost in the depths of south Devon in England two centuries ago, when men spoke far slower and with much elaboration. They were much given up to the weirder sects that have flourished in Africa —particularly the "Amboteka", an off-shoot of the Watchtower. They refuse all medicine, European or African, all meat, bananas, and all beer or even tea, and listen to lengthy sermons from their preacher who builds his shaky pulpit up a tree. An existence which must have few consolations, in this world at all events.

The Jiundu was a peaceful place, where the paths between the villages ran over tiny streamlets, with miniature bridges built by the local people. In great thickets of green trees the birds sang all day long, not just at sunrise; and the constant noise of the running water was pleasant to the ear.

Headman Kaindu sat in his village, a small, shady place, a man of importance in his own area, but with only about four males with him. He had his native ukelele beside him, and had been playing peacefully before we came up and put the village in a bustle of preparation. He was a powerful, bent figure sitting before me, with grey hair, and trusting, faithful eyes. The rigmarole of administration must first be gone through, perhaps the more thoroughly for all the temptation to sit and drowse the day away in that peaceful paradise.

But then: "Play to us, old man, we would like to hear you." Without a word he picked up his *Jinsense* and began. It was a high mournful lament of long ago, before the European had come, and his mother had been taken away into slavery by the Arabs, and his brother had died in the Congo. He knew that he would tempt us, the old man, and he did. It was over an hour before he had finished: and the other villages must wait until tomorrow. The Chief, Musele, a tiny, birdlike man, who had an absurdly elongated little-finger nail (for taking snuff), and I, rewarded the old man fittingly and departed. One felt in a medieval kingdom—that every day should be like this! The tiresome formalities of accounts, administration, roads, progress in general, should be abolished and extinguished forthwith, and we would sit for ever and a day, listening to the old man plucking at his single string.

All too soon the old man was to be supplanted by unemployed youths with guitars with naked women painted on them, singing debased songs which they did not even understand, without pleasure, decency, or tradition: and no doubt the old instrument thrown away on the rubbish heap. "Ye mid burn the old bass-viol that I set such value by."

But administration must continue. The Chief took me to see a man who lived, cut off from his fellows, in a hut within the shadow of two hills. He was something of a curiosity, the Chief said, for he appeared to be changing from a man into a woman: his relatives had deserted him and his wives had deserted him. Doubtless he was bewitched in some very powerful way: no such case had been known in the country before.

The unfortunate creature was cowering inside his dark hut. He had exhausted his savings on the witch-doctors, and all that he desired now was exemption from tax. I gladly made out the form. He would not come to hospital and I had no heart to make him. I doubt whether he lived very long. Interesting, to find in the middle of Africa, the self-same physiological change that brought such publicity to Roberta Cowell and to a number of other unfortunates.

The Jiundu is the last reported haunt of the pterodactyl, or *Kongomato* as the Kaonde call it. Melland relates how when he was there he learned from the Africans that this creature still existed. Its wing-span was four to seven feet across and its colour a dull red. Its body was covered with skin, not feathers, and in its beak were teeth. But one could not be sure of this, for no-one had seen a *Kongomato* and lived.

Mr. Melland sent for books that he had in his house, featuring prehistoric animals, and the Africans at once identified the pterodactyl as the *Kongomato*, without prompting—but had never seen any of the other creatures. But all knew what the *Kongomato* was like, though none had ever seen one. In his opinion the Jiundu swamp is a place where they might conceivably still exist, if anywhere. He pointed out that the area extends over fifty square miles, a high inland delta, interlaced with numerous small streams, many vanishing underground. The vegetation, thickets and trees, are dense and tangled, and the soil constantly wet, overlaid with decaying vegetation. African memory for things seen and experienced in those days was excellent; it is still good today. Melland believed, and stated in his book *In Witchbound Africa*, that the *Kongomato*—pterodactyl—or some such large reptile—existed recently, within living memory. He should not lightly be disregarded. In my brief stay there in 1952 I found the memory still alive among the older men, but no deaths from it had been reported for years. Melland reports the last case as in 1911 but states that the river where they were said to have been taken was in flood, and that there were no witnesses to the people's death. Two expeditions went to the Jiundu in the 1930's but they found no trace. So the mystery, and the opportunity, remains open.

My own belief after a brief visit to the country is similar to Melland's. I believe that some mysterious and unpleasant creature existed in the Jiundu within living memory when Melland wrote in 1922. To sceptics who laugh at any such idea I would simply extend an invitation to visit the Jiundu swamp. I do not believe that their scepticism would survive the journey.

Though the terrors of the living world are bad enough, the terrors of the dead are worse. *Kayewela* was, and is, the dread of the Kaonde: both in his village, and in the garishly lit towns of the Copperbelt, the horror and the possibility remains. What is a *Kayewela*? In a word it is the most horrid creature a Kaonde can conceive—of human shape, some three foot high with protruding stomach and legs turned backwards. These horrors do not range about freely, no, they are owned by people and they live outside the villages in the bush. In the middle of the night they creep into the village and visit their owners in secret.

So long as their owner treats them well they bring prosperity and good luck. The crops grow well, the shot goes home, and enemies die off one by one, while the owner and his family are protected. All is set fair : but the *Kayewela* are bloodthirsty and malevolent creatures. One day they wish to add to their number, and they set about doing so. With a hollow stalk of grass they creep up to a sleeping man and, placing it in his mouth, they suck out his breath. He dies, soon after, of illness. After the funeral the *Kayewela* return to the grave, and blow back his breath which they have sealed up in the stalk, into him. They rub him down and revive him with warm water, and he slowly emerges, like Frankenstein. But he emerges not as a man again but as a *Kayewela*, one of their own number. He joins them, and the three, banded together, go from strength to strength. The owner has now lost control, and is thoroughly frightened. He would get rid of them all if he could, but now, instead of being his servants, he is in their power. He can do nothing. . . .

At last the deaths around him grow too numerous, and his own immunity becomes sinister. His fellow-villagers will not look him in the eye, or greet him in the little hut in the centre of every village where the men gather in the evening. His wife hears whispers, not pleasant ones. At last he is called for divination : he makes no effort to escape as he might, but accepts it, like a man hypnotized. He knows his own guilt. The results of the test are adverse : and still acting like one in a trance, he is taken, and killed. His body is burned. A report is sent into the Boma. Regrettably "so-and-so" has died of a snake-bite, or been drowned in such and such a river in flood. Or it is simply reported on the next visit of the District Officer. "What did he die of ?" "Oh, stomach trouble." Or—"T.B." A row of faces, completely impassive, and a neat line is drawn through the name in the Tax Register. "Dead 1952, T.B. ?"

I do not write of the early days of the century, but of the present day.

In 1957–58 an outbreak of witch-finding took place in the

Kalabo District of Barotseland. Similar cases were brought in, some going back twenty years, when unfortunate women were burnt alive before large numbers of people. Now that village-to-village touring is no longer carried out by administrative officers from the Boma can it be believed that such cases are likely to decrease?

It was Mr. D. B. Hall, later Sir Douglas Hall, last Governor of British Somaliland, who was the real architect of the North Western Province. The old Kaonde-Lunda Province had been closed down in 1946, and the whole country attached to the territory of the Senior Provincial Commissioner in Ndola. He already had the Copperbelt and the Luapula Valley to look after, over 500,000 people, and the area could not receive the attention that it deserved.

At that time the Government had the very sensible policy of sending round experienced senior officers to take the pulse of the country, and report back to Lusaka. As a result of Mr. Hall's report he was sent back to Solwezi as Officer-in-Charge with the same powers as a Provincial Commissioner. He inherited a loose conglomeration of Districts and staff, neglected and in some disarray. Two years later he left a flourishing Province in its own right.

He was the ideal to all of us of what a District Officer should be. In appearance distinguished, his manner was exactly the same to junior clerks as to senior officers, always equable and courteous. Always he seemed in complete control of every aspect of the work, of every corner of the Province. His conduct of the office, so often neglected by the officers in the field, was meticulous: his personal approach always easy and cheerful. In all that he did or said, he was an example and a friend. By the pure force of his example he turned the Province from the backyard of the territory to an ornament of happy, peaceful progress.

Men like him built the territory of Northern Rhodesia over twenty-five years: it is only sad that they were not followed to the end by others of equal calibre. Under him the Boma, from Provincial Commissioner to cadet, clerk, District Messenger and Kapasu were a "band of brothers" as in Nelson's day. There was an ardour and spirit in the way they did their work never seen again. A posting to Lusaka was not an object of ambition, but the equivalent of being sent to the rear in the Army, or ashore in the Navy.

The ghost of a copper-mine stood on a high hill ten miles to the north of Solwezi. George Grey had discovered it, and years before it had been worked by the Kaonde under the Arab slave-traders. Heavy rough Maltese crosses of crude copper were still to be found in the villages: the price of a slave. The old workings stood abandoned, the shafts, on top of the hill from which one could see for miles, measureless, bottomless and full of water. Only the cemetery was kept up, with about twenty graves of all kinds of names, English, Greek, Norwegian, Afrikaner, who had almost all died of blackwater fever. In one corner a stone with plain "Matabele Boy" upon it. In the early days he had held the Mine together and died there with the others.

The Mine, though of particularly rich copper deposits, had died in the depression of the '30s. The cost of moving the un-refined ore was too great. The works closed and the employees scattered. All that were left were gigantic iron-wheeled steam engines used for hauling, abandoned by the side of the road. Like huge extinct animals they stood, rusted and inter-twined with creeper, the only memorial of European enterprise: and the re-minder, too, of how easily it can be forced into retreat in Africa.

Later in 1952, in a barrage of rumour and counter-rumour, the Mine re-opened. The shafts were cleared and great engines thundered night and day to pump the water away. Electric light was installed, new houses built, the road improved to Chingola. Then disaster struck. A hidden stream or river, of much larger proportions than was thought possible, was broken open. The waters flowed back into the Mine with an irresistible force. No-one was killed, but all was over within two hours. The shafts were closed, the engines taken away, and Kansanshi stood alone once more. Nature had won again: the place was left to ghosts.

Chief Mujimansofu, senior of the Kaonde Chiefs in Solwezi District, had been stricken by cancer while away on a course in

Lusaka. The doctors could do nothing for him: the disease had taken too firm a hold, and the poor man could no longer eat or swallow food. It is important for a Chief to die at his own village and so he returned there, to die. On his way through, the lorry which carried him stopped outside my house, and he lay on a mattress surrounded by a litter of crates and tins. He had left Solwezi as a fat, jolly man, but now no longer. Under a sheet of white calico lay a living skeleton, who had just strength to raise a claw, in greeting and farewell. I took it and held it as I knelt beside him. So he passed on his way to his fathers; the lorry driving on through the night reached his capital just in time, and within a few hours he was dead. He was uneducated in the sense of formal schooling, but before he succeeded he had seen the world outside his village in the towns, and he knew all about his people. He was jovial, shrewd and energetic, and his people missed him when he had gone; a good man, a typical Chief of his time.

When a Chief dies he is not buried in a grave by an anthill like an ordinary person, but placed in his own house. A *Chitala* or small hut or platform is constructed in the middle and the Chief's body placed on it, covered with clothes and blankets. The floor and walls of it are mudded and plastered and the house itself carefully closed up. When Chief Kapijimpanga Mandwe was buried, and he was a very powerful man, they placed a helmet on his head, and buried him in a sitting position. When the house has been sealed a white calico flag is attached to the roof: and so all remains until time crumbles the house and it falls. And it is the custom for such of the people as own guns to fire a last salute at the funeral. All then return, laughing and joking to shake off their gloom, and resume normal life. The *Muchinko* dance indeed, that follows the funeral, is so suggestive that it is a frequent cause of domestic strife and quarrel.

After the funeral a year or more may elapse before the appointment of a successor. This, unless some obvious man stands out, gives ample scope for discussion and intrigue until a general concensus of opinion is arrived at. There are usually a large number

D*

of younger brothers and maternal nephews (for succession is through the female line) who are eligible, and to be a Chief is the summit of a man's ambition. Too often when he succeeds, it proves to be a crown only of care. Some take to it as if born, but not many. As no Chief can be appointed without the formal approval of His Excellency the Governor it is the duty of the D.C. to be informed of how matters are going, and at many Bomas there are elaborate family trees, and lists of those who are in the right degree of family relationship.

But Government moves with discretion : it would not intervene unless some obviously unsuitable person were to be chosen —a drunkard, an adulterer, or a thief. The Chief often is the tribe in his person. He is the land : in him are all their fears and hopes : he is to every man what every man makes him, and what he makes himself. He is infinitely more than the elected chairman of a county council : he is the morning, the noon, and the night. He is youth, and age, and death. Though it is difficult to become an African in imagination and to "feel" him as they do, one quality they desire above all others. They desire a Chief of calm and equal temper who was the same yesterday as he will be to-morrow. They do not need necessarily a conqueror or a war-leader, but a pillar on whom they can lean, a rock to whom they can turn, and whom they may touch. He may be cheerful or morose by nature : but it is his sameness that they will value. It is easy enough to see the reason for this. The whole world, the crops—roads through the hunting forests—wells—dams—villages—government—new customs, and the respect due to age from youth—is changing at such a fast pace that the peoples need a landmark, something and someone who will not change, but like the vast majority of them will look all changes in the face with an unfrightened eye, and choose only the best of them for their people. This sufficiently explains the attitude of almost all the Chiefs to the new African political parties, until in the end they were shamefully abandoned and left to make what terms they could with the sweepings of their own tribe.

Under the circumspect eye of the Government the search for the right heir goes on. A word from the D.C. may put paid to an unsuitable candidate's chances, but that word is almost never spoken. Meanwhile, during a year or more, the Regent or *Mumbelunga* reigns, with all the respect and prerogatives of the Chief.

At last when there is general agreement on the man from among those eligible, the heir selected will send a present to his superior Chief. The Headmen of traditional importance, the bearers of historic names, the Mwanaute, the Commander of the Flank, the Mulopwe, the Commander of the Rear Guard, and the Mutonyi, and the men of weight and standing in the community are gathered, in outward amity at least. But first the heir must undergo a test. He goes, appropriately, to the hunt. If he has killed his predecessor by witchcraft or poison, or if he has slept secretly and adulterously with his wife, then he will kill a male animal. In that case his claim to the succession naturally falls to the ground, and the next heir undergoes the same test. Happily, there are very few instances of a prospective heir who has failed.

Now the female has been killed, all is plain sailing. There are no more obstacles in the way of installation. On the evening following the confirmation of the heir the meat from the animal is given to the people. That night the *Chibwankata*—who fulfils the function of the Archbishop of Canterbury—"catches" the heir and says to him: "You are the *Swanamumi*" (heir apparent), and places the leaf of the *mulembu* tree in his mouth. When this is done he is indeed the heir, and can succeed to his predecessor's widows. And a Chief, keeping proper state, will have at least three, often more.

On the following nights the wives are taken to the shelter where the heir is staying, with their gifts to him, such little things as beads or cloth. These are the *Via u Tuzhi* or the gifts of widowhood. They stay the night in the shelter with their new husband : and the senior wife co-habits with him. If she is too old, as well she may be, a younger and junior wife is chosen. The spirit of the dead Chief is released from them all by this co-habitation, and the older wives are permitted to return to their home villages. Those that stay rank in precedence above those already married to the heir.

The three stages of preparation for the heir are now complete. By the hunting test he has proved himself worthy : he has been hailed by the Chibwankata and given the leaf. Finally he has inherited all the widows. The stage is set for the public installation.

Each Chief has a Headman, traditionally known, who installs him. For Kasempa it is the Headman Kalela. In front of all the people he and his followers gather at the new Chief's house. He hands to the sister of the dead Chief—the Inamfumu—the insignia of office, the *lukanu* or metal bracelets, and a bell (*lubembu*), or a ceremonial gong of metal. Chibanza of Solwezi has the *Kalongo* or red feathers of a bird from the Congo, Kasempa *Mpande** shells in a circlet. The Inamfumu takes them and gives them to their heir, placing the bracelets on his arm, after which she takes two small iron hammers and strikes them together over his head as he sits. Then, in a form of anointing, she puts white powder, *mpemba*, in the centre of his chest and forehead. The new Chief is then installed.

Immediately this is done the new Chief takes over the goods of his predecessor, his blankets, his guns, his furniture. Still before the people the new Chief faces east, with the Mumbelunga, who has had custody, to the south facing his right side. He presents the goods to the Inamfumu, who hands them over to the new Chief. The ceremony is at an end.

The new Chief is now acclaimed by all the people. The women set up their own special noise, *Mikunda*, trilling, and cupping the hand over the mouth and quickly removing it. The gong is beaten, guns are fired off, the drums begin and the little children caper and dance about as the beer is brought out. Seated on a chair or stool, with his brothers by him on a mat, the new Chief receives the ceremonial hand-clappings of his more important men, then gives himself to rejoicing. The next morning begins a service, or servitude, which only ends when death or extreme old-age and infirmity remove him from the stool. By far the greater number die in harness. There is no leave for Chiefs, no comfortable retirement or pension scheme. There is never complete peace, or complete equilibrium. Always, Sundays and holidays, they are at the service of their people, the importunate, the poor relation, the man with a grievance from long ago. And as though this were

* These are round shells, white in colour, are known in Barotseland; and were awarded as insignia by Mushidi in the Congo.

not enough, the great changes from the outer world, and the steady lights which had guided them for over fifty years, flickering, and then fast dying away.

The whole ceremony is finally completed a few days later, when the new Chief and his Headman pay a visit to the important official who has installed him. With beating of drums and gongs they present him with a second gun, or in olden days a slave. Then the Chief's people come with their guns and pretend to fight the host's men. His people line up and hide him behind them, until the new Chief's brother comes up, presents them with beads, at which they draw aside. Further gifts are exchanged, and rejoicing follows. "Now do you become as big a Chief as I am," says the Headman to the new Chief, and the compact between them is sealed to their mutual satisfaction.

The abbreviated, and by Kaonde standards simple, family tree, will serve to illustrate some of the complexities in the succession to the Chieftainships. (See p. 106.)

It is easy to see from the chart overleaf how complex a succession to a chieftainship may become, and how far divorced is matrilineal succession from our own simple ideas of inheritance from father to son.

By the end of 1953 the accent was on development: and as always happens with a change in the form of Government, a good deal of money which had accumulated against a rainy day in the Treasury chests, was distributed around the country. A mechanical grader appeared in Solwezi, throwing up dense clouds of dust, but the road got better. The first motor-car, driven or piloted by the famous prospector, Raymond Brookes, had left Solwezi for Kasempa at 9.30 one morning in 1926. It had arrived at 6 p.m., eight and a half hours, while a man on a bicycle would have taken one and a half days, travelling as hard as he could go. Now it took four hours to travel the 120 miles, and in a few years more it would take three.

The District Commissioner, Mr. Fred Passmore, a kindly man who had spent over twenty years in the country, took the trouble to show me over my new house on my arrival from Kabompo. "You will like it here," he said, "and I am sure that you will be

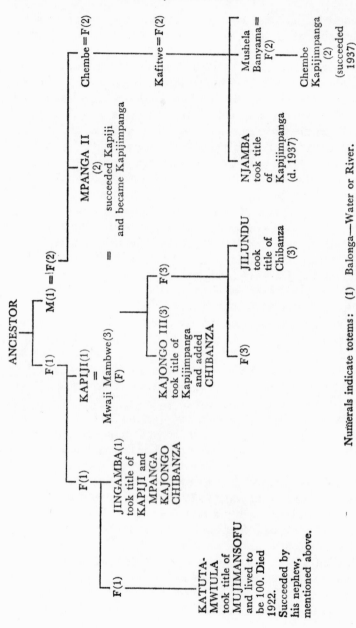

Numerals indicate totems: (1) Balonga—Water or River.
                           (2) Chulu—Anthill.
                           (3) Mutembushi—Lion.

comfortable," As he said this he tapped the top of the door frame with his hand. The whole frame fell away into powder round our heads, revealing a great honeycomb of white-ant passages. Progress had not yet achieved a universal triumph. Comfort was relative : but, after Kabompo, a tent would have done very well.

In Solwezi two Missions contended politely for spiritual mastery, the South African General, composed of non-conformists, and the Franciscan Fathers. The non-conformists, however one respected them personally, seemed slow, ill-organized, and dependent for doctrine on the vagaries of their own Biblical inspiration. The Catholics were a religious engine of tremendous power, well financed and with a discipline that demanded and received all. Even a man's personality must be trimmed to serve the needs of the Universal Church. Their leader, Father Bede, a missionary cast in heroic mould, may have been judged in this way. He was removed from Solwezi, and was sent to minister to the Indians in the deserts of New Mexico. Though the Catholic Church has the same methods of treating its servants as the Colonial Service, it has, it seems, an even greater scope.

To say good-bye to the Kaonde oneself was to leave one's own family. The inner world, so lonely and so desolate, had grown to be loved. For ever after one would feel a little lost in the towns, away from the villages and the Boma where one took one's own place, and however ineffective, misguided, and sometimes rashly self-confident, tried to help the people. To organize them perhaps, to push them on, to reward merit and punish crime, to resolve their quarrels, and at times to bandage their wounds. To build to last, and to enjoy what was true friendship with so many of them. Whatever else the Government was, it had no malice, no hatred, and in the field there were no ulterior motives. It strove only to do good, and to defend the right.

CHAPTER VI

COPPERBELT—THE MELTING POT

IT was as though on a Crusade that I arrived at Bancroft in 1954. Bancroft,* the newest and smallest copper-mining town, fourteen miles from Chingola, was the end of the line. At that time Africans and Europeans who did not fit, for one reason or another, into the larger towns, gravitated there, and there they stayed, free from direct Government administration, and from all supervision except by one European and six African police.

At that time, near the end of Sir Gilbert Rennie's tenure of office, there was a slackness and a lack of drive in the administration of the Copperbelt. A Provincial Commissioner, nearing retirement, and a poor D.C., had allowed themselves to be caught by surprise and, as a result, the Government found itself stared in the face by a sizeable town, composed largely of the most disorderly elements of the population of the Copperbelt. No Government facilities existed—no Boma—no school, no houses, clinics or even roads, which were not made by the Mine. Not even a flag. For all their fourteen miles from Chingola the people there might have been living in a foreign country. The Europeans were self-consciously tough: their women went about in stetson hats and leather trousers and talked of the rigours of living in the "bush". It was apparent that they had never been to Kabompo: they had electric light, a cinema and many other luxuries. But the magic distance of fourteen miles from Chingola gave many of them a freedom from civilized restraints which was an unfortunate example to the Africans living there.

They were of all tribes in the territory, with a strong contingent

* Or *Karilabombwe*—'the croaking place of frogs', as it is called under the new régime.

of Ma-Chusa from Tanganyika, and another of Kasai women from the Congo, whom I regret to say were almost all prostitutes. It was quickly clear that a proper administration was required.

A tent and a flag, the traditional apparatus, were acquired. Three Messengers, headed by Kasosa from Kasempa, and a District Officer, and the Boma was established. The condescension and patronage of some of the Mine officials was irritating, but it was appalling, after Kasempa, to see Africans who had never heard of a District Officer, or a District Messenger, and had no intention of beginning to listen to either. No doubt they had left their rural arears originally to be free of such irksome restrictions. But at Chingola all was *laissez-aller* and cynicism : after a little the Government party was withdrawn and only allowed up for fleeting visits. Bancroft continued for some time in the gloomy state of non-government, disorder and neglect. The Crusade ended in recrimination, a not uncommon end.

The Crusade at Bancroft had failed. The Boma had been established, but no more. At Chingola confusion prevailed, and odious family quarrels among members of the Provincial Administration. It was impossible to continue in such an atmosphere. Bancroft, that should have been called Fort Churchill in honour of the great man's eightieth birthday, was left to moulder, and I was transferred to Kitwe.

The Mining Companies, then as now, were veritable weathercocks. They were free with advice at both director and local level. They pictured themselves as tough, practical men only intent on getting the copper out of the ground : men with rolled-up sleeves and hairy chests, men who had come up the hard way, while University dilettantes fiddled with minor matters of administration. They failed to grasp that copper cannot be mined entirely by machine, and that they had to contend with great numbers of human beings, living close together, not scattered in villages, and fertile ground for new ideas, good or bad. Irascible and inflammable also.

Yet the Mine Personnel Branch was junior in status in their hierarchy, and thus, individuals apart, of poor quality. It was obligatory for its members to pass an examination in an African language, but few of them bothered to speak it. The use of an interpreter was standard practice, and as a result Mine Personnel Officers never thought in it. They seldom left their offices, and seemed largely concerned with the issue of boots, rations, and similar routine details with one or two exceptions, their distance from the ordinary worker was measureless, their interest in him, minimal. Once the miner's material needs were met, in the form of food, pay, medical attention (good), cinemas, the Company was satisfied. The Churches, or the welfare workers, or anyone, could take care of the rest.

Of course it was the African Mineworkers' Trade Union that did so, and its hold on the loyalty of the vast majority of its members became absolute. Loyalty to the Company there was none : the Company had treated them as machines, as fodder, not as human beings.

The Companies lacked the courage to introduce an outright paternalist policy, with tribal compounds and a tribal background, as in South Africa. The experts proclaimed that this would cause more trouble than it prevented. Judging from the years 1954–57 it is hard to believe so.

Such was the power of the European Mineworkers' Trade Union, covertly backed by the United Federal Party, that for years, until the late 1950's, they were able to blockade any substantial industrial advancement by the African. So, while their policy remained in a state of uneasy suspense, or rather non-existence, the Companies laid out hundreds of thousands of pounds on football stadiums, beer-halls, and more useful, hospitals. But they lost the Africans as human beings. A good master knows his servant. They had no idea about theirs. The Trade Union had them in its hand. As has been said, "there is nothing so timid as a million dollars" : and I would add, nothing so obtuse. In the ordinary way this would not have mattered, might indeed have been fitting even. Unfortunately the Mineworkers' Union at that time had become the prey of adventurers and demagogues who had never worked there. Accounts were in complete disorder or never kept, funds vanished and kept on vanishing. Such a situation could have but one result, a series of strikes, not for a good cause such as African advancement, but for a series of ridiculous minor ones, such as the compulsory wearing of leggings. These duly occurred.

But the Union had one great leader, possibly the greatest African that Northern Rhodesia has produced, Lawrence Chola Katilungu. He was my friend: to him I was *Bashampundu*, the "father of twins" in Ci-Bemba; to me he was *Chola*, which means the third child who follows twins. He was a man apart, almost alone. He was sufficiently intelligent to see far ahead, when the African would inevitably be given his chance in industry and education: in addition he had few illusions either about his Council or his rank and file. Closely allied to the Paramount Chief Chitimukulu of the Bemba, he regretted the laxity and disrespect of the Mine Compounds, and the divorce of the people from the good habits of the villages—politeness, respect for authority, care for one's family and loyalty to one's Chief and tribe. Yet, surrounded as he was then by worthless men, he had to move with care. Often, when a crisis approached, he would be found to be away at an important gathering of International Trade Unionists, in Paris, or Stockholm, or Brussels. He was the most human of men—his failings also were human enough. He was a big burly man, of fine presence. He laughed often; and most often at himself. His death in a motor accident in the late '50's was a tragedy: he could have been Prime Minister, and a great one. With his death and the exile of Tshombe passed two of Africa's greatest men, both related to and in sympathy with the Chiefs, and big enough to reconcile the best of the old world with the good in the new—not merely mountebanks swept along by forces they could not control.

Early in 1955 the African Mineworkers came out for the first time. All had expected the strike: none had made preparation for it. The wiseacres, who had been in the Mine for twenty years, were confident that the Ma-Chusa from Tanganyika would never join. They disliked the Bemba, it was said. They struck to a man. Not only did they strike, but they were among the most enthusiastic of its supporters. Since no-one in either Mine Personnel or the Boma could speak a word of their language it was completely impossible to approach them. Hunger too, said the experts, would drive the workers back. On the contrary the Union, financed by the Mineworkers' Union of Great Britain, gave evidence of remarkable powers of organization in distributing free food. To their chagrin the Mine Companies saw lorry loads of meal being brought into the Compound and served out by the enthusiastic Union officials to enthusiastic strikers.

The whole influence of Government was thrown into the scale against the Union, and in vain. Repeated advice from the Labour Department was spurned. Once people are on strike they acquire an obstinate frame of mind and a feeling of solidarity, and are doubly difficult to shift. District Officers and District Commissioners were drafted in from the outstations, together with the Messengers. They spoke to the men from their own Districts, as we did, in terms of the village. The Government wished them to return to work, while their leaders negotiated. Therefore they should do so.

All in vain. Like a soap box orator, with a couple of Messengers in attendance, one would call: "To me, Ba-Kaonde, hear me now." They would gather round, laughing, smoking, talking, a very different attitude from the respectful attention of the village. One would be heard, but with no effect. No-one would return, and after a week this had become apparent. It made one think: indeed it made Government think. Once in the Mine the men would obey their Trade Union, rather than their own District Officers and Messengers, often well-known to them.

The Mine Companies determined at first to take a strong line, "signed off" the strikers in their books and in the men's Identity Cards, which meant that they were no longer in employment. Under the legislation of the time if they were no longer employees they were no longer entitled to Company housing, or indeed to be within the Mine Compounds at all. Eviction was therefore the logical and final step, but both Government and the Companies shrank from it. Yet it was the only course of action that could have broken the strike. A different section of the Compound could have been wired off daily, and strong forces of Police posted round. The families within could have been ejected as trespassers and they would have billeted themselves on their relatives. The initiative would have been regained over

the Union, and no section of the strikers would have felt safe. I
do not necessarily advocate this strong, even brutal, course of
action, yet it is the only one which would have caused the strike
to collapse. Trade Union solidarity, which withstood the pressure of short funds and general disapproval, could have crumbled
under the inconvenience of doubling up in quarters already full
to capacity.

The strikers struck for more money, but also for something
more : they had a general feeling that, although they were paid
more than other Africans, they were second-class citizens of their
own country. Although it was suspected, they were not Communists, nor had the Trade Union officials the slightest understanding of what Communism meant.

After all, Will Lawther was their mentor, Professor Tawney
was their landmark, and they went no further. What, fundamentally, they protested against was that they could not go and
drink in a bar of a hotel in Kitwe. They would have been ejected
at once. If they went to a shop, well-dressed and respectable, to
spend their money, they would either be ignored by the female
European shop-assistants, and left to stand about, or told, in
abrupt and discourteous tones, to go round to the hatch (reserved
for Africans), at the rear of the shop, leading off a lane filled with
rubbish and filth.

I remember Lawrence Katilungu coming to me in a rage on a
Saturday morning because his wife, who had a baby on her back,
had been refused service at the butchers. The man or woman
behind the counter had said that she might begin to suckle the
baby at any moment, and told her to leave.

Fortunately at that time Mr. Katilungu's position was sufficient
to reduce the butcher very quickly to more civilized behaviour,
but there must have been many others who suffered comparable
humiliation and who never complained. I cannot wonder that
when the time came for Europeans to offer friendship and real
equality, it was rejected except on terms of African superiority.
Nor could an African at that time obtain a gun, unless he had
served for over twenty years with a blameless record : even then
there was a quota, and that quota was too often full up. European youths, working in the Mines, aged 19 or 20 and earning up

to £2,000 a year, would come in and licence their rifles without difficulty. The African, who had worked for twenty years and earned, say, £350 a year, would have the very greatest difficulty. The Mining "camps" in the late 1950's were certainly a European's world. To own a shotgun when he returned to his village from the Mines was the thing nearest to the African's heart. It was more than a weapon, it was a "status symbol" which marked him above and apart from his fellows. Too often it had to be refused on the ground that the quota was full, or that he had been away from his village for so long that his Chief had forgotten who he was, and gave only a tepid recommendation.

As for a rifle, it was beyond the scope of imagination of most Africans; later, in 1961 a start was made and a few permits were given out. This was one of the points where the Provincial Administration failed to measure African opinion. Faithful servants of the Government of up to thirty years' service were refused, while European youths of very little merit were permitted freely.

Almost every European on the Copperbelt kept his dog, or a number of them. They were badly trained, or worse, trained deliberately to bite Africans. In 1954–55 there was no redress for an African who had been bitten even on the public highway, no redress that is, apart from a dab of iodine from the Police. However the number of such cases grew so large that some action became imperative.

The dog-owners were summoned to the Boma and forced to disgorge, not much, but even a little helped. A list was kept and the more vicious dogs were destroyed. Great was the outcry at the time. "Even one's dog wasn't allowed to bite a Kaffir. It was a free country wasn't it?" At last a courageous Magistrate gave a ruling in court, and large numbers of European-owned dogs were either controlled by their owners or were destroyed.

Cases would occur also, tragic cases, when a European motorist, by accident, knocked over and injured or killed an African cyclist or pedestrian. In a large city such cases were fairly frequent. However it often happened that the Police, uncertain whom to blame, would refuse to prosecute the motorist. The insurance companies would then evade liability by standing on the letter of the English common-law, and as their client was not held to blame they would refuse to pay.

As the essence of African customary law is the payment of compensation to the person who is injured, whatever the rights and wrongs of the matter, this led to much bitterness and mis-understanding. In fact it was rank injustice that should have been corrected by legislation, but it was not. Month after month, year after year went by, and nothing done.

All this, and the normal accidents of life as well, was blamed by the people on the Federation, and to a lesser degree on the Northern Rhodesian Government. "Government", to African eyes, was still all-powerful. Why then did it not act to remedy the crying abuses and humiliations of the Copperbelt at that time? Had it become old and weak, or corrupt? What could an African do? On the Mine he had the Trade Union, which was militant enough : but outside that, nothing. No doubt, in the Compounds, the African National Congress made deep inroads underground, though to be a member was then to be a marked man.

The European Mineworkers, at that time, were enjoying a Copper bonus of over 100 per cent, that is, over double their mine salary, and which often, for mere routine jobs, totalled two, three or four hundred pounds every month. Unfortunately this privilege did not extend to servants of Government! And as two or three firms had been granted a monopoly of trade as an in-ducement in the 1930's, they could raise their prices without fear of competition. They did so.

Perhaps this only added an edge, if that were possible, to our sympathy with the broad mass of the Africans. We were in a sense, in the same position—the under-privileged, the under-dogs.

Kitwe was then the centre of the Copperbelt, and had at least eighty thousand African inhabitants, the Europeans about ten thousand. Line after line of neat little houses stretched as far as the eye could see in Wusakili and Mindola on the Mine. Their administration I have described : it was not enough. The Union had the workers in their grip, and the Union was irresponsible, mal-administered and full of anti-European, and of anti-Government animus. Week after week the workers were filled with hatred against the system for which they worked, in public assemblies, in the great, disgusting barrack-like beer-halls, in their houses. The Union was at that time the focus of all discontent against the Government, much of it justified on grounds of discrimination, but much of it made up of self-interest and self-glorification on the part of the Union leaders.

If one caught them "off-duty", Nkholoma, Chindele, Namitengo, and the rest, they would laughingly come to terms. And they were often "off-duty". But "on-duty" they were the embodiment of all the hatreds and frustrations (and terror of separation from the family and tribe) that modern industrial life had raised up. They were nothing in themselves, but formidable in all that they represented. How to break the grip of the Trade Union on the workers, that was the question. I could gauge the atmosphere on the Mine by the weekly tax collection. A great crocodile of people, many of whom had already visited the beer-halls, would collect their pay at a hatch-way, and file past the waiting tax-collector clerks, reinforced by half a dozen District Messengers. Most would pay willingly enough, or show their receipts, but a few would try to shoulder or elbow past to the Union office.

The Messengers would take them gently by the arm and guide them back. Often there would be two or three fights in an afternoon, but in almost all cases the Messengers would be too much for their man. Only in one case do I remember a tax-payer getting clean away, with swerves that would have done him credit at Twickenham if he had had a rugger ball in his hand. Sometimes the other workers would be on the verge of joining in to help, or to rush the barrier of Messengers, which they could do easily. More often they would be simply passive, as the great mass of people are all over the world, not looking for trouble but willing to submit to what is apparently the greatest force on the ground. Ours was transparent bluff, but as far as it went, it served. Tax was collected, just: the outward and visible sign that the power of Government prevailed.*

* Government tax, the Poll Tax, was the successor of the tribute that the people paid their Chiefs in pre-European times. The greater proportion of it was repaid to the rural Native Authorities.

But, how to break the grip of the Union? It was clear, since 1955, that tribalism was not enough. Trade Union solidarity was real. Nor would the Mining Companies divide up the Compounds into tribes. What was needed were centres of Government influence, sub-Bomas, in the middle of the Compounds themselves. An excellent idea, but with but two District Officers impossible to man them. Simply an African clerk was no good: he could be overborne. And in the evening and at night, when the bulk of African workers were off-duty and might have come to talk, the District Officer and the Messengers were off-duty as well. So this experiment, conceived on the most correct lines, had little effect.

Then, the rural Chiefs were mobilized. It was thought that if the older and more conservative workers received visits from them, another focus of loyalty would be created in the Compounds, and that the men would be less likely to strike for the sake of a minor grievance thought up perhaps as an act of policy by the Union leaders in one of their week-end speeches. There were plenty of major grievances awaiting remedy without these distractions. So for fourteen days each a succession of the major Chiefs of the territory, accompanied by the District Officer, visited the Mines and talked and listened to their own people. They did their best, and even had some effect upon the more mature among their people. But these were in a minority, and it was a strange and different world that they entered. Fourteen days was not enough, and their people were scattered in hundreds, thousands, of houses. As the Companies would not, dared not, divide their townships into tribes they had in fact little effect. Was it even right to try to break the grip of the Union? At that time it was.

The Union had excessive power. At the whim of a completely irresponsible clique it could halt the production of the country's main wealth, the taxation upon which provided for the greatest amount of funds for rural development, for all the amenities, not to say the necessities, that the rural Districts lacked. When one thought of the hungry children in Kasempa, or the old people dying without cause for lack of medicine, I had no scruple about undermining them in every possible way, and I became impatient for the day when the Government would at last decide that their teeth must be drawn.

Besides, at that time, the village, the Chief and the tribe was the focus of loyalty to the people. A grown-up man who had been born on the Copperbelt and had never known his village, was a curiosity, a phenomenon almost. Poor man, what he had missed, to grow up in a purely materialist atmosphere from birth! But the great majority were adrift in a new world, a mechanical world of industrial revolution, a world far removed from the village. That world was a cruel world, sometimes perilous, and the life was hard: but it had its affections and kindnesses, it certainties even. The Chief and the Boma were first of these. Can it be wondered then, that we sought to break the power of the Union over the people's hearts and minds, and to substitute our influence for their's?

In charge at Kitwe for years before, and for years after, was John Bentley, D.C. Stiff, formal, upright and unapproachable, a cartoon figure almost. When he made a joke, and this occurred once or twice a year, the earth shook, then remained still for a second, before his audience broke into delighted laughter. Every day he was there, punctual to the minute, ready for anything that might, or could, happen. No crisis found him unprepared, he was always on duty, always at his post, calm and unruffled. He did not pretend to any great intellectual ability, but he was there, and always the same. The Africans admired him, and as the years went by and he was still there, a little greyer, they came to love him. He was a man who was always on duty, because he lived for his work, and for his people.

At the Boma an African could always get a hearing, something which at that time he could get hardly anywhere else. He could get a hearing, too, in his own language, and in a court to which he was used, being based on his Chief's courts at home. Not many Solicitors and Resident Magistrates were interested in African cases: solicitors at that time because Africans could not pay their fees: magistrates because they wandered and rambled far from what seemed to them to be the point, and because no interesting points of law were involved. So they came to the

Boma, where Assessors from their own tribes dispensed justice according to customary law with decorum and equity, and at very low fees.

Each case was reviewed by a District Officer, and out of some two thousand or more every year the average number of appeals was under twenty. The fiercest of the Trade Union leaders at the time, Matthew Nkoloma, recognizing what a weapon the administration of justice was in our hands, himself stated that he could find nothing to complain of in the conduct of the courts. At that time this was a rare tribute.

The professional Magistrates then were touchy about their prerogatives, perhaps realizing how their own work was dwarfed by that of the Urban Courts under the control of District Officers. No District Officer could adjudicate a lunatic, of whom there seemed a great number wandering at large. One of these nuisances started a disturbance outside the Boma one day, and all that could be done was to commit him to prison for a brief interval until he calmed down. The local hospital wisely refused to have anything to do with him, and the Magistrates were already in court.

For this I was rebuked, which I received with a becoming humility: but I did wait for the next lunatic. He came soon enough—the Boma attracted them like a magnet—gnashing and straining at a pair of handcuffs which had been forced on after a struggle. I ascertained that the particular Magistrate was on the Bench. I regretted that I had no jurisdiction in the matter, and forwarded the lunatic with his large and by this time excited escort, to his court. I received no more complaints: it was even intimated that the Magistrate would be grateful to be saved the inconvenience of having his court cast into uproar by whatever action the District Officer might think necessary.

It was appropriate at that time to tour the town and Mine Compounds by bicycle, accompanied by two or three Messengers and dressed in khaki. Even if people took no notice it served to remind them of the Boma and the Government. We were, after all, the "Queen's men" and if we chose to be a little old-fashioned, perhaps it was fitting. It was the sight that the people were used to in the villages. Besides, we could take the temperature as we rode along, and enter to some extent into the African's feelings as we were borne over to the side of the road by a succession of badly driven motor-cars coming up behind us. The Africans had no cars, or, if they did, they were crazy second-hand models sold without warranty. "Caveat emptor"—let the buyer beware—was the rule, and it was a rule that the African found hard to understand in such cases.

In 1956 the hot season began particularly early, on August 2nd, a full six weeks in advance, and it never let up. By the time people with their cases reached the Boma they were usually in a very bad humour with each other. Cases between the races, the most difficult and unpleasant to handle, began to increase, as always in the hot season. A European woman, well known in the town, committed suicide by shooting herself outside the Boma. A lovers' quarrel had led to her shooting her friend in the stomach in his office. Convinced that she had killed him, she turned her pistol on herself. There was a loud report nearby.

The Messenger, in the middle of the case said :

"Bwana, someone has shot himself."

"Nonsense, a car back-fired."

But it had not, and there was a thunder of feet as hundreds of Africans ran to investigate this extraordinary thing. It was indeed true, and nothing could be done for that unfortunate woman. Her lover, happily, recovered. This incident marked the beginning of a particularly trying period. The heat continued and tempers among both races grew sharper. The local newspaper printed a headline saying that all Europeans were permitted to carry fire-arms, which they were not, with the strong implication that they should use them if necessary. Squabbles and brawling increased at the Beer Hall, always a good barometer of trouble. A small riot occurred, dispersed by the Police with a fine display of pyrotechnics. I happened to be present when a man who had been hiding in a ditch climbed out bewildered by the smoke and noise, in the middle of the Police. He received a swing which went off like a report, from an open hand, on the side of his head. I was moved to protest, and the Officer in Charge checked the Constable. It is difficult to protest in such cases, surrounded by excited men, but it is one's duty to do so when the man is defenceless and is either a prisoner or a bewildered spectator.

The Mineworkers' Union chose this time to call a series of what they called "rolling strikes" for trivial causes in one Mine after another on the Copperbelt. Lawrence Katilungu was away, some said in Brussels, others, Stockholm. The other leaders had become the slaves of their own rhetoric. Even if they had wanted to go back they could not now : they were as corks tossed on the top of the wave. If they retreated they would become the laughing stock of the Compounds, or worse, the target of the undefined discontents of thousands of miners whom they had worked up into a high state of irritation. The Union leaders had no objective, or none at least that could be reduced to coherent terms. As they strutted from town to town and from Conference to Conference it became apparent to all who saw them that their sole object now was to display their power, and to proclaim that they, not the Mining Companies, nor the Government, held control of the workers. Stories of beatings and night visits to houses began to come in.

The Provincial Commissioner on the Copperbelt at that time, a man of great determination, G. S. Jones, who was later Governor of Nyasaland, had been present at Luanshya in the disturbances of 1935. Then the Police had had to open fire, and he had distinguished himself both beforehand and after the shooting, by walking about among the Miners, and by helping the wounded. He was able to convince the centre of Government at Lusaka that a dangerous situation was building up as minor incidents grew. He feared that if it grew worse a similar incident, arising out of small beginnings, would occur. He was helped by the presence of an acting Governor who had been D.C. Kitwe for seven years, and who knew the people and the ground. We were fortunate.

Meanwhile the strain on the Boma became very great : calm and conciliation became an overtime job, and at times it was difficult to make one's limbs answer the commands of the brain, to wash, to walk about, to eat.

It is always difficult for Government to gauge exactly when a dangerous situation must be faced and tackled to save it from growing worse. To us, on the ground, the danger-point had long been passed by the beginning of September, and we began to wonder how long the situation could continue without an explosion. Unfortunately the Government decided to take Mine Managers into their confidence and to tell them their plans, without properly covering the security of the operations planned. The Mine Managers told their subordinate staff, and soon the Personnel Offices were a-buzz with rumours, founded on all too solid fact. I felt a sense of shock when a subordinate official told me that the Mineworkers' leaders would be arrested, and even the code-word which would give the signal. In fairness, however, it may be said that there was so little contact between them and the Africans that none of their leaders had an inkling of what would happen. They had worked themselves into such a state of power-hysteria that they could not believe that Government would dare to touch them. This was not the case.

As usual on these occasions the code-word was given out, cancelled, and two hours later given out again. In accordance with plans already made we went with a strong Police escort to arrest Matthew de Luxe Nkholoma at midnight. He had built himself, and been built up, into such a figure that all half-expected armed resistance. In fact he was sound asleep in bed, and appeared a different, a frightened and forlorn figure, in his dressing-gown by the light of torches. The house was of course surrounded. It was very small, and crowded with bulky furniture.

As always one was sorry for the man at the moment of his disaster : after all I had known him quite well. There was no real animus in his character towards Europeans. He was a round, bouncy little man. He had an impertinent tongue and almost boundless self-esteem—not founded upon just and right. Indeed, he was good for us, though we did not realize this at the time. His crime, or at any rate the cause of his arrest and removal from the scene, was that he had unloosed forces he could not control. He was before his time : today he would be Prime Minister.

So he was led away to detention and in due course to trial. The search of his papers and documents began. What a disappointment! Instead of the Communist Manifesto, Professor Tawney. The worst that we could find was Hewlett Johnson's

Socialist Sixth of the World. If there were secret instructions from Moscow, they were kept elsewhere. Besides which, every room was hung round with oleographs of the saints and the Virgin Mary: not a convincing background.

Some two hours later we returned to the Police headquarters with two suitcases full of documents. So far as an arrest and search can ever be a friendly proceeding, this had been. I believe myself that Matthew Nkholoma was secretly glad to be arrested and removed from the scene. Whatever happened now, the responsibility would not be his. Irresponsible as he was, he had begun to fear the forces that he had set in motion, the huge masses of the mineworkers all over the Copperbelt, all their frustrations, and their buried dislike of modern European industrial society, which had seduced them from their villages and treated them as part of a machine. He dared not go back now: he could only go forward. And he feared what would happen when he did.

When Matthew Nkholoma had been removed, and his fellow Union leaders all over the Copperbelt, the night's work continued. Clerks and Messengers had to be roused out and gathered at the Boma. Violence was expected in the Compounds when the men heard that their leaders had been arrested. Strong patrols of Police were maintained and relief D.O.s and District Messengers were hurried in from remote rural Districts.

At first light, armed with powerful speaking trumpet and accompanied by a Clerk and District Messenger (an ex-askari* sergeant), we made the proclamation around the Compound. We told the people that the Union leaders had been arrested by the Government, which had reasserted its power in the Mines, and that all should return to work without delay. If we had expected stones, or abuse, there was none.

But Nkholoma's removal struck home at the men, one could see it in their faces. They had not believed it possible. They hurried away to consult their friends, and sat talking in little groups. It was clear that the Union had no plan prepared for such an eventuality.

With constant patrols of Police in the Compounds, foot and motor, the men had a free choice to return to work if they wanted

* Soldier of the Northern Rhodesia Regiment.

to. There was a steadily increasing trickle, which we tried to turn to a flood. We did not succeed. We were again confronted by the obstinacy of men on strike. It was a choice between evictions, and getting the Union to order a return to work : but, as all the higher Union officials had been removed, this was difficult.

However, the Joker remained, Lawrence Katilungu. Summoned back post-haste from Brussels and from talks of World Trade Union solidarity he was invited to Government House. The result was an order within 24 hours by the President for the men to return without delay. With few exceptions they did so. We begrudged the saving of even the remains of Union face, and would have preferred to see its whole organization struck down and shattered, and the Compounds quite re-shaped with their loyalties on tribal lines. Quite apart from its poor leadership, we recognized its existence as a threat to all that we stood for, a benevolent, paternalist autocracy built on village, Chief and Boma, with a prosperous, responsible, conservative middle-class of Africans gradually emerging. Yet it was too late, although the restriction of the ruling clique of officials enabled the Union to purge itself and select new leaders of a better type, honest men who had actually worked on the Mine.

At Matthew Nkholoma's subsequent trial on comparatively trivial offences connected with Trade Union administration, his Counsel was a retired Judge of the Transvaal Supreme Court named Blackwell. He had a fearsome reputation as a cross-examiner of innocent lay witnesses and affected to be much shocked at a trivial slip in legal drafting which had, according to him, made the arrest of Nkholoma illegal.

Nor was the Prosecutor* of any assistance : he had, he said, "to sacrifice me for the sake of his case". Under cross-examination in such cases it is always best to tell the truth in an unembarrassed manner, as there is nothing to hide. A District Officer is not accustomed to question the orders that he receives from his District Commissioner, and Mr. Blackwell's forensic thunders passed me by. In the event the unfortunate Matthew was convicted, and subsequently restricted to a hot place. He returned briefly to

* The Crown Offices were filled by the Colonial Office with Dublin Irish lawyers. Such men were seldom warm imperialists.

7. The Source of the Zambezi, near Mwinilunga, with District
Messenger, Piton Mamfuka.

Trade Union life but his place had long been filled. New loyalties and new animosities had formed in the ever-shifting jungle of Union politics, and he soon retired again to private business where his energy, tempered now by experience, earned him just rewards. I have often wished to meet him again, and discuss affairs in the amicably hostile way that we used to do before his arrest at midnight.

The strike had ended, but the miners continued to be volatile in their behaviour. On a quiet afternoon, tax-collecting, not even in front of a crowd, a tall youth in a tie began protesting in fluent English against the payment of the tax.

The Messenger, in the tolerant way that they had, ushered him towards the payment window. "Don't touch me," he screamed, and it ended in the usual way, a night's confinement in the lock-up. We were tired, the Messenger did not understand English anyhow, and if one person could push his way through, so would all the others. But Alois Miti was a more interesting character. Brought up and educated at an Anglican Mission in Southern Rhodesia, he was hopelessly out of place in the middle of a Mine. He should have been at Oxford: and indeed in his exaggerated accent, learnt certainly from some High Anglican Parson in the south, one caught the unique echo of the quadrangles, with the sun throwing its long shadows on the lawns. Keble. . . . Cuddesdon. We talked: and I released him after a paternal lecture. He became attached to me: he sent me his poems, and I lent him books. An innovation, and a daring one, in Kitwe of those days, he came to tea.

But it went no further, and we drifted apart. One had one's own family, friends, and Kitwe always upon one. The effort was too great to sustain. But the failure was my own: I felt that I had failed Alois and that I had silently pushed him back into the Mine Compound where there was no poetry, only machines. Alois Miti, poet: I wonder still what became of him.

The Copperbelt was an inhuman place. It paid laborious lip-service to culture, good causes, racial harmony, welfare. But what it admired, respected, worshipped, was money. It was swept by rumours, scares, ghosts, and stories of leopard-men from the Congo, which would put thousands into a state of violent hysteria

E

within minutes. It did not matter, as the Mine magnates would tell their shareholders later, whether the country was ruled by the Colonial Office or by an African party Government : it was an autocracy in any case.

Yet it mattered to us : we were the trustees. And in time it will strike even the magnates that an efficient, thoroughly benevolent and mild autocracy is preferable to a disordered and capricious one, manned by the outcasts of African society. Our task on the Copperbelt was a ceaseless struggle to get the Africans treated as human-beings, not as counters, or non-beings used for mechanical functions. Dog-bites, guns, odious treatment in shops and even post offices, poor education, insurance, housing, lack of social equality, Federation even, all hung round the African's neck. We were helped there by men of good will, but they were scattered and we were few, too few to turn the tide from the mass rejection of European paternal Government. Yet had Lawrence Katilungu only lived, what changes there had to be would have been accomplished in peace and not in violence, in friendship, not hatred. Had he but lived.

CHAPTER VII

INTERLUDE AT KING'S

HIGH summer at King's. The flowers were out in the courts and it was nearly time for the bells to ring out for evening service. Within Chetwynd Court one looked down from a high Gothic window. Nothing could disturb the immemorial peacefulness, what one had sometimes imagined, but never dared to believe would be one's own for a little while. A sudden noise, shouts, scuffling, disturbed the tranquillity. Surely the unthinkable had occurred? Two youths, dressed in black drain-pipe trousers, were rolling over and over in the flower-bed, fighting over a girl. On the other side of the court, just a floor or two below, and directly above the contestants, a bent and famous figure approached the window, and looked out in wondering amazement and distaste. Then slowly, firmly, the author of *A Passage to India* withdrew, the thick curtains were drawn, and the unpleasant, the incredible was shut out. Soon a porter appeared, dressed in a frock coat, and stood silently above them for a second. The two contestants got up, shook themselves, and departed with bowed heads. The flowers that had been rolled upon straightened themselves, the curtains breathed, and peace, protected by centuries, returned to the court. The bells began their lovely call. But the peace, after all, had depended upon the stout porter, and not so much on the innate *goodishness* of mankind.

The bees drone round the flower-beds in the courts and the stone is warm in the sun. There is a smell of new-mown grass, and the great mulberry is laden with fruit. Surely the most beautiful place in the world. And all the day long the talk of the Conference goes on until the human-beings have been blown up into an enormous abstract balloon fit for an Official Report. The subject is forgotten now, and only the dreary self-assertion of the coming

127

men is real. The arrivistes arrived in due course, but they found no more than a heap of ashes.

The Americans attached to the Conference watched us from behind thick spectacles. They were to give a party. The cream of the administration of fifteen colonies gathered to drink beer and whisky and to put off inhibitions. But the jargon, the rugger-club atmosphere and the quick return to school become oppressive, unbearable. Out in the clear night air one could be a deserter, a renegade, an escapee. No longer in the Colonial Service, one became at will a bus-conductor, a clerk in the gas-works, a milk bar attendant—and wished one was!

For we were all exiles in England. England was home, but long absence had made us alien. We stirred uneasily in suit and collar and tie. On our arms and legs we could always see the brown-white contrast where the khaki drill had come to an end. We went about together, drank together, as though for our own safety. We imagined misunderstanding in the vacant faced crowds who had never heard of our Colonies, not to mention our famous Chiefs and tribes of whom we had such special, intimate knowledge. The need to explain ourselves, the essential rightness of what we were doing, common to every European in Africa, clung round us like a blanket. Yet to do so would have involved such detail as to lead to but one result—complete boredom. So we were at ease only among our own kind: only there could we hear our own language—Askari, Boma, Ulendo, Bwana. We had gone away, to govern and civilize Africa in the name of England and the Empire. We longed only to be received again at the fireside: and the Family looked on us as remote, eccentric, slightly doubtful cousins.

"Cousin John who went to the Colonies and came back once in 1939: haven't heard from him for years." The English had not changed.

CHAPTER VIII

MWINILUNGA—THE UNWEARIED SUN

The unwearied sun from day to day
Doth his Creator's power display,
And publishes to ev'ry land
The power of an Almighty Hand.

(Joseph Addison).

SIR ARTHUR BENSON, who ruled and governed Northern Rhodesia from 1954 to 1959, was the greatest Governor the country ever had. He had begun his service as a cadet at Gwembe, had been promoted to District Officer, and after the war, when he had touched Churchill's mantle, he returned from Whitehall to be District Commissioner at Luwingu.

He knew more about the rural African than any Governor before or since : he had his knowledge at first hand from the villages, from the tours where the slope was always up-hill, from the carriers, and the camp-fires sending up their showers of sparks on a cold night. His love was for the African, every African, and for the real African about to be submerged in a mass proletariat behind a façade of progress and freedom. He looked the politicians in the face, and they would slink away.

Governor Benson realized as no other Governor before or since, that the struggle was for the soul of the African people, whether they should become a people in their own right, or a herd baying at a dictator. So he would project himself larger than life, and this this magnificent presence fitted him to do. On his visits, or progresses, even the office orderly would be given a hand-shake. The Chiefs, the base on whom the whole of African society rests, were his special friends, and the District Messengers, so many of whom had served alongside him. He knew the people, knew them not as units or statistics or problems, but as men and women. In effect, he knew them as a District Officer. He succeeded, not always assisted by some of his senior officers, but he succeeded. In 1959 the battle was won. With one hand he developed the country and advanced the rural Africans, with the other he had sedition by the throat. How his work was shamefully cast away will be the story of the second half of this book.

Governor Benson's first task was to re-animate the Provincial Administration, the back-bone of the country. To this he brought Churchillian fire. He advanced merit, so that able and devoted men came to the fore. The old and worn-out were gracefully retired from the Service, for men do wear out quickly in Africa. They lose their flexibility of mind, and the ability to accept new ideas. The time-servers whom he remembered from the past were left to moulder as they deserved. Their smooth advancement ceased.

Within six months the Provincial Administration, which had run down into a poor state of morale in the last tired years of Sir Gilbert Rennie's administration, jolted and shaken by the Federation was re-animated to a force second to none. Proper equipment and dwellings were provided, the African staff paid decently, and the subsidies of the Chiefs, on whom so much depended, were increased from £3 to £5 a month to between £20 and £40, in keeping with the great power and responsibility they wielded after nearly sixty years of British rule.

The increased efficiency, the surge forward, the greater contact with and understanding of the Africans, was felt in every Boma in the Territory. The District Officers, a force of less than three hundred men, upon whom in the last resort everything depended, were re-animated. They were not tired Civil Servants, poor relations of men of higher attainments in the Secretariat, but the vanguard, the *élite*. Every District Officer, Clerk and District Messenger knew that the Governor's eye was upon him—whether engaged in dim routine work or in a position of splendour and responsibility at the head of a Province—he knew that the Governor was there. He knew too, like one of Nelson's Captains, that if he laid his ship alongside that of the enemy, whether it was sloth or sedition, if he did his utmost, he would not much be blamed whatever the outcome. Zeal for the Service, that was what Sir Arthur Benson demanded, every time and all the time. And like all great leaders, he got it. The Secretariat groaned and chafed under his peremptory demands: but they obeyed. He was the Governor: and on the Africans' behalf he would gladly stand up to the Federal Government, Sir Roy Welensky, and the serried ranks of the Colonial Office, not to mention the Fabian Society, and the Africa Bureau.

If Sir Arthur had his faults, they were faults of greatness. He had his detractors, who gathered strength and courage in the ignoble period after his demise, when they crept back to positions of power. True, he bore down hard on some individuals, and seldom forgave those whose paths he had crossed. He was much criticized for his attempt to develop the Northern Province on a grand scale with a £2 million loan from the Mining Companies. But the idea was boldly and properly conceived. Rural townships, with agricultural projects near, were to be built in the countryside, equipped with all amenities, water, light, power, wherever possible. Around these nuclei, development would take place, people would gather and industry begin. The obstruction of one or two Departments of Government itself frustrated this scheme: but it was the failure of the Bemba which caused it to collapse. The Chiefs had lost much of their old power through nepotism, idleness, and intrigue for position which had less meaning as their power decreased. The people preferred to sit in their villages and live as they had always done, and to grumble along in their huge rural slum. Not Alexander the Great could have made men of them. Their history shows them as cowardly and cruel. They earned, and retained, as a tribe, the well-merited dislike of every other tribe in the Territory. Lawrence Katilungu was the greatest of them, and there were others who stood out. But these could be counted on the fingers of one hand.

Always a traditionalist, the Governor withdrew the Northern Rhodesia Police from certain outstations where they had led a peaceful bucolic existence, and put them to work in the towns. This caused some resentment. The Governor held, rightly at that time when consent was freely given, that the District Commissioner had no need of Police to enforce his authority. He had his prestige : and for the occasional violent case he had his force of District Messengers. That was enough. As usual, His Excellency was right. It happened in the past, and it happened then, that inexperienced Police Officers would know more about the Africans than the District Commissioner, and by maladroit handling could disturb delicate balances. The sudden manner of their withdrawal caused for a time some resentment against the Provincial Administration among a fine force.

It was not many years before Police and Provincial Administration were dragged down together into a common ruin. But it is beyond question that had the administration continued on the lines that Sir Arthur Benson laid down, this policy was entirely correct. Police were not nedeed in peaceful rural Districts, and at that time the overbearing attitude of a few junior officers disturbed the continuous, intimate converse between the officers of the administration and the rural African emerging bewildered into a modern world. That this exchange has now ceased for ever is no fault of the survivors of his administration or of the great man who governed over all, for more than five splendid, memorable years.

All who served as District Commissioners under Sir Arthur Benson were honoured. They were in the front of the front line. So long as they did their utmost to help and guide the African, to cherish and support his Chiefs, to develop where possible—crops, roads, bridges, hospitals, schools, and toured far and wide over the District, all would be well. I was fortunate, at the age of a little over thirty, to get a District at all.

To be appointed to Mwinilunga, the remotest and the most interesting District of the Territory, was indeed good fortune. It was the upper tip of the North Western Province, bounded upon the north by the Congo, by the west, Angola. It was reached by a single road which ran 180 miles from Solwezi over wooded hills and wide empty plains on top of the plateau, skimmed by tiny birds. Over a long racketing bridge of trees and planks crossing a plunging river, the road ran up to a house commanding the most majestic view in the world, a range of hills like a great moor curving away into limitless distance. That was Mwinilunga.

The District was bisected by the West Lunga River. To the

west lived the Ndembu, under Senior Chief Kanongesha, and to the east, Senior Chief Sailunga and the Lunda. The Ndembu were the most "African" of Africans, worthily headed by their Senior Chief. They lived an inwardly haunted existence, vexed by innumerable adverse spirits whom it was important to placate, compensated by some, inevitably fewer, who were the bearers of good luck, health and safety. Over this chaotic Pantheon presided the dim figure of *Nzambi*, the "Supreme Being", who was quite ineffectual and had lost control centuries ago. Villages, even schools, were moved to avoid ghosts. Roads were directed to skirt forgotten graveyards and in every village and near every hut stood groups of little sticks as guardians. The taller hunting shrines on stilts had thatched roofs and pieces of bloodstained white cloth and beads hanging inside. Their guns had small bags of pellets or charms tied to the trigger-guard. The successful hunter was the ideal of what every Lunda wished to be. Privileged even above Chiefs at their funeral, hunters were buried in a sitting position. They were regarded with the same sort of adoration as W. R. Hammond or Bradman were by the schoolboys of the 1930's. They were hero-worshipped.

The Lunda represent a later wave of invasion than the Kaonde, and they have kept their tribal cohesion to a remarkable degree. They are closer to Mwatiamvwa, the Great King, and their Chiefs wear the beaded head-dresses presented by him as a mark of Chiefly recognition on ceremonial occasions. Kanongesha stems straight from Mwatiamvwa, while Sailunga is from Musokantanda who lives close by across the Congo Border. Amid scenes of great enthusiasm Mwatiamvwa himself twice visited Mwinilunga, and there is no doubt that both the Lunda and Ndembu are far closer to their brothers in the Congo than they are to any other tribe, even to their cousins the Kaonde in Northern Rhodesia. Although there is some doubt about the validity of the present Chief Kanongesha's claim to his position, there being a rival claimant in Portuguese Angola, it appeared to the British that he established his right; he was, after all, admitted as Kanongesha by Mwatiamvwa on his cross-border visits from the Congo. It all hinged on the possession of the *Lukano*, a sausage-like bracelet said to be made of human fibres worn on the left wrist.

E*

Both Kanongeshas claimed that theirs was the genuine and original. However that may be, it is clear that the Lunda—with some reason—consider themselves superior to the surrounding tribes in Northern Rhodesia, the Kaonde, the Lamba, the Lovale and others, and it is not until they strike the Lozi that they recognize their equal. Coillard,* in the 1880's, recorded that Shinde, who had fled from the Portuguese, entered Lealui in the time of Lewanika with drums beating and in full ceremony, something certainly not permitted to any other Tributary Chiefs.

It is likely that the Ndembu and Lunda entered Mwinilunga in two parallel waves late in the eighteenth century, not as conquerors, except no doubt that they chased before them a few wandering Nkoya down the rivers. But space was plentiful and only the fittest survived the hard village life of those days. Men, women and little children were sold off as slaves to the Ma-Mbundu slave-raiders, huts were of grass and sticks thrown together, and even when there was peace, witchcraft or witch-finding thinned the ranks. Even today at Kalene Hill Mission there is a small but flourishing village of women accused of the black arts who have taken refuge there. In their villages, their lives would be forfeit.

In this state the two tribes had lived for just over a century at the advent of the British South Africa Company's Administration in 1907. Mr. Bellis was sent up from Kasempa, then established six years, to found a Boma in the sub-District. The attempt met with disaster. A skirmish developed with some villages, and Bellis, a brave man, was shot with a muzzle-loading gun. With the greatest difficulty he was rescued by two District Messengers, Nswanamumi and Kachinka, both of whom received tax exemption for life for their good conduct. Nswanamumi, a Kaonde, later became Chief Ntambu, and lived on to a great age, dying in the late 1950's, full of honours, and a mine of information on the past. Mr. Bellis recovered, but contracted sleeping-sickness and died of it in England in 1916. His assailant, from Kasanga's village, is said to have walked in to Mwinilunga, an old man, to give himself up in 1920. Very shortly after he died of pneumonia.

* François Coillard: *On the Threshold of Central Africa. A Record of 20 years Pioneering among the Barotse of the Upper Zambezi.*

The new administration found the following Chiefs in being:

Ndembu.	*Lunda.*
KANONGESHA	SAILUNGA
CHIBWIKA	KAKOMA
NYAKASEYA	KANYAMA
IKELENGE	NTAMBU
MWINIMILAMBA	KATAMBI
NTAMBU SACHITOLA	MPULUMBA
MUKANGALA	KANGOMBE
KAFWEKU	

In addition the following Lunda were recognized traditionally as having been Chiefs in the past, but had been degraded for having slept with the wives of their father Sailunga : Makangu, Iamvwa, Fundamukanwa, Kakungamalwa and Mukanganya. The descendents of these scapegraces formed the five senior and revered Headmen of Sailunga's Court.

The Administration that followed, that of Mr. Macgregor and Mr. Pound, was unsuccessful. They drank, and beat people. So all the people ran away, they could get no clerks, no Messengers and no carriers or servants. They were discovered on the banks of the Lunga River doing their own cooking and washing. The Lunda's reply to their oppression had been effective, as Mr. Macgregor was recalled to Headquarters and his resignation asked for and given.

Mr. Bruce Miller succeeded them, a wise and humane administrator who established relationships on a proper footing and came closer to the Lunda people than any of his colleagues before or probably since. Like Melland at Kasempa, he recorded many of their customs in the District Notebooks, and their work has lived on after them as an inspiration to those who followed. It is clear that both men were just, kindly, and determined.

Previous to the Administration, Kalene Hill Mission had been founded in May, 1906 by Dr. and Mrs. Fisher and Miss Darling. They were Plymouth Brethren, and settled on top of a high hill in the northern tip of the District. Doctor Fisher was a surgeon of outstanding skill,* and a successful operation on the important

* A characteristic inherited by his son, Dr. Walter Fisher of Luanshya.

Head-woman Nyampasa (mother of twins) opened the door to medical and evangelical work. Though it is true that there are still shrines to propitiate the spirits within a mile of the hospital, and that their missionary work has not made the impact that it might after nearly 60 years, the amount of human suffering and life that Dr. Fisher and his devoted successors have saved must be immeasurable.

Missionaries, like clergymen, are tempting targets for criticism by lay-men, especially administrators jealous of power. They in their turn, see them come and go, the idealist, the plodder, the careerist making a brief sojourn. They continue their work, and though we may be critical, they no doubt have even greater cause to be. Their achievement of a modern hospital built in the middle of Africa, three hundred and fifty miles from the railhead, is a monument to their faith, and the fruit of many years of hard work and self-denial. If their lives and doctrine appear to us sometimes sombre and narrow, they can only be judged by their fruits : and these are worthy of high respect.

After all, who can tell whether he will be remembered by the people after twenty years? It is true that we all have our "nick-names" which are recorded faithfully in the old District Note-books. Few are descriptive, and others purely onomatopoeic, such as "Pom-Pom" for a long dead Popham. But are they the true ones? We cannot tell. Some D.C.s are flattered by the "man who keeps his word" or the "man who walks straight", but one sus-pects that, as Africans have one name for everyday use of con-ventional sort, and another of their very own kept secret against the spirits, we too have our second name which indicates the true feelings of the Africans towards us.

From Kalene they have preached and taught for nearly sixty years, but the spirit-shrines still stand. Are we to expect remem-brance and gratitude when we have gone? Never. To expect gratitude here is to lay oneself open to a life-time of disappoint-ment, ending in tears. How often one hears the complaint : "Look what we do for them." That is hardly the point. Rather, look what they do for us. And sometimes it comes, as a delightful surprise, a flower in the desert, a letter from a teacher or a small present from a Headman, long after whatever one had done, or refrained from doing, had been forgotten in the press of day-to-day affairs.

One thing is certain: no rural District can be run by a Committee, however earnest, however well-intentioned. Thirty thousand people, living in clumps or villages of about fifty or so, scattered and far apart, demand someone, or something, to act in any circumstances that can arise. A bridge is swept away by a flood, a woman is murdered, a dog goes rabid and bites everybody within range, smallpox breaks out. It is little use summoning a body of leading citizens to examine the problem in all its aspects. Action is required: and at once. That is the reason for the District Commissioner, for his deputy the District Officer when he is on tour, and for his staff of District Messengers who are never, so far as I know, all in the Boma at once during their whole service. They act through the Chiefs, their Court Assessors and *kapasus*, and they in their turn through the village Headman, who is personally responsible for his own village.

That was Sir Arthur Benson's conception of how the territory should be governed. The District Commissioner was allowed the widest scope, but one thing above all he must do, he must honour the Chiefs: in his day the Chiefs were King. A few abused his trust in them, but the great mass showed that, uneducated as most of them might be, they could lead their people out of the dark void of the past forward to all the opportunities of the modern world. Here, Sir Arthur addresses the Legislative Council on 7 April, 1959:

"In any nation old or new, homogeneous by origin or welded together by history, and in any community which feels itself to be a Community, there is, and there must be, one central form of loyalty. If there is not, the nation or community or tribe will always be in danger, under great stresses and strains, of falling apart. The form of loyalty cannot be a purely material one, it must have something of the idealistic, indeed the spiritual, in it.

"I have never been able to understand why, amongst so large a proportion of the population of the United Kingdom, the people who joined themselves together by such unbreakable bonds of loyalty to the Queen are so slow to understand that the indigenous people of tropical and sub-tropical Africa found their focus and continue to find their focus in the persons of their Chiefs, and in their chiefly institutions which we have today in Northern Rhodesia called the Chiefs-in-Council or Native Authorities.

"It is the Chief who, in African religion, holds in his person the entire spiritual welfare of the tribe, and therefore its material welfare.

"Look to your Chiefs. During the past five years my Government has done so and the Chief's position today is stronger, while at the same time being no less democratic than it has been since British rule first came to Northern Rhodesia. On the other hand, during the past fifteen years of my service I have seen the power and position of Chiefs elsewhere broken, not by the British Administration but by the failure of the British Administration to recognize that emergent commoner politicians can persuade the people themselves to destroy what is vital for them to preserve if they are to remain Africans.

"A great administrator, under whom I had the honour to serve in Northern Rhodesia, once said: 'What does it profit the Africans if we preserve their soil and destroy their soul?' Great powerful Chiefs in the Gold Coast and in Western Nigeria have been swept away. Where Chieftaincies remain, the traditional popularly chosen Chiefs have either been reduced to mere names if they have been content to permit this, or have been supplanted in their Chieftaincies by nominees of the political party in power, who during their rise to power, fawned on them and flattered them, or when the Native Authority itself saw the dangers looming ahead and refused to put its head on the block, mounted the strongest attacks on them it could by creating disaffection against beneficial and progressive but unpopular Native Authority laws.

"The result is likely to be that without the final sheet-anchor, without the age-old forces of loyalty, without the final determination between what is right and what is wrong, without the soul, all spiritual sanctions which deter a man in the last resort from crime and skulduggery vanish; and support is transferred, most often through fear of the consequences, to a central point which can be nothing better than a dictatorship, if indeed it be not a band of Nazi-minded lieutenants who are yes-men to a central Führer.

"The Chiefs in Northern Rhodesia preserve the essential characteristics of being traditional Chiefs : that is, Chiefs chosen out of a small group of potential traditional successors in due form by recognized elders who, for all the tribe, represent the will of the people.

"Being traditional, not all are good. Some of our Chiefs are lazy, some are incompetent, one or two are bad. But it is not the person of the Chief that matters, any more than the person of the worst King of England mattered : it is the concept of Chieftaincy, just as it is for us the concept of the throne. Surrounding the Chief is, and always has been, his Council, and great strides have been made over the past decade, while preserving the essential and vital element of the traditional, to have included in the Council well-educated, progressive and sound young men who supply the equally important modern outlook which form the machinery on top of the solid, because traditional, foundation.

"Our great task in Northern Rhodesia is to graft the new and modern and efficient on to the well-tried, traditional and old. We must never allow the foundation to be swept away, at least until there is something equally sound, equally acceptable to the African population, equally understood by them, and equally enjoying their confidence.

"Mr. Speaker and Honourable Members, I say to you, *Look to your Chiefs.*"

Prophetic words today, when the Chiefs all over the Territory have been either deposed, or stripped of power and surrounded by "elected councillors" composed sometimes of the lowest and worst elements of their people, sometimes criminals and men who would have been virtual outcasts from African society in ordinary times.

No Chief that ever ruled, no government that ever governed, has done so without opposition. To imagine this, is to live in an imaginary past, in a Golden Age that never was, to live in an illusion. The records of King Lewanika's Court, with their story of intrigue, rebellion and dreadful punishment, are sufficient to dispel it for ever. They ruled by strength, in spite of all that could be brought against them, as every government in history has ruled, be it monarchy or republic.

The fallacy was later to be that Chiefs should not rule because opposition existed, even of the most despicable kind. It was brought to the point that government must abdicate because opposition existed, a feeling symbolic of a perverse guilt-complex, born of Hobson's "Imperialism" or the perverted "humani-tarian-ism" that justifies murder in a "good" political cause. That particular Golden Age may have had no substance : but after over half a century of British rule there existed something enviable in Africa. A man and his family could go to bed at night without fear that his house would be set afire, and walk along the paths from one village to another without being set upon on the way. Apart from his tax, the money he had was his own, and there was no forced levies by gangs of youths armed with clubs and axes. And that was something to be thankful for. The system was like an old, worn, farm-house chair, knotted, rough in places maybe, and with one leg which always seemed shorter than the others. But it was there, so that when it was suddenly snatched away the bare ground seemed cold, hard and wet, to the ordinary man.

The Lunda are spoken of by the early administrators as being a timid race, but that is not so nowadays. True, great numbers fled into the Congo during the administration of Macgregor and Pound, and at the first introduction of Tax. Now, they have come to know the European, the great majority administrators and missionaries in their own District, and in the Congo, where they were humanized by Catholic culture and kept under strict, not to say rigorous control, by the Belgian administration. Some Lunda, particularly those from the south, who have an admixture of Kaonde blood, display powers of forethought and organization which one did not then expect from an African. And in ex-President Tshombe they have produced one statesman of inter-national stature, only possible in a tribe with cohesion, tradition, and centralized authority, with the potential of a nation as we know it.

The material condition of the Lunda people had improved strikingly within the five years from 1953 to 1958. It was the custom of District Officers on tour to enter every hut or house, and thoroughly to inspect each village. At times one would discover people who were gravely ill, and whose lives might be saved by going to hospital, at others the dying, to whom one might try to give comfort as they looked up with frightened eyes. But the increase in blankets, clothes, furniture, pictures, trunks and other smaller comforts, gladdened the heart. In some villages even, there was the feeding bottle for the baby, often I fear, more of a danger than a benefit, because not properly washed, and again plastic pants, too hot for the climate and not removed often enough. But still, a start. In the overhanging eaves round the hut was the family medicine chest, more replete than ever. Cock's feathers, little calabashes, beads, and occasionally, at the better-known physicians, the set of cupping-horns, of *duiker* or sometimes larger, which was indispensable equipment among the Lunda. Headache, backache, stomach-ache and any other ache, were relieved by this old-fashioned method, and the very numerous tiny scars on almost everyone testified to its popularity.

Senior Chief Kanongesha, as he had been for twenty years, typified his people. He was more "African" than they, and even less predictable. A sad obstacle to orderly administration, and when times grew rough, a nuisance. In peaceful times, a worthy opponent against whom to fence, to match one's wits, as successive District Commissioners had done since 1942, when in the course of six months, through the unexpected deaths of both Chibwika and Kanongesha, he was translated from village Headman to Superior Chief. All the cunning and evasiveness of the old Africa were his, all the obstinate conservatism and resistance to progress in any form, all the delusions of grandeur of petty authority over a few thousand people. And, when he had once again evaded the net, the snare set out before him (set entirely in his own and his people's interest), then he would laugh, and behave in a particularly courtly and pleasing manner. His voice would deepen and mellow, and his gestures, beautifully pointed, would bring to mind a benevolent statesman of the old school.

Coillard records of King Lewanika in his early days that his younger brother aspired to the throne. Lewanika had him swathed round and round in yards of cloth so that he could not move. Then he decked him with the ornaments of royalty, shells, beads, etc., "that he might go to his fathers in a manner worthy of his rank". He placed him under a shady tree within his court. A high pallisade was built round him, and he was left to starve to death. This medieval jest would have exactly suited Kanongesha: but by ill-luck the British Administration had already arrived. There is no doubt that he thought it a pestilent nuisance.

Chief Kanongesha claims to be the "Chifwankene" to Mwatiamvwa himself: it is he who takes, in Lunda custom, the leaf from the *mulembu* tree and places it in the mouth of the heir. He it is who issues powder to the hunters, who are told to go and shoot the female: if a male is killed then, as with the Kaonde, the heir is unsuitable; or a hartebeeste or warthog or zebra. They are *kahonga* (unclean) and they count as males. It follows, therefore, that he has much influence, one might say almost a veto, on the choice of the Mwatiamvwa himself.

It is not recorded whether, on the choice of the new Mwatiamvwa in 1963, Kanongesha attended his functions in person. Probably not, since he was ill. The royal capital, some two hundred and fifty miles to the north-west near Dilolo in the Congo, is, or was, like a town, with even electric light. The courtiers, sub-chiefs with no areas of their own to administer, surround the Mwatiamvwa jealously. Like the courtiers of Versailles in its most affected period in the eighteenth century, they clip the vowel sounds off the ends of their words, and their esoteric language is now unintelligible to any ordinary Lunda who has not made it his special study.

One brilliant stroke of Sir Arthur Benson, when Governor, was to persuade Mwatiamvwa to send his representative, in this case his own daughter, to govern Chavuma, a chronic trouble-centre at the Portuguese border, the under-world of Balovale, an ulcer incapable of cure. The immigrant tribes, Lovale, Luchazi, Chokwe, had wrested it from Chief Shinde of the Lunda, and the

Government had fumbled with the problem for years, contenting itself with direct rule and the despatch of police when this rude Soviet broke into open disorder.

> The Jews, a Headstrong, Moody, Murm'ring race
> As ever tr'd th'extent and stretch of grace;
> God's pamper'd People, whom, debauched with ease,
> No King could govern and no God could please;
> (Gods had they tr'd of every shape and size
> That God-smiths could produce or Priests devise).
> *(Dryden—Absalom and Achitophel).*

Since all the tribes, it was generally agreed, stemmed from Mwatiamvwa, he sent his daughter Luweji to rule over them. In proper custom at the installation all important people file past the new Chief and drop a present onto the mat in front of him or her.

These are given to a second important official known as the *Chimankata.* They say then: "You must now know me, and if you hear my cases, treat me well," something akin to an admonition at a Coronation. But these Chavuma people, perverting the custom, passed Luweji with a stream of foul abuse, which as her husband was a Methodist Minister, was as unjustified as it was disgusting. After this, which passed unnoticed at the time, "her heart was not good towards them", and after five years of unavailing effort she abandoned them to their own evil devices and returned to her father in the Congo.

Apart from Chavuma which could be contained but never governed—unless by an iron despotism of which the Colonial Service was incapable—there had been a change in the people since 1950. Rightly they had grown more independent, more ready with their own views. Then, they never even had a view, and the outer world was a closed book: now even the people in the villages, mostly the younger men, had things to say, out of tune with the respectful greetings and requests of the old régime. While this was both inevitable and right, there was a crudity in their expressions at village level that made one not always receptive.

It was the custom in Mwinilunga to sleep while on tour on a "Kadidi" or Lunda bed, made up from a base of solid tree-trunks built up to a framework upon which a huge palliasse of grass was laid. This superbly comfortable edifice, warm and soft, was built up anew each night by the nineteen or twenty carriers who accompanied the touring officer.

At a village called Nyani in Chief Chibwika's country the word had arrived that passive resistance to touring officers had begun. They refused to supply water to the camp that evening. Nothing was said, and the carriers brought up the water themselves. But next morning, very early, the village was visited by the whole cavalcade of District Commissioner, Chief, and District Messengers. In the cold light of dawn the village Hampdens regretted their rashness of the previous day. They had been discourteous. Would they accept the punishment I would give them, or would they prefer that the matter should go to the Chief?

They agreed to accept my verdict. Very well: my carriers were tired from carrying water: in their turn they would carry my bed, and they could see to it that it was completely assembled at the new camp when I arrived. So it was: about ten miles down a hot, sandy road, complete as though it had been lifted in one piece. One had no wish to make oneself a nuisance on tour, but custom and courtesy were to be observed in future. If there were to be changes, it was the Chiefs who would have to agree to them first.

Or there was the man who asked me, in the middle of a village in Chief Nyakaseya, why I was going about looking in houses. I was astonished at such a question: I had looked upon it as a part of duty, and a service to the people, to tell them how they might improve their buildings, not to say their complete household arrangements. The opening was too good to miss in Mwinilunga. "Looking for witchcraft, of course," and I had my laugh, but all the same, it made me reflect. Shortly after, the rash and unfortunate man was striken by a disease which caused his tongue to swell up and loll out of his mouth like an idiot. This, I affirm, was none of my doing.

The exaltation of the Chiefs as leaders of the African people was accepted by them, so long as there was nothing else. Many of the best still stood by them long after party politics were rampant. But they had not captured the younger men. The edifice was magnificent, yet with uncomfortable echoes of the Habsburgs: it presumed a static society, or a static enemy. The Austrian armies were too fond of standing in one place and waiting for the enemy to make the mistake: Napoleon swept them up, and even Napoleon III managed to beat them.

The young men were the danger, and they should have been headed off early into the administration where their energy and new ideas would have made them excellent District Officers. Instead, in the climate of Federation, and even of the old Colonial Service, they were thought "unsound", and by an act of folly permitted to travel to India and to other places, and return as bitter enemies, not as allies. Are Prime Ministers necessary in Northern Rhodesia? Clearly not: and there were at least five prospective Prime Ministers in Mwinilunga alone.

Stanley Tepa was the first of them, and at that time the most dangerous. There was a new constitution—the first of a long and weary succession—in 1958. The "intellectuals" were invited to discuss it. I saw then that he was not to be reconciled to anything lower than an African Government of men of his own kind. Partnership and "gradual-ism" in his eyes were nothing but an obstacle in the way of the right of he and his kind to rule and govern in their own interests the District, Province and Territory. Federation then was a side-issue, a half-forgotten grievance, and later a stepping-stone to power.

Stanley Tepa had the fixed glare of the fanatic: he had the mad eyes, the beard, and some of the character, of Rasputin. Unlike most of the Lunda, he had travelled far afield, and seen the sea at the Cape. He was quite well educated and a skilful mob-orator. The Lunda feared his fixed stare and his refusal to accept the established order which they had always known and which seemed a part of nature. He was the one man who had the following, the organizing ability and the fanaticism to set the District afire. It soon appeared that he was determined to do so, and I, equally determined, that if he should start to do this, he would be broken.

Under the Constitution of 1958 one African and one European member was to be returned for each rural Province. The

Liberal Party was formed, under Sir John Moffat, Mr. Alfred Gondwe and Mr. Harry Franklin. They stood for partnership in fact, for equality of opportunity, and in a word for human decency between all men. The attraction was that all races could join and work together for the same good ends. Though Federation was already in fact past saving, the Liberals had ideas as to how it could be made to work more decently, more fairly and more cleanly. The best of the educated Africans at that time joined with enthusiasm : others, who already had ideas of racial victory through violence refrained.

No-one is more the target of the bitter hatred of the African racialist than the Liberal, and no-one, especially if he has any following, a greater danger to them. By his example and conduct he holds up a mirror to themselves, and his presence, to the last, is a challenge. With no ideas of superiority or inferiority, yet firmly suppressing violence, he is the greatest obstacle against dictatorship and mass-Führer worship. He is the ultimate peril, the man with the open, sceptical, even mocking mind. He is the challenge to all the chicanery of modern party politics, and may, by his example, by his presence even, puncture the glorious Animal Farm euphoria in which the people are plunged. He is indeed the enemy of the new "nations" of Africa. Their rulers fear him far more than the caricature armed with a sjambok. "Sjambokkers" change remarkably quickly when they realize where the power lies.

Before a man could stand as a candidate for the Election of 1958 two-thirds of the Chiefs in the Province had to counter-sign his application, and certify the following :

(a) Is he a man intelligent enough for the Legislative Council?

(b) Does he have peaceful intentions, and will he not try to threaten peace, order and good government?

(c) Is he a responsible person who will uphold the customs and laws of that area?

(d) Will he not try to undermine the Chiefs and Native Authorities?

(e) Does he want to work for the good of all people in the country, regardless of race or creed?

(f) Is the man of good character?

This was paternalism with a vengeance. The Chiefs of one District or tribe, if they were so minded, could eliminate an African candidate. In the event they did not do so, but allowed all the candidates, who approached them in person, to go forward.

Only two parties stood, the United Federal Party and the Liberals, with a Dominion Party candidate or two on the line of rail. The African National Congress, at that time a mere collection of misfits and malcontents, announced that the Election would be boycotted, but in his masterful way the Governor personally demanded from every D.C. that his estimate of Headmen votes and others on the Roll, should be attained. His Excellency had his quota, and it was attained in ways which would give a profound shudder to constitutional lawyers, and no doubt to the Colonial Office.

Aged Headmen, who could just write their names and no more, were cornered in their villages and gardens and badgered, cajoled and guided until they had completed the form. Trembling old hands were guided, and guided again, until all the details were correct. Puzzled, they went off, until the time came to vote. Then they all appeared, anxious to do their duty and in their best clothes, leaving their muzzle-loaders behind outside the Boma.

"Where do I put the cross", they would ask looking worried.

"Opposite the man you want to vote for."

"Yes Bwana, but who do I vote for please; I don't know these people."

"You know I can't tell you that", the unfortunate District Officer would reply—"but Franklin was a D.C. and you know William Nkanza, who is of your tribe".

"Oh, thank you, where are their names please, on this bit of paper?"

"There, and there." And so was registration and voting completed.

Both Liberals, I am glad to say, gained their seats with a thumping majority. One is thankful that at the time the future was hidden from us.

The houses in the villages in Mwinilunga were cosy-looking cottages made of mud-brick, thatched with golden grass that turned to silver grey with age, and more often than not provided with well carpentered doors and windows. Often there would be little flower gardens in front and occasionally Bougainvillaea bushes cut into clumps or an arbour. The Lunda would build like this from pride, a sense of superiority, and because the Chiefs had made it a rule that villages should be properly built. Perhaps this was the deciding factor. Only the boys recently from school would build little shacks of poles and mud, from indolence and as a gesture of anti-social protest. They would graduate within a few years to membership of the political parties' Youth Brigades, and to terrorize the ordinary village people.

Senior Chief Sailunga was the first of the Lunda Chiefs, and the best of them. He was a stout man, of fourteen or fifteen stone, with a jovial expression and a great wheezing laugh. He knew the people, not only the Headmen but the villagers, the men on leave from the Mines, and the young men who hung around the stores. He had many wives and children, and treated them well. He loved to drink the honey-beer in the evenings. He was a man, and he led his people. In his person he embodied all the virtues of strength, solidity and unchangeableness that the African people respect. He had one idea at a time, and once he had grasped it, he held on to it. He knew where he stood, or thought he did then.

Later, in 1962, the unfortunate man, deprived of support, wrote me a letter which I showed to the Minister of Native Affairs. He could say no more than that I should reply "according to my conscience". I gave what comfort I could, which was little. Chief Sailunga was of the kind of man on whom a new Africa could be built, solid, kindly and good, without empty gestures, without rancour, without the appearance of victory or defeat for one race or the other, without hollow political

triumphs and inflated images of the "Leader". For him orderly
progress was enough, a new road, a dispensary, a school. What
did the headlines matter where he lived, the posturing on the
steps of aircraft, if it meant that the school was burned down
with all the desks and books, or the road closed by bands of
youths with sticks?

His sub-Chiefs and Headmen too, would have nothing to do
with subversion. Katambi, a sub-Chief, had joined as a Messenger in 1924, and served over thirty years : he had a little Court
at the Boma where he settled the domestic squabbles and petty
crimes at the station. Sawana, a tall, distinguished Headman
of his own group of villages, who would carefully correct my
Lunda; Kadyata, the huge, gentle *kapasu* who was never
angry.

The villages were poor by our standards, but were growing
more prosperous. Kamusanye village with the Watchtower
Church had a great peach-tree in full flower, round which the
bees buzzed in clouds. It had grown from a single stone.

Makangu, the old rascal, where honey-beer was always to be
found. Nyakaponda, ancient, with his *Lubembu* or small brass
double-bell, the sole remaining trace of his vanished importance.
Chitondo, with his small library of blood and fire gospel books :
"You May Survive Armageddon." Having borrowed this in my
camp I took steps to ensure that I should, if Armageddon took
place at any time.

Cattle could be kept in the great empty plains, where they
were free of tse-tse fly. The owners would borrow a small herd
from the Government, and return their debt over the years with
the progeny. Beside wealth, cattle were a status symbol, much
valued. Salt-lick was brought up from Lusaka, great lumps of
what looked like dried grey mud. At evening the cattle would
gallop home from grazing to taste this, and they flourished.
Wealth increased under one's eyes, and under the eyes of the
people.

The honey trade was revived. Instead of destroying the hives
for honey the Lunda were taught to preserve them. Bees-wax,
in large yellow balls, was extracted and sold. Cash began to
come in : Mwinilunga might become a land of milk and honey.

There were the peaceful, contented people, order, and the increase of wealth : that was one side of the picture in that remote country. It was the most hopeful side, and it was our job to see that it was not darkened by foolish or evil men. This we strove to do.

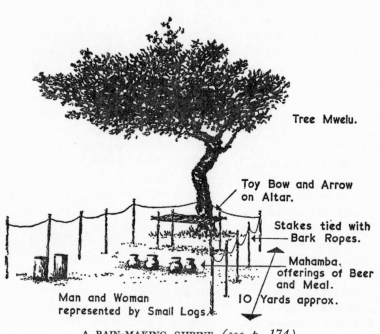

Tree Mwelu.

Toy Bow and Arrow on Altar.

Stakes tied with Bark Ropes.

Mahamba. offerings of Beer and Meal.

10 Yards approx.

Man and Woman represented by Small Logs.

A RAIN-MAKING SHRINE *(see p. 174)*

CHAPTER IX

THE WRITING ON THE WALL

CHIEF NYAKASEYA, who governed the area round Kalene
Mission, and where the three borders of the Congo, Angola
and Northern Rhodesia met, typified one chietainly virtue, that of
solidity, in an excessive degree. He was a block, and by remaining stationary, failed to influence his people or events. Yet, if he
was lazy and ineffective, he was there, and his presence gave
some focus to his subjects. They might grumble and complain
and go their own way, but his square, inactive form was always
to be found near the side of the Zambezi. Everyone knew where
to look. From near his Court the last roads went off through
the trees to the secret places of the Congo and Angola, where
administration was far less direct and the people were left even
more to work out their own devices.

A Headman along one of these roads had died in 1949. No-
one at the time had taken any notice, and a new Headman was
written in the Register in his stead. In 1958 Kabungu, a man
from Angola, appeared in Court to sue Headman Kuchaya for
£2 : Kuchaya had killed Kadavwa with medicine concocted
by Kabungu, and he had not received the promised sum. After
nine years he went to the nearest Court, and brought a case
which appeared to him an ordinary breach of civil contract. He
had supplied medicine for an agreed sum : and that medicine
had worked its purpose. Now then, where was the money? His
position was entirely logical, and it was a matter of civil debt.
However, such contracts are contrary to public policy—*ex turpi
non causa oritur actio* . . . and he lost his case on my intervention :
he went away genuinely bewildered.

Living in such an atmosphere from day to day, one cannot
help but absorb some of it. European conceptions of justice begin
to crumble and phrases like "contrary to public policy" to lose

their meaning and become mere alien pedantry. Until, that is, one is brought up with a jerk against the practical implications of unfettered African custom at work.

In Nyachikanda village, within ten minutes' walk of Kalene Hill Mission, lived a single Christian convert, the woman Nyachisochi. Nyachikanda the Headman was a tall good-looking man, middle-aged, respected and a traditionalist. Then his wife died, to whom he was much attached, and he began to look about him for the person responsible. Inevitably, Nyachisochi stuck out, and inevitably his choice fell upon her. People began to "look at her sideways", and after preliminary tests were made in the village, the accusation was made.

It would have been better for her safety if the woman had gone straight to Kalene Mission and reported the matter : she might have found refuge in the "village of witches", or have gone to relatives in another part of the District until the matter had blown over. Instead, with the curious fatalism that comes over Africans on these occasions, she stayed where she was.

Soon after an expedition consisting of almost the whole village set out for a witchdoctor living near the Angola border. Nyachisochi the accused with them, passed by Kalene Mission.

The *Mwaji*, a chicken test, was carried out. Each chicken stood for a person in the village. Each was given meal and medicine and the results were observed. On both occasions, Nyachisochi's chickens were seen to stagger and die : the others remained alive and well. This, in the eyes of all the people, was conclusive, and there was a "true bill" against her. But what none of the people knew at that time was that the witchdoctor, in consideration of a fee paid by Nyachikanda, had doctored the meal given to Nyachisochi's chickens, which were fated to die, and did.

After the test, which had been faked in advance, the party returned on the way to Nyachikanda. Nyachisochi was shunned by the others, and fell behind the group. In their minds, and perhaps in her own, she was the guilty woman who was responsible for the death of the Headman's wife, and she did not anticipate a pleasant reception when she got home. She was a widow, and had no relatives near, and as she walked through

the drizzle which sometimes falls for days together in Mwinilunga, she must have felt singularly alone.

She never reached the village. On the path back she was way-
laid, dragged into the bush, brutally strangled, and hung from
a tree by a cord of bark-rope. It was natural that the Headman
should fall under suspicion for this murder: and he and a
simple-minded villager named Bernard were arrested after a
fortnight. Although the woman disappeared within two miles of
the Chief's court, it was a week before Nyakaseya heard about
it, and another week of intensive search before the body was
found.

After exhaustive preliminary enquiries the Crown entered a
nolle prosequi on the eve of their trial for murder. In any case
where there might be the slightest element of doubt the Crown
lawyers would not bother, and refused to prosecute. Instead of
leaving such doubts to be resolved by the Court they would content themselves with sending a brief telegram and returning the
accused to their home District.

Too often persons who were clearly guilty escaped the penalty
which they deserved, and this was specially true of poisoning
cases. The number of vegetable poisons in use in Africa is very
large, and by far the greater number leave little or no trace a
short time after death. By the time that suspicion has been
aroused, the body exhumed, and parts sent for analysis, the trail
is long since cold. Even when people have confessed to adminis-
tering poison, which they do quite freely, no action can be taken
unless the cause of death can be established, scientifically, by the
medical authorities.

However, Nyachikanda and Bernard were not the confessing
kind. They returned, only to be re-arrested and charged with a
breach of Native Custom in their compact with the witchdoctor.
They each received six months imprisonment. I, and everyone
else in the District, thought them most fortunate. But that will
not be the end of the matter: Nyachisochi's family will now
be concerned, and the cycle will go on, until it is settled by large
payment and counter-payment between any parties surviving in
a few years' time.

Unquestionably there is a very great deal of fraud in many

witchcraft cases. As Lewanika said grimly to the French missionary, Coillard, "the bones say what I tell them to". In the mind of many Africans the witchdoctor is a benevolent figure, the only protection that the people have against the malign influence of witches and evil spirits. Several authorities, including Melland, have sympathized with this view.

It is not mine. On many occasions my experience has been that he is an unmitigated fraud, who gulls and milks the simple people by a mixture of chicanery, ventriloquism and local knowledge. This standpoint is shared by the missionaries, whose view is narrow, but correct. I have never met a witchdoctor who was not fraudulent. Yet, though their ideals are far from those of the General Medical Council and the Hippocratic Oath, they do in their peculiar way suit the African and are most effective when an illness is in any way of mental origin.

One doctor, Kayikesi, near Kalene Mission, had a most remarkable record in the cure of mad people. Heredity, witchcraft, and still more, the stress and strain of adaptation to European twentieth century life produced a disproportionately high number of mad-men and mad-women in the villages. No European doctor could get near them in their minds, and the Lunatic Asylum at Ingutsheni was simply a secure prison for the maniacally dangerous. Their life in the village was miserable, and often cut short by lack of food and care : for in an African village there is, simply, no room for passengers. The treatment of mental illness among the Africans would, with its overtones and hidden causes in custom and witchcraft, provide a lifetime's work for a devoted man. There is, alas, all too abundant material.

The gloomy, tree-ridden area of Chief Chibwika was part of the old outlaws' refuge, the Lukwakwa. The people were still untouched, close and secretive : the village Hampdens who had suffered under the weight of the Lunda bed were from there. Chief Chibwika himself, frightened of his own shadow, and of many others, presided ineffectually over an area which stretched from the Boma to the Kabompo border.

The slow spread of literacy from the three schools in that area had resulted in a spate of anonymous letters, written usually by sympathizers of the African National Congress. Usually I threw them away immediately, but one in particular had an interesting touch in accusing Chief Chibwika of living with a human head under his bed as a sovereign specific against evil spirits. Though I had never looked under the Chief's bed I was convinced that there was no truth in this particular allegation, and sent the letter on to him. He was indignant, and the writer of the letter was searched out and found. Quite rightly, he was imprisoned for a term by a combined court of justly incensed Chiefs who thought that the honour of their order was being impugned.

Chibwika's country was sinister. The attitude of the villagers in 1959 was passive and watchful. The long years of peace were over, and the villagers were waiting for something to happen. After touring and inspecting hundreds of different villages one would be a fool if one did not develop sensitive antennae for trouble. It is the general atmosphere that counts: one bad Head-man can be ignored, but after twenty or forty "doubtful" vill-ages, relieved only by the occasional good one, then one must be on the alert for trouble—soon—and near. Many of them were almost ostentatiously well-swept and clean for one's arrival, but there was no heart, no warmth in their welcome, and a half-humorous, half-fearful watchfulness in their demeanour. The Chief was no help, for he knew little of what went on: the Head Messenger, faithful Kasosa, was from Kasempa and recently arrived, the others puzzled but certain that something was in the wind.

The Boma under Sir Arthur Benson lived on its prestige. That prestige was maintained by the personality of the District Com-missioner, the reflection and representative of the Governor him-self. There was no Police nearer than at Solwezi, 183 miles away, and a D.C. who called them before anything had hap-pened, on a vague "hunch", would be suspected, rightly, of having lost his nerve. True, in the event of serious trouble, over-whelming force could be brought to bear: it was there, in the Copperbelt and Lusaka, but the secret was never to use it.

It followed, therefore, that any trouble or disorder must be dealt with within the District and by one's own resources. One would never be much blamed, one understood, if one laid one's ship alongside that of the enemy. On the other hand, "prestige" is a fragile web and once lost can never be regained in its original pristine form. Therefore, if one should be beaten from the field with one's Messengers, one's own usefulness at least, was at an end. That also was understood.

The tour continued up to Kamapanda on the Angola border, near where Stanley Tepa had been born. It was apparent that the Congress had made deep inroads into the village population, by a technique of fantastic promises, such as a motor-car for every villager once they came into power. This laudable object, or its equivalent, could, we considered, be attained more expeditiously if we remained in power, and continued our steady and painstaking efforts to better the standard of living as a whole. As Chief Chibwika had in no ways consented to the operations of the Congress in the area. Messengers were sent out and had considerable success in "cleansing" the villages and in bringing in numbers of party cards surrendered by the people. On one side was a picture of Harry Nkumbula, on the other an attempt at a coat of arms made up of spears, axes, shields and other impedimenta, bearing the motto, "Freedom Now".

At Kamapanda there was a Plymouth Brethren Mission staffed only by three old ladies, Miss Clara Perkins, always cheerful despite a crippled thigh, Miss Whyman, a quiet saint who did the nursing, and Miss Kelly, a lady from Northern Ireland, manager of schools. All alone they lived, each in their separate cottage, with little money, through bad times and through good, fifty miles over bad roads from the Boma, and hundreds of miles from civilization. Two of them had first arrived in 1923.

It was when I was at Kamapanda that the crisis exploded : and as so often when one is somewhat tired. A Land Rover drove up, one could hear it approaching for miles, with a worried-looking driver and a hurried letter from the District Officer describing the events of the morning of 3rd March, 1959. A Congress leader of the District, Mwinilunga, Bernard Mashata, had been due for

9. A Leader of Youth : Mr. Haydn Dingiswayo Banda. (Minister, 1972.)

10. Alice Lenshina.

release from prison. He was an amiable mountebank with a love of publicity and some gift for repartee. In due form he had been let out after breakfast, to find a procession of his followers awaiting him, led by Stanley Tepa. The procession had marched in formation through the Native Authority and the Township, past the Boma, and back again. At its head was Stanley Tepa, flanked by two standard-bearers with a cardboard banner bearing as inscription a long offensive tirade about the Government, ending "Get Out You Stupid Government—We Want To Rule Ourselves".

At that time, political meetings and processions were allowed on a permit from the D.C. countersigned by the Chief, and no such permit had been asked for or granted. A meeting had, however, been agreed for the following day. The District Officer very properly took notice of the illegal procession, of about one hundred people, and as they passed the Boma took out the few District Messengers that he had and confronted them. He pointed out that they were acting illegally, and after a scuffle, managed to take their banner away. So, after abusing him, they moved off again, still singing and still in formation, down the road to their headquarters. The District Messengers were too few either to break up the procession or to make any arrests.

Reading the letter, which gave a terse account of the proceedings above, it was clear that Government by consent, and by prestige, had been challenged in the rudest and most direct manner, short of actual assault. It was, it was meant to be, an insolent and studied demonstration that the Party had taken power in the District, and that the régime of Boma, Chiefs and People was at an end.

It was a challenge, a gauntlet flung down, which left no choice. A breach of the law had taken place in a public, flagrant fashion, and the District Officer and Messengers had been abused outside the very Boma, the centre of all authority. Stanley Tepa, as he marched off down the road, thought that his hour had come. He would be the real power in the District, the Chiefs would do his bidding and the District Commissioner come to him to take advice from the Party.

F

At that time there was only one reply possible. The challenge rudely put, must be faced and answered. Kalani Funda, the prince of Messengers, was away in the villages, but the tent was left standing as the rest of us started thirty-five miles back to the Boma. The Chief, Chibwika, worried but for the moment resolute, Head Messenger Kasosa, two Messengers and a Chief's *kapasu*, enough to slow up the Land Rover as it laboured over the sand-hills between the trees, enough time certainly for reflections of one's own.

One was alone with the responsibility, one must plan what to do and put resolution into one's own forces to do it. Any appearance of doubt, of hesitation, would be fatal: the moment would be lost in a discussion of pros and cons, and the blow would end by being suffered. The decision and what followed must have the appearance of being pre-destined and inevitable. With the Nyasaland disturbances in progress a defeat in Mwinilunga, which would become known very quickly in Africa, might have evil consequences, not only in the Province, but even throughout a large section of the Protectorate.

There were three choices open: first the easiest, to do nothing, to wait for the Party to make a move, and if they did not, to smooth over what had happened. Second, to call in the Police from Solwezi, who would arrive a day later, and make any arrests necessary. But the psychological moment would be past, and the Lunda, a clannish people, dislike as a tribe any intervention from outside. Third, to settle the family quarrel on the spot with what Messengers we had available, and trust to their discipline and the prestige of the Boma to carry the matter through. The risk there was that we were heavily outnumbered and might be beaten from the field. Subject to this one question, as to whether Congress was in quite overwhelming strength, I had already decided in my mind on this last course.

As we neared the Boma we passed on the road two of the best and sturdiest Messengers who had been sent down to keep the Congress meeting under observation. Fortunately, they were cheerful, which raised my own spirits—"we will all be back", and we continued. At the Boma we encountered the first of those distractions sent to throw events off their course at moments of crisis. A parliamentary candidate had reached Mwinilunga in order to canvas, and courtesy demanded that having travelled all the way, he should be treated politely. But issues of grand policy seemed abstract at that moment, and I took the staff away from him into my own office.

Never before had the Boma drum been beaten in the middle of the afternoon. The Messengers on the Boma were quickly brought together, and they, with the D.C., the Chief and the Kapasu, amounted to under twenty. For the first time I used an interpreter, since a measure of assured calm was necessary. We were going down to arrest the people who had led the procession in the morning. We did not want to fight: but if we had to fight, we would win: we were not going back to the Boma without those people. Two of the strongest Messengers, Solomon and Loti Power, were detailed to arrest Stanley Tepa. So we set off, leaving the Cadet and one Messenger on the Boma.

There was, luckily, little time for reflection and doubt. Our Land Rover and the lorry rolled down the hill in the direction the illegal brigade had gone from the Boma, with its peaceful views over the river, and two miles away came upon a single house on a gentle rise with a large thatched shed beside it. There the convoy halted. There were numerous people about, who stared at us in curiosity. Here was the Boma, headed by the D.C. whom everyone thought on tour, in the fullest possible force. What would it do?

At first even the Messengers seemed uncertain, but they were fallen in and they marched up the hill in single column, with the Head Messenger, Messengers Solomon and Loti, and myself at their head. At the entrance to the shed we halted: it was packed with people. At one end was a raised platform over which hung a picture of Nkumbula surrounded by leaves and branches, and an inscription, "Your Government in Waiting". Well, it would just have to wait.

I called out, "Stanley Tepa", and he came through the crowded benches to where we stood at the entrance. He was a tall bearded figure, like a prophet with staring and excited eyes. The Messengers half feared him.

"What do you want?"

"You are under arrest for leading an illegal procession this morning."

Then a flood of Lunda, which one recognized as the beginning of a tirade, or a continuation of his speech at the meeting. But things had gone too far to go back now; I moved behind him to cut him off, and with a gentle push ejected him from the building. Perhaps I pushed harder than I should, for he shot out like a cork out of a bottle into the arms of Solomon and Loti Power. He at once began to struggle like a maniac, for he had boasted often that Government dared not touch him, and it took three men to subdue and handcuff him. Once that was done he began to demand that he be allowed to go freely to the lorry, but by then it was too late.

Within a matter of seconds there was an angry buzzing sound like a hive of bees disturbed, and people began to pour out of the shed from all directions to the rescue of their leader.

Three Messengers were engaged in conducting Stanley Tepa down the hill, the others stood in line where they had halted. As the people came on at a run down the hill I realized with a sense of dismay that our bluff had been called, and that the mystique of the Boma which had served for so long, was confronted by a rival—the Party—something much more powerful than a handful of malcontents who could be dealt with under customary laws with the general consent of the people as a whole. As I spread out my arms widely, half in appeal to them to listen, half in an attempt to stop their progress, I felt a clubbing blow on the left ear. The world went dark. Then a low growling, worrying noise as Kasosa was on to the man: he had seen his own D.C. with whom he had served since Kasempa hit, and could not contain himself. Long forgotten boxing lessons come back at such times, and after a moment I caught the assailant with a left counter before he vanished back into the shed. Round one was over.

By this time the crowd was thoroughly roused, but Tepa was nearing the lorry. To get the Messengers in a line to face them was the one thing to do, and this was accomplished to the accompaniment of further scuffles. However, past experience had taught that so long as one can talk, people will listen, and they will not hit a man making a speech, if only out of curiosity to hear what he will say next. There was plenty to say, and I said it, with the hopeful intention of calming the people. It appeared that I had succeeded: the shouts and screams died down and the people listened in sullen silence. Tepa had been lawfully arrested, and the people must respect the laws, as they had done in the past.

However, it would be imprudent to remain too long with but a thin line of Messengers and oneself between the crowd and Stanley Tepa, by now sitting in martyred dignity on the lorry. It was necessary to move on. It is never easy to retire down-hill, particularly with an untrained force: but we wheeled about and slowly began to move back.

Unfortunately the best educated of all the Messengers, in pursuit of some plan of his own, broke into a run, and before he could be stopped the whole crowd, led by the women and particularly the sister of Stanley Tepa, a fierce virago, had surged forward through the rear-guard, and picking up any stick that was handy, again set about the District Messengers. It has been rightly said, and by Clausewitz himself, that a truly intelligent army would run away.

The Messengers were of course unarmed, and caught at a disadvantage, but they turned and grappled with their assailants. Two were wounded, one badly, and the Chief himself was struck in the chest. The habit of assaulting District Messengers with sticks had been growing in isolated cases, and I had thought it well to bring a supply of stout pick-helves on this expedition in case it occurred here. Now they were needed, and quickly put in the Messengers' hands. They were of far heavier metal than anything in reach of the crowd; they were not not used, but they were enough to cause them to draw off as a whole, leaving individuals in combat with the Messengers.

By this time the Messengers had their backs to the lorry, and it was time to go, accompanied by seven further prisoners, including Stanley Tepa's sister. Had the crowd, a good two hundred strong, made any sort of a concerted rush at the Messengers we should have been quickly overwhelmed. But their training was worse than our own, and they wasted their strength on a dozen futile single combats : we at least had some small cohesion and a very definite aim, which we had carried out.

As we drove back I had a sense of failure. We had not dispersed the disorderly mob, but it had continued in being, shouting insults as we drove away up the road. Surely they had, to that extent won the day. For the size of the crowd made renewed force impossible, and they certainly would not listen to persuasion. However, we had achieved our objective, and taken Stanley Tepa from the middle of them, besides other prominent and troublesome characters who had assaulted the Messengers. The man too powerful to be touched had been carried away struggling in handcuffs. We had cause for sober satisfaction, but the assembly must be dispersed the first thing tomorrow morning. This little affair had seemed like three hours : in fact, it had taken exactly forty minutes.

The parliamentary candidate was waiting for us on our return : and since the wireless had broken down, kindly carried a message to the Provincial Commissioner at Solwezi. The situation was in hand, but the Police should stand ready. There was no sleep that night. Would the Congress organize and make a stand, or would they disperse quietly? One prayed that they would disperse.

Happily, at first light the next morning it was raining, a steady persistent drizzle which would take the heart out of a revolution. The sleepy Messengers were warmed by cups of hot tea from a field kitchen at the Boma, and once more we drove down the hill. No-one was astir : the Congress Committee were roused from bed and left sitting under guard.

Strong parties went down the roads where the villages were full of people.

"All is over, put your blankets on your bicycles and go home."

This they were glad to do, riding or walking off in the rain to their own villages. It was complete success. All was over, and the Party "putsch" had been quelled with our own small forces. It was unnecessary to call the Police, and the doctrine of the "D.C. and a few Messengers" keeping order in the traditional manner, had been upheld in its purest form. All the same there had been some very disturbing moments, and the courage and endurance of the Messengers had been severely tested. They had lost two wounded: but from that day they became a magnificent force of men, their internal dissensions and jealousies forgotten, completely confident in themselves and the Government that employed them. So far as Congress was concerned, it sank away to a despised underground movement, and for a brief golden, Indian Summer, the Boma and the Chiefs reigned supreme. Yet there was no real reason why their rule should not have endured for years. A good government, a sound government, which made the utmost economy of gesture and parade, and which hid its achievements rather than trumpeting them. It gave few medals, but it did its work.

There was no need to pursue Congress to the limits of the District. Contrary to what is often supposed, the Africans, though unsophisticated, have a shrewd idea of political realities and an acute sense of where power lies. The vast majority of silent uncommitted people in the villages who had been watching these affairs, swung decisively over to the side of Government and Chiefs. Some eight or nine people were sentenced by a Magistrate for their part in the disturbance, Stanley Tepa receiving nine months' hard labour. It was thought wise to send him to serve his sentence in a large central prison in the Copperbelt and to let the District have a rest from him.

Unhappily, these large prisons were political forcing houses, and no attempt was made to re-educate the prisoners. Indeed they were in a state of legalized anarchy within, and seemed to be run more for the benefit of the prisoners themselves than of society. At the end of his sentence, therefore, Tepa returned not repressed, nor reformed, but refreshed. However, he was soon sentenced to another term, which he served at Mwinilunga, for refusal to surrender his shot-gun, of which he had been deprived as a consequence of his first conviction. This seemed for the time being to neutralize him so far as politics were concerned.

If it had the appearance of persecution, it was a unique case, and it achieved its object in keeping the District from turmoil and allowing it to go forward in peace. Each month, each year, small steady gains were made as well as keeping the machine going, an achievement in itself. It is a well-worn subject of academic discussion whether one, or a few, seeking to change the order of society, should suffer for the many. In fact, in the circumstances of Africa, where law, order and the whole fabric of society rests on such slender pillars, I have no doubt at all that it was justified to hunt and harry these people on every possible occasion until they sank exhausted into impotence. There could be no qualms, and there were none. At the same time one's actions must be kept within the strict framework of the law, which constituted the rules of the game.

On 11 March, 1959 the Zambia African National Congress was proscribed as an unlawful organization by the Governor, Sir Arthur Benson. Its branches and offices over the country, from where unemployed clerks and other misfits were busy spreading sedition and plotting murder, were shut down in a night. This time surprise was complete, and the operation went off with clockwork smoothness. The Governor denounced the organization in a broadcast as "Murder Inc.", an accusation justified by information already known to the Special Branch, and even more by subsequent events.

The leaders of the organization were deported in groups of two or three to remote stations of the Territory, mainly to Barotseland and the North Western Province. Mwinilunga was spared because of its recent troubles. This dispersion in the event proved a cardinal blunder. No doubt it was thought that their removal to out-station conditions off the line of rail, denied the luxury of political meetings, would reduce them to their proper size.

It quite failed to do so, and indeed the adherence of the two quietest Provinces almost solidly to the United National Indepence Party (Zambia A.N.C. under a new name), can be traced directly to the effect of the detainees.

These men had a sinister force. They behaved with an odious self-assurance, a truculence against which the Messengers and other staff seemed powerless. They wandered about at will, and did what they liked. With Hola Camp in mind, the Government issued instructions that made it impossible to discipline them.

They were provided with ample allowances and given good houses, bedding, plates, knives and forks, etc.

What was not provided they demanded at length from D.C.s. They would enter their offices without permission, sit themselves down in a chair and begin a lengthy rigmarole of complaint before these busy men had recovered from their surprise. As to enter usually meant formalities with the Head Messenger, and to take a chair, not a mat, was a privilege granted to people of importance, this cool assumption placed them in a category by themselves. A chair once granted cannot next time be taken away, and they knew it. They could not be controlled unless by the actual application of greater physical force, which Boma staffs, accustomed to rule by universal consent, were reluctant to apply. They feared letters of complaint to the Governor, or far worse, to Members of Parliament and questions in the House.

So their unpleasant, sneering figures wandered about at will in home-made togas of blankets, and their detention, which was meant as a lesson, developed into something nearer to a series of local triumphs.

The difficulty could have been got over quite easily by holding all these men in one camp, under a special staff, or limiting the allowance strictly to necessities so that they would have had to look for work. As few of them had done any manual work before, this would have reduced them to size beside their fellows. In the event fifty miniature Lenin's spread their poison unchecked in twenty peaceful rural Districts, and they did very great harm. The same purpose, to relieve pressure on the line-of-rail, could have been achieved with closer thought, and a little less anxiety for uninformed opinion in England.

It was a pity that we missed years of opportunity to bring Africa and England closer to one another by an exchange of people and ideas. The Paramount Chief of Barotseland had been there for the Coronation in 1936 and was surrounded and fêted by his old friends. An Army contingent marched in the Victory Parade after the War, and a lone Bemba had set up his own system of *Chitamene** cultivation in the heart of the New

---

* The Bemba system of lopping branches, burning them and cultivating on the ashes.

F*

Forest. There were so few others. Yet loyalty and friendship could have been stimulated and built up by a simple system of exchanges as soon as air-travel became a commonplace event.

English towns could have adopted Districts in the Territory as they once adopted warships and aircraft squadrons : not to advise the commanders on navigation and tactics, but to provide a visible link with home. The surplus wealth of the towns, always poured out in good causes, could have been used to finance two- or three-week trips to England, for Chiefs, Councillors, farmers, District Messengers, Policemen, Clerks, and vice versa. Old D.C.s would have emerged from retirement as hosts on these sight-seeing and educational tours. Town Councillors and important men from the cities would have returned the visits and touched the edges of the complexity of Africa.

True, a fortnight is not long, but it is better than nothing : or even nothing plus the *Guardian*. It might have been possible when the project had got under way for the English towns to give such things as ambulances, dispensaries, libraries, on a more personal basis. The exchange of visits would have supplied the personal touch so lacking in Christian Aid, Oxfam and others. Pemmicanized aid may keep people alive, but it hardly satisfies anything else. We did little : we might have done far more. A fairly large body of solid loyal men who had seen and enjoyed England at first hand, would have done much to counter the lying promises of little men when the testing-time came.

Chief Ikelenge of Mwinilunga was typical of all that was best in Africa. A large, jovial man, who filled his robes with unselfconscious dignity, he had proved his courage by shooting a man-eating leopard shortly after his succession. Thanks to his drive and energy everything about his village was of the best; the modern post office, welfare hall, court house, water-pump and the buildings round them.

All were neat, well-kept, and a model of what a Chief's headquarters should be. Nor was it a matter of outward appearance only, for his own area, densely populated, was well administered, and crime of all kinds was the lowest in the District. There was order, progress and happiness. Nearby Mr. ffolliot Fisher, the son of the great Doctor Fisher, kept his patriarchal state surrounded by his family and by a herd of valuable pure Jersey cattle. Sakeji School, next door, for the children of missionaries from all over the Congo and Northern Rhodesia, had over one hundred European pupils. All was sunshine, and a wonderful example of what might, what should be done, by African and European working together in friendship over fifty years.

Chief Ikelenge, in his modern car, or if necessary by bicycle, skimmed round his territory, and found time to lend his ability in the District, the Province and the Territory. In the north the Apostles, a bearded, fanatical and cheerful sect, astonished people with their feats of fire-walking, and the Sakeji Stream, flowing over weirs through wooded banks, looked like nothing so much as the River Itchen. Meanwhile the birds in the thick woods set up a clamour at morning and evening, so punctual that one could tell the time by their start and finish.

Camping in Ikelenge was solaced by a variety of extraordinary books found in the villages—*The Manual of Roman Law,* the *Danish Army Manual* of 1909 (in Danish) and Gladstone's *Irish Speeches.* Following the perverse logic of the last we were roused by a report that Mwatiamvwa, the Great King, was touring the southern border of the Congo. We wished to pay our respects to him, and being bound by no strict time-table we set off, together with Chief Nyakasaya, in Chief Ikelenge's car. It was an excellent opportunity to see the Belgian type of administration at ground level, shortly before the débacle of 1960.

It is true that the Belgians have been much blamed for their alleged failure to prepare the country for its independence. The unlikely theory has been advanced that they withdrew at such short notice in the hope that in the resulting disasters they would be invited to return with some sort of mandate from the United Nations. If so, they misjudged. One is never invited to return : it is almost as though a country which has its own trumpery flag and ridiculous insignia would rather slaughter its inhabitants to the last man, woman and child, than admit it was unready, unequipped and incompetent to perform the first basic function, to preserve some sort of peace and order. And no-one knows, or may ever know, the strength of the pressure exacted by other countries on Belgium to withdraw. There may have been, of course, one of those sudden failures of nerve and fibre, similar to that which overtook the Belgian Army in 1940, or Great Britain in 1960.

The Belgians, a legacy no doubt from King Leopold II, were far more authoritarian than ourselves. No Welenskys arose, and no African politicians, though there were doctors, managers, and an *élite* which had official recognition. There was no colour-bar as such, and the contrast to the Copperbelt was striking. Africans would dine at the Hotel Leopold II unremarked. There were no harrassing pass-laws : and there was a strong flavour of real estate about some of their development schemes. Large profits were taken out, but the workers received substantial benefits also. Public order was maintained in the last resort by heavily armed African troops with European officers—the *Force Publique*— thought to be a rampart, but which later mutinied and became a menace.

The Fonds du Bien-Etre Indigène spent some $600 million per annum from 1947. In ten years they had completed :

  28 hospitals
369 dispensaries
118 maternity hospitals
124 children's clinics
  15 orphanages
   5 sanatoria
  17 equipped medical centres
   3 malaria elimination campaigns
242 ambulances into service

and spent 60 million francs on leper colonies. This was on the medical side alone. It is a good record.

The railway line from Elizabethville to the coast skirted the north of Mwinilunga. There were junctions, actual towns, within striking distance. The occasional house of brick and corrugated-iron roof would stand out, and one or two bridges. But the approaches to the bridges were much like ours, rough and worn, and the generality of village houses of poor quality, many still of grass. Grass houses had been outlawed in Mwinilunga since the 1940's. A more "continental" atmosphere prevailed. Beer was sold freely from small bars, and so, it seemed were muzzle-loading powder guns of modern manufacture. There was a pleasant freedom and lack of formality in African-European relations: the crowded bars hummed with friendly life. Independence was already in the air, and the *evolués* expatiated in bad French on what they would do with freedom.

Tshombe, the son of a rich trader, was a product of this environment, yet his French was the purest and most musical that I have ever heard.

The Belgian *Chef-de-Poste* sat smoking a cheroot, and failed to rise when I entered the office with Chief Ikelenge. We explained our mision and he became more cordial. We even lunched together: in a matter of months he would have to return to Belgium. He would be replaced by a District Council elected by Universal Suffrage. He had become cynical. He had no faith that this arrangement would work, and I am bound to admit that his gloomiest forebodings were more than justified by events.

Mwatiamvwa outstripped our party, and we returned to Northern Rhodesia and the curiosities of Ikelenge, through a "beaten zone" of Portuguese Teritory along a fine road equipped with magnificent concrete bridges, but naked of all signs of human habitation. The inhabitants had long since infiltrated across the border where they clustered along the roads and paths. There, above all, was a chance to sell whatever they could produce, and to live under a regular system of Government, not exposed to the whim and caprice of the administrator or his African staff, but subject instead to the law.

The first double-storey house in Mwinilunga looked out across a large plain. The ambitious proprietor had excelled his fellows, but since his wives refused to sleep upstairs, he had become the butt instead of the envy of the people around. Nearby Dimas Kambungu, a joiner, produced exquisite chairs from local wood, superb carpentry, worthy of the best of the English cabinet-makers' work. His family were dressed complete to shoes and woollen booties for the babies, and his manner was that he was as good as any European who might come to see him. No doubt he was, but it was necessary to tell him that he must continue to make good chairs.

In a remote village there was once a man with a peculiar illness—he wanted to be a European. So strong was this mistaken urge that he fell ill, and consulted a witchdoctor. He specialized in the therapeutic treatment: the man must dress, behave, and generally conduct himself as one for the space of one month. Towards the end of that month the District Officer came upon him sitting gloomily by himself in the village, dressed in sweltering clothes, collar and tie, and suit, surrounded by cups of tea. The other people in the village had become bored with him and left him severely alone. He suffered. But soon his term of penance would be complete and he could return to the freedom of everyday life again. In a few days he did so, perfectly cured of his mysterious disease.

Kapelembe, the official circumcisor of the youths, was waiting to perform his ceremony nearby. An ex-medical orderly, his instruments were sterile and his technique sure. He was maintained by the Lunda Native Authority in the teeth of the hostility of Kalene Hill Mission who disliked all pagan ritual.

Long ago, in Lunda legend, the child of the first woman, Nyachibanda, went to the river to draw water. Her male child, crawling after her, accidentally scratched his penis on a sharp blade of grass. The Chief, for some reason, thought this good, and ordered that all male children should be circumcised as they approached the age of puberty. It became, with its camp surrounded by high wooden stakes, forbidden to women, its masked dancers, master of ceremonies, and singing in the night, an ordeal by which a youth proved his right by his stoicism to be treated as a young man. But it was undesirable in the twentieth century that boys should be damaged by brutal techniques and unhygienic methods.

Therefore, Kapelembe, the official circumcisor-in-chief, who visited the camps in turn and saw to it that all was well. The Missionaries denounced this official recognition of paganism from their pulpits : but the Lunda were the Lunda and had no more intention of abandoning circumcision than the Jews. It was apparent that a broad eighteenth-century tolerance was the order of the day. After all, no Government can afford to be unpopular every day of the year.

To the north-east of Mwinilunga, eighty miles away along the Congo border, was the last administrative outpost, that of Chief Kakoma. The border ran along the water-shed, the ridge between where the rivers rose and flowed north and south. Huge empty plains stretched to the horizon to the north-west, without a tree, and crossed by minute solitary figures. At sunset it was a huge, forgotten world.

Chief Kakoma was a simple man, who guarded his tribal relics in his house, hung also with pictures of Queen Elizabeth, Prince Philip and King George VI. Modern life with its problems puzzled him greatly, and he disliked undue activity. His people loved him, for he was all that they were themselves, honest, well-meaning, slow.

At his elbow, living only a few miles away, was his tormentor, Rhodes Mapaipai Mwangangu, a highly sophisticated man owning a model house and with a following among the youths, the storekeepers and the disenchanted. He was the perfect example of a man of complex African character who had encountered European civilization, seemingly adopted it entire, yet who remained more "African" than most in his unpredictability. No-one could follow the tortuous workings of his mind. He had occupied a responsible position at Roan Antelope Mine at Luanshya, but had not found it satisfactory : he had become a British citizen entitled to vote, but the constitution did not quite suit him : he had been an assessor at the Urban Court, a most responsible position, but had found his fellow Justices lacking in wisdom and common sense.

So he had departed. Always impeccably dressed, fortified by boundless self-esteem, far better educated than anyone for fifty miles around, he conducted a war of nerves with unending eloquence on the unfortunate Chief and his staff. They returned his contempt with cordial dislike. Later Rhodes went to England as an Adviser to the African National Congress at one of the many Conferences. That was the apex of his career, which petered out in internal political quarrels.

Mwinilunga, far the remotest District in the Territory, had its share of confirmed individualists and men of destiny whose only possible role was that of Prime Minister, without an opposition. At that time the fabric of society was stable enough for them to be suffered quietly, and even with a measure of wry amusement. The Lunda had a proverb for everything, and their comment on them was: *Chikunulu Wadingi Kalamba, Wadisenda Wukaleni*—"the owl was a Chief, but he threw away his chieftainship". That is to say that the owl appeared to have great wisdom as he sat still in the tree, but once he started to talk, there his reputation ended.

Long ago, in the 1920's, there was a forlorn attempt at European settlement in this high forgotten corner of the country. Land was cleared, fenced, and brick houses built and a store. Men from the local villages had work as cattle-herds and farm labourers, and over two thousand cattle grazed over the wide well-watered plains. Only the chimneys stood now in the long grass, these and a few rusty pieces of iron. One could make out what had once been gardens, and quarters, and cowsheds. Hidden in a thicket were four hummocks surrounded by stones, the graves of Hunter, Shipley's child, another, coloured, and of Larsen the Dane, the only survivor who had lived alone there for years and married an African wife. Now she was living with one of Chief Kakoma's Court Assessors. I asked that these pathetic relics of men who had died forgotten should be cleared, and left sufficient funds to see that this was done. The small cemeteries of about a dozen at such places as Kasempa give a feeling of sadness, but at least they are tended and are recorded. There seemed a quite peculiar additional pathos in lying abandoned and forgotten so very far away.

As Senior Chief Sailunga was the Chifwankene to Musokantanda in the Congo, so was Headman Kasontu to Chief Sailunga: the Chief-of-Staff or second in command, a position of great traditional importance. A stately, upright old man over

six foot tall, he advanced towards Chief Kakoma and went down
on his knees. With much deliberation he produced a small bag of
white chalk from within the folds of his ample blue kilt, and
began his full greeting: *Evuleyi* clap-clap-clap—*Kalombo*—
clap-clap—*Evuleyi*, etc., with his village behind him joining the
clapping. One white line he drew up the middle of his stomach,
then another up the Chief's stomach (he opening his shirt to
allow it), then sprinkled himself with dust over the head, neck
and body. His ceremonial greeting complete, he drew up a small
stool in front of the Chief: his people sat, as custom required,
on the earth.

It was clear, even then, that this distinguished old gentleman
was looked on with a half-smile as sadly out of date. Politically,
he had no following and was a spent force. Schools, mines,
motor-cars, had left him hopelessly behind. Yet, someone will
emerge, in different form, to perform his ancient function—the
installer of the Chief, and a leader in war—even though expressed in modern western terms, the echo of the idea will live
on.

Meanwhile the villages were at peace. Little summer houses
of bougainvillaea cut into decorated shapes marked the most
enterprising. The medicine chest was busy in the evening:
"stomachs there, coughs there, then malaria and wounds". The
drums beat through the night where there was honey beer, and
at the camp-fire the burning logs shot up showers of sparks to
the stars.

"Government is God," said a flattering Headman. No, it was
not, but it had some reason then to be satisfied with what it
had created in the last sixty years.

Chapter X

THE LAST YEARS OF PEACE

A man that looks on glass
On it may stay his eye,
Or if he pleaseth, through it pass,
And then the heaven espy.
                    (George Herbert).

CHIEF KANONGESHA, Senior Chief of the Ndembu to the west of the Lunga River, was the custodian of all that was conservative and the great enemy of progress in Mwinilunga. Improved roads and bridges he looked on with scepticism, schools he regarded with a marked coolness, and Missions he secretly abominated. When African medicine and treatment had been tried and had failed, he would resort, with open distrust, to hospital. His watchword was *Chisemwa Chetu Cha Lunda*—"the customs that we Lunda are born with", and these were a sure rampart and defence against anything new, or rather, anything new that he disliked.

In his area custom was King, and the witchdoctors went about openly as respected citizens. Nfunji, their leader, would wander past officers on tour, hung with charms and with his hair in long ringlets like an Orthodox Jew in Jerusalem, on his way to some illegal ceremony. The old Chief would gesture with his arm, the one ornamented with the bracelet of human sinew—*Chisemwa Chetu*—and give his most gracious smile.

Rain, if it were late, was summoned by the building of a special shrine :

Here the people would gather to pray for rain : "Oh God, give us rain." Similarly the Kaonde long ago would gather round a whitened tree or pole and address *Chakapanga*—God—*Wishoo*—the rain falling in torrents.

But the villages had whole collections of shrines for the sufferers from varied complaints. *Kamwadji*, or the loss of sexual power and pleasure, *Karombo*, or the spirit to be placated on a run of ill-luck hunting, *Chintemu*, the thief. . . .

A *Chintemu* was a man who could turn himself into a spirit, and by so doing acquire his neighbour's goods. Painted with a faintly luminous medicine he would fly about on moonless nights, in appearance similar to a shooting star or small rocket, though five miles, at the very most, was his range. He would abstract the food from gardens or from storage bins, and if spotted, turn quickly into an innocent village pig or dog. Should he be shot, the man himself would die in his hut soon after. A man would become *Chintemu* voluntarily, and was usually the type who would have bulging grain bins and stores in time of dearth.

But there were other worse creatures in the background, again the *Kayewela* of the Kaonde, shaped this time like a hunting dog, and which killed its owner's enemies by hitting them on the nose with a stick while they slept. It carried their bodies to the owner who cut them up secretly and ate them. They were despoilers of graves, and, a descent to the mundane, stealers of cloth from stores.

The *Ilomba* had the shape of a long black snake with the face of a human-being. The owner fed it on chicken. He was immune from witchcraft as he could transfer himself to the Ilomba : and if he was shot or speared the Ilomba would lick his wounds clean and he would live. He was invulnerable. He would take his creature at night round the huts of his relations, and dig a little hole near each hut. Then the Ilomba would hide there and could report all that the owner's relatives had said. If the owner had an enemy, and everyone has enemies, the Ilomba would go and eat him. If a witchdoctor found an Ilomba he would kill it, but otherwise the owner, guarded by his immunity, would live to a very old age. When he died, the Ilomba would die also.

Yet another, the *Nkala* or crab, fat, bloated, about four feet high with long talons, which would catch a man's shadow in its teeth and carry it to the water to devour it. At the same time the owner, deprived of his shadow, would die.

Ihamba was a comparatively harmless ceremony of expelling illness from the body. After a day or a day and a night of constant drumming the patient would be brought from his hut and the noise would rise to its climax with all the people of the village joining in. The sufferer, laid on the ground, would feel a sudden sharp pain at the seat of the illness. Then, by a sleight of hand, a tooth would be produced from the place and held up in triumph to the crowd. The illness had been cured : and it is natural that the patient often experienced a marked, if temporary, relief.*

Near Kanongesha stood Matonchi, a forlorn and abandoned European farm. Great terraces had been built up with a view for twenty miles at least into the trackless wastes of Angola : others, falling away to the side, had been planted with orange trees and vegetables, with careful brick furrows running down to a deserted pool.

The house still stood, inhabited by ghosts, with arm-chairs, and hunting prints on the wall—toothpaste solidified in the tube, and Gordon's gin in a half-full bottle. The proprietor, a man of great courage, and skill as a carpenter, had set out from the Cape after the 1914–1918 War in an ox-wagon with his wife. They had gone on till they found themselves in this forgotten corner of British territory, had settled, and then after some years he had died.

In a corner of the farm, by a grove of eucalyptus which sighed and rattled in the wind, his wife had built his tomb, looking out over a measureless horizon, a great square of stone.

So for years he rested in peace and in state. However, this was not to be the end. Independence approached, and his wife, living far away, heard rumours of graves being violated in East Africa. She interposed : she disinterred her late husband and cremated his body, whose ashes she scattered in the Indian Ocean. The farm was abandoned, and will soon be overgrown. No-one will have tea on the lawn again, and look over a view

---

* It will be understood by those who have studied Dr. V. W. Turner's masterly work *The Drums of Affliction*, that I merely touch the surface of these things as an interested amateur.

that seemed to take in the whole of Africa, so that one could imagine that the rollers of the Atlantic were just over the horizon.

Even in Mwinilunga the modern world would occasionally intrude. Peter Matoka* was born the son of the D.C.'s cook in about 1930. By hard work he had risen to a university graduate, joined the Government and returned to his home village to spend his leave. One could hardly require this charming educated man, of higher academic standing than oneself, to sit on the ground and clap his hands in greeting. In fact, he and his wife came forward and shook hands, in a way that removed any awkwardness that there might have been. But it is necessary to remember that even so late as 1959 this was quite an innovation on both sides.† Others, far stiffer then, went much further later.

The contrast came two days later. Kabonzo, a famous "doctor" from the Congo, appeared in the camp dressed in skins, and his assistant carrying his divining basket, skins, rattles, bells, and other paraphernalia. He asked, a bold request, to hold a session that evening to make sure that everything was well in the camp, and that no-one was, unknown to himself, engaged in bringing ill-luck or disaster down. I had a good idea that in my own presence his performance would be ineffective, and thus demonstrate his impotence : I had also a curiosity to observe a witchdoctor in action.

The performance was quite tame : all the carriers were drawn up by the light of the fire, half-laughing and half-nervous, like the audience at a horror-film. One by one they went forward, and Kabonzo rattled his basket and flashed a sliver of broken mirror in their eyes. Not one bearer of ill-fortune was found, and all retired peacefully to sleep, some perhaps even relieved. He appeared a fairly harmless charlatan, and I gave him a letter of introduction to the Chiefs, saying that I had seen his perform-ance, which appeared to be innocuous. But I was much mistaken.

Without the presence of the District Commissioner events took

---

* Entered politics late. Minister of Information, 1965. High Com-missioner in London 1970.

† It was always the custom to shake hands with Chiefs, Councillors, Teachers, etc., but not with the villagers—there were too many.

a more sinister turn. In front of a large crowd Kabonzo held a further session at Chief Nyakaseya's village: medicine was applied to the eyes of the people, and one old Headman, whose misguided curiosity had led him over fifty miles from near the Boma, was blinded by it. For this I was to blame: a little fore-sight should have told me that what was a silly joke, a charade, in my Camp, would be quite different out of sight. But living in a place such as Mwinilunga one begins to accept witchcraft and witchdoctors as part of the normal pattern of existence, and to relax one's vigilance, until quite suddenly an incident, or a death, brings one back.

As I have said Senior Chief Kanongesha was foremost in up-holding ancient custom. One day he arrived, out of breath, and at his most charming. Usually his visits heralded a stream of querulous complaint, his wives had run away, his ancient privi-leges had been curtailed, or he had run out of petrol. But today, he was at his most amiable. He had just lost, by ill-luck—and no doubt witchcraft—a favourite nephew, a young man whose body lay at the Boma.

By an extraordinary stroke of luck two famous doctors, a man and a woman, had arrived from Kabompo: they could restore the dead to life, and had numerous testimonials of their success. Only after a year and a half at Mwinilunga would one have even listened patiently to this nonsense, but the day had been a long one and the old Chief seemed genuinely affected at the death of his nephew. After all, it would only mean a few harmless passes over the body in private, failure, and the discrediting of the two charlatans. I weakened and I fell—I agreed.

A while later, at my house, some sixth sense called me back to where the raising ceremony would be held. It was as well that I went. The Chief was nowhere to be seen, but people appeared to be pouring in from all over Mwinilunga, on bicycle and on foot, the women running with the babies bouncing up and down on their backs. Many were members of various branches of the Government, but they all had the peculiar lowering and glazed expression that meant trouble. Who and what would start it I did not know, but it was there.

The only thing to do was to cancel the ceremony forthwith, as within two minutes it would be under way, and nothing would have then dispersed the crowd. In the hut there was darkness, one could just see the body lying on its side on the bed, as though asleep.

"Who killed you?" asked the man.

"Witchcraft killed me," the woman answered.

"Name the witch," the man went on.

That was the time to terminate the proceedings at once. Calling a Messenger in the crowd, who came forward like a man in a trance, I ordered him to tell the people to go home and to lock the door of the house. The ceremony was ended with effect from now.

The couple returned to Kabompo under escort, on foot, the next day. A message was sent to the Senior Chief regretting that it was not possible after all to test their powers of resurrection. However, he was offended, and left the Boma without bidding good-bye. He wished, I believe, to demonstrate his power to hold what would have turned out to be a witch-finding pointing-out ceremony in the Boma itself, which would have been followed by a whole wave of similar meetings—no doubt attended by deaths —over the whole District.

And the ultimate responsibility would have been pinned on the District Commissioner—who else—who had sanctioned the first pointing-out under his very eyes. Quite correctly. One is led into some difficult situations by interest in native custom and sympathy with people, or, should one say, human weakness.

Nineteen-sixty was the year of the Monckton Commission. Far from seeming an instrument of fate, it was welcomed by the responsible members of both races. Lord Monckton, unlike Lord Devlin, had the capacity and experience to take more than a purely legalistic view, and to avoid loose phrases such as "Police State". He, and his distinguished colleagues, were welcome as evidence that we, and the Africans, were not forgotten by the British Government; that the Queen, and the British people, still indirectly, had concern for us.

For years we had watched the advance, step by step, of the

Federal Government, towards independent sovereign power, sometimes slow, sometimes with a bound forward, as when the African Affairs Board was over-ruled in 1957, and the Constitutional Convention established in the same year.

It ran as follows :

"The United Kingdom Government recognized the existence of a Convention applicable at the present stage of the constitutional evolution of the Federation, whereby the United Kingdom in practice does not initiate any legislation to amend or repeal any Federal Act or to deal with any matter included in the competence of the Federal Legislature except at the request of the Federal Government."

So we were alone.

Few realized at that time that the Monckton Commission was the watershed. The Federation had to move forward, and quickly, to Dominion status and independence, or to perish from the dead weight of inert opposition of, by that time, the complete African population of the two northern territories. It must go forward, or meet the fate that overtook it in the end.

Once again the spectre of Southern Rhodesia joining the Union was raised, though this time with less conviction, as the continuance of aggressive Afrikaner Nationalist Government made union with self-consciously English Southern Rhodesia less likely. The best that could be hoped for, we thought, was the return of such subjects as directly affected the Africans, such as Health and Post Offices, a halt to constitutional "advance", and a less bullying tone from Salisbury. We did not realize then that much of the heart had gone out of the Federation. Those who detested it for what it had done, and they were the majority of the Provincial Administration, imagined it as part of the fixed order of things, imposed in ignorance and folly, but to be lived with as a disagreeably necessity. The Queen's Government must be carried on.

One thing we thought would serve the interest of nobody was violence and boycotting. Violence would give the Commissioners a poor impression of the African's responsibility, and boycott would prevent their case being heard. Indeed it might go by default, and there was no intention of permitting a few irresponsible, unemployed riff-raff silencing by fear what the great mass of Africans had to say through their Chiefs and Councils.

The possibility that the Native Authority might refuse to give evidence was not mentioned in Mwinilunga District, and so it did not arise. Attention was focused from the start on what they had to say, with excellent results. A most sensible document was produced, full of concrete examples of matters to be righted, and reminding the Commissioners that they were the true representatives of the people.

The Chiefs, in full ceremonial robes and head-dresses, caught the imagination of the Commissioners, and they were listened to with close attention. So far as Mwinilunga was concerned both the boycotters and the Federals were answered with calm assurance by men who represented both the tradition and the wisdom of the District. Unfortunately, after Sir Arthur Benson's departure, there were already signs of some slackening of purpose, and entirely unrepresentative figures were allowed to gain much-sought publicity, and even to confuse weak Native Authorities to refrain from giving evidence by their antics.

The Commission reported that "intimidation and violence had been organized on a considerable scale by nationalist parties against their political opponents, and even against those who had failed to give their active support, with the general aim of stifling the expression of moderate or pro-federal opinion". They could have said no less: though it was not pro-federal opinion that it was sought to stifle, but moderate opinion of any kind. But on the whole, at that time, it was still strong enough to speak.

To suppress moderate opinion, there was the key. To present a crude choice between Welensky and Federation on the one hand and an African Government on the other, of whatever kind; however thrown up, that was the object of the small group of malcontents, at that time plotting by candlelight, a few years later driving triumphantly about as "Ministers of the Crown".

Their conspiracy succeeded. Already just sufficient funds came in from India to keep it alive. In a little while, as soon as they achieved cohesion, they were to pour in in a flood from Tanganyika, Ghana, Egypt, and Russia. Though much remained in the hands of party officials, there was enough surplus to buy vehicles, rent offices, to maintain agents abroad and to conduct propaganda through the Press. Nineteen sixty was the vital year, the watershed. If the Federation could not move forward, it would perish. The Monckton Commission threw the whole question of its existence open to debate, first in England, then in Africa. The tragedy lay, not in the weakening of the Federation, but in the surrender by the British Government to extremists who used the grievance as a stepping-stone to power, in its failure of will to treat them as what they were, and to give moderate and responsible Africans a fair chance to take control. In other words, a collapse of will.

Meanwhile Samundenda, the African carver with crippled legs sat in his village working. He, and another in Angola, were the only two wood-carvers left. Fifteen years ago he had produced excellent, delicate, humorous work, much sought after. Then an anthropologist had arrived, armed with quite proper ideas of fair payment for work, and promised him larger sums than he had dreamed of for anything he produced. Naturally he arrived at the solution of mass-production : the quality fell away, nails were used for a join, the limbs became larger and crude, and his work was no longer worth buying. But the price, once attained, did not come down, and the laws of supply and demand failed to operate. Samundenda had once received £10 for a table, and from then on, £10 was the price. The anthropolgist was Dr. Turner, of Manchester University, who spent two years in a village just north of Mwinilunga Boma, living as an African, keeping to a diet of cassava meal and fish. No-one in the world knows more of the Lunda than Dr. Turner, the author of *Schism and Continuity in an African Society*. In Mwinilunga he was known as "Samunyati", or "the seeker into the past".

The African banking system is all too like our own, twentieth-century style. What in Victorian times was called a debt is to them a "credit". To hear, therefore, that a man is in credit is to know that in fact, he is deep in debt. *Kilimba*, or the swapping of wages month by month is practised almost universally between men of similar income. Mbelwa gives all but the bare subsistence minimum to his friend Mwanza the first month, and he,

Mwanza, spends the surplus on desirable objects. Meanwhile Mbelwa finds towards the end of the month he has not sufficient to feed either himself or his family : he proceeds to incur various debts at stores or with other friends. The next month it is Mbelwa's turn to be rich and Mwanza's to go hungry : but instead of paying off his debts Mbelwa spends the surplus cash on other desirable objects, and the debts remain. Now Mwanza repeats the process and he incurs various other debts. This, very African, response to a cash economy, is the result of too many and too tempting consumer goods in a country of low cash wages. It creates debt, not wealth, and the debt is born not so much by the trader but by African society, which, too often, means by hungry African children.

Chief Kanyama, in whose country Lake Chibesha was included, was a quietist, a Quaker almost. Whatever he did, he did quietly with a silent, smiling rubbing together of hands. His people were the same, they made little stir in the world. The rivers flowed peacefully between their wooded banks and the people continued making reed-mats, a patient occupation. They were descended from the hereditary mat-makers at the court of Mwatiamvwa and had achieved remarkable abstract and *trompe d'œil* designs, of very ancient date and evidence of old established civilization. The older women still wore copper and lead bangles* round their ankles, which weighed them down as they walked and caused the ankles to swell. There were strange happenings in the outwardly placid villages, the deaths of children being investigated by cutting a chameleon in half, and examining the entrails.

Lake Chibesha, in the centre of the country, had been rediscovered as recently as 1949 by a District Commissioner who was fond of fishing. No villages lived near, or even drew their water from it, because it was haunted. The wind soughed gloomily through the reeds by its side. Once Headmen Chibesha had been a great man in the country, and had prospered. His pride had turned to witchcraft, and one day suddenly the waters had rushed down upon the hollow where he lived, and engulfed him and all his people. Since then it had been shunned, and all the paths on

* Ijingu.

the busy way between Kanyama and Kakoma give the place a wide berth. Fortunately, witchcraft and ghosts do not affect Europeans, though it is true that three prospectors who camped nearby were struck by lightning and nearly killed. There was a time when motor-boats skimmed the lake with powerful outboard engines. But now the road has been closed, condemned as "uneconomic", and the lake is left alone again, to the wind in the reeds, to the legend.

The spirit of the Provincial Administration in the early days of 1960 equalled that of a first-class regiment at the height of condition. To bicycle over 50 miles in a morning was an achievement, but something that could be, and was done, over the rough, sandy paths. Europeans and Africans drove themselves hard, together. They felt they had so many years of history to make up in their own lifetime. The Provincial Administration was a band of brothers, and every District Commissioner had friends everywhere he had served in the territory, and among every class. There was no snobbishness, no patronage, and the post sought after was the "field". There were some clever men "on the staff", in the Secretariat in Lusaka, but they were, quite rightly, treated with a certain condescending pity at their undoubted misfortune. But with Sir Arthur Benson's departure on retirement a more narrow, calculating, negative era began, and the spirit of the service began to change and wither.

Self-interest replaced *esprit de corps*, and expediency slowly became the order of the day. Had the men in the field been certain of support they could have remained both strong and liberal for ever, and until sufficient trained and responsible Africans were in position to take power, and govern a country both strong and free. But this was not to be : lesser men had gained control of a well-night perfect machine. It remained for them only to destroy it. Within a few weeks of the dissolution of the Ministry of Native Affairs in January, 1964, the hoarded experience which had guided the territory for over fifty years was scattered to the winds, ironically to the sound of applause. It was not needed by the new régime.

One of the signs of wobbling and loss of nerve at the centre, even in 1960, was an increasing distrust of officers in the field. If a crisis should arise in a District it was thought better to have an officer who knew nothing of it, so that he could obey instructions to the letter, without views of his own. The Congo situation was increasingly serious, and tribal fighting had already broken out in the towns near the border. Large numbers of Europeans were packed and ready to leave, and headquarters received reports of all this with increasing distaste. Of course there would be no disorder : the transfer of power had been worked out to an exact schedule, and would take place in an orderly fashion. Anyone who believed otherwise was an alarmist—indeed he might be said to have lost his nerve. Since the most circumstantial and alarming reports emanated from Mwinilunga, which had District Messengers dressed in plain clothes across the border in touch with actual events, it seemed an opportune moment for a change of District Commissioner. Further reports could then take the form of a bromide, not a stimulant, and record what had happened, rather than what was going to happen. Prophecy, particularly accurate prophecy, was unpopular. Some six weeks later three or four thousand refugees descended on Mwinilunga on a public holiday, all in crying need of food, water, petrol and the necessities of life.

So it was good-bye, to the gardens, to the great view over the hills, to Sailunga, Ikelenge, Kanongesha and Unpredictable, to faithful Kasosa, Makina and the Messengers, to old Katambi who had served forty years, honest Joas the builder, and Mundia the Medical Assistant who had tended us like a family doctor. We left a world of its own, with its own standards and its own sanctions, at a moment when it all seemed to be in peril. To be sent to the rear, to Lusaka, at such a time, seemed no compliment from my superiors. It was only years later that I found that there was more accident than purpose in this move. A need to fill a gap in a minor branch of the Secretariat had been thought more important than any first-hand knowledge and experience of Mwinilunga District.

Clearly the safe men were now in control, and in turn they wanted safe men in the field. Unfortunately, safe men are not the men for any kind of emergency : the Congo, as it developed, was certainly beyond them. It was sad at that moment to drive down the familiar road, saying good-bye at every bridge, to leave the streams and the forests and the little villages with their cooking fires, behind for ever. Yet however perverse I thought them, orders, after all, are orders.

There were men who had stayed in Lusaka for fifteen years, with regular routine and plentiful local leave : they grew plump and white with lack of exercise, and their eyes shifty with office intrigue. Usually they ended in some outwardly important position, and usually they were fumbling, ineffectual and rooted in the past. Their horizon ended at their desks : and Sir Arthur Benson was their scourge. Some had served as District Officers years ago, but their manner towards Africans was odious, until Africans attained political power, after which it became unpleasantly subservient. When the Colonial Service is caricatured, as sometimes it is, these are the figures that the caricaturists have in mind. They are quite right. It was this class that for years laughed to scorn the idea of promoting young educated Africans to responsible administrative posts : so many of them went off and became the most rancorous of the politicians, the most infected with racial hatred. Theirs is the responsibility. Placed in positions where their task was to look into the future five years or so ahead, they sat sunk in routine and intrigue. Most had left before the end came : for they saw to themselves first, and the country afterwards. After them, indeed, the deluge.

Luckily in such places as Mwinilunga one accumulates a store of local leave oneself. There are no holidays on out-stations, or very few. Fuming in a job little more than that of a clerk's, I felt able to indulge myself, to head north to the Congo with a Minister of the Government who was also correspondent of *The Times*. So, disguised under the umbrella of that august, omniscient newspaper, I set out. "It can't be true—it isn't in *The Times*", as the English governess is reported to have told an excited Frenchman on 4th August, 1914. Unfortunately, in the next few years Africa was to experience revolts, famines, outrages and massacres, not reported in *The Times* but all too true, nevertheless.

Arriving at Elizabethville in the middle of a hot morning, the street hung with blue national flags, but deserted of people. Had the seige begun? We slowed down and edged forward to where the noise of drums and bands could be heard. It was the *Défilade*, or march past in celebration of Congo Independence. The Ministers, Monsieur Tshombe in the centre, stood on a high platform, dark-suited and surrounded by uniformed officials. Army units, Red Cross, Boy Scouts, Catholic Youth, filed past in formation. A row of uniformed Belgian officers stood in line beneath the platform. They did not look pleased, or happy.—"How long do you give it?" "Two months." Before we could continue this interesting discussion the parade came to an end, the Ministers drove off rapidly in their large black cars and we retired to lunch at the best hotel.

Next day the correspondents saw M. Tshombe and his Cabinet in private : *The Times*, the B.B.C. and the *Daily Mail*, and an independent District Officer, still masquerading under the umbrella. One felt though, that one had an equal right to be there : after all, one spoke the same language. M. Tshombe's command of French was complete, and the sentences flowed out in mellifluous harmony. We fell, like so many others, under his spell. He had his policy : peace, development, friendship with all, and he meant it. It was a revelation after our own politicians, whiskered, bearded, matted and uncouth like the crew of a pirate ship, to meet a statesman—who was not only clean and at ease—but not filled with race hatred and mouthing stale rhetoric like old garlic. It was the difference between the civilization we had brought; and the return of Africa to a perverted version of its primitive past.

For a while he held us, then retired. We relaxed, and felt that we had been listening to a great man. M. Munyongo made a speech : a man of rude force with recently acquired polish : a good Interior Minister for a new country. He spoke French, then we fell into Lunda, at which the other members of the Cabinet looked more interested. I conveyed, I hope, the good wishes of the British Government and people without committing them to any alliance or even arrangement. I was not aware that anyone else had done so, or that our Government had yet heard of M. Tshombe. Certainly Whitehall had not. It was right and proper that this should be done. Also, of about equal importance, the greetings of the Chiefs and people of Mwinilunga to the son-in-law of the Great King, Mwatiamvwa. I felt I had the right to do this also. The atmosphere warmed appreciably. At that time Katanga stood on its own, while the antics of Patrice Lumumba, a convicted ex-post-office clerk, now Prime Minister, almost caused the collapse of the "Independence Celebrations" at Leopoldville.

If ever a people in Africa gained independence with good hopes for the future, it was the Katanga. They had an outstanding Prime Minister, a true statesman, great wealth, and an abundance of Belgian technical experts who were willing, anxious, to stay on to help the country. The country was at peace, and only wanted to remain peaceful. This was of course, before the days of Conor Cruise O'Brien, Dr. Bunche and the Ethiopian troops, before the days of the dive-bombers on unarmed civilians, and the falsification of news and history. No-one, after all, is more ready with the use of force than the frustrated Professors of politics. Yet nothing in the end can thwart the true wishes of the people in such a scattered and unprofitable country as Africa. They can be held down for so long by force, and then the bayonets begin to waver and it all ends in withdrawal and retreat. The country resumes her sway and chooses her own leaders.

For the moment all was set fair in Katanga, but in a matter of weeks the apparently well-armed, well-disciplined troops upon which the whole structure depended, had broken into bloody mutiny, and the first wave of refugees, frightened women and crying children, with a few possessions bundled into their cars, drove southward for their lives.

Tshombe might have returned; but he died in captivity, far from home, an African martyr. He might well ask, what has the United Nations achieved in the Congo or Katanga? How many dead to satisfy its *amour propre* : how many millions squandered by those ignorant of Africa? And how many bridges built, how many hospitals, how many agricultural schemes and training schools? Where are they? For it is certain that if they had built so much as a mud-hut, it would be weighted with a brass plaque proclaiming that it had been built by the United Nations, together with the names of the engineer and architect. The United Nations was used as an instrument of personal spite and inter-

11. The Boma at Mwinilunga.

national aggression, and its policy was carried out by persons whose ignorance was only equalled by their foolish irresponsibility.

* * *

By 1961 it was clear that the Empire had ended. Round Fort Jameson, the capital of the Eastern Province, the planters' houses were deserted and their roofs caved in. The Provincial Administration went on, without fear but without hope. The little town was built in an airless hollow in the hills, it seemed by some misguided descendant of Macdonald of Glencoe, who had somehow escaped, while the well-stocked cemetery testified to the unfounded optimism of the pioneers at the beginning of the century.

Fort Jameson Church (Anglican) was a red brick building with a square tower and a thatched roof. It had just the air of an English country church, though it would have been hard to place it in any one county.

Within were dark pews, lectern and pulpit, and round the walls elaborate brass memorials, mostly commemorating officers in the cavalry who had died of malaria and enteric while hunting elephant long ago.

When the Archbishop came the congregation filled the Church. The Wardens would urge those who had brought their dogs to remove them from the aisle, where they lay panting to escape the heat. For the rest of the year the Anglican spirit slumbered.

The fabric of administration held together, but only just. On 14th June, 1960, the new Governor, Sir Evelyn Hone, had addressed the Legislative Council as follows, referring to the recent elections:

"By that time 'Zambia' had already done a major disservice to their fellow Africans. By dissuading so many eligible Africans from registering as voters, they severely limited the part that Africans were able to play in the election of this Council. During recent months we have witnessed the formation and growth of a new political organization which early this year came under the control of many of those who had previously been officials of the prescribed Zambia African National Congress. As a result of the activities of persons connected with or

G

inspired by this organization—the United National Independence Party—a most threatening situation arose on the Copperbelt just over a month ago, which again faced my Government with the necessity to declare branches of a newly formed African political organization to be unlawful Societies.

"I and my Government are resolute that violence in all its manifestations in this Territory shall be stamped out and that the right of law abiding citizens to go about their business peaceably and without fear of intimidation and unprovoked attack shall be preserved."

Quoting Mr. Macleod : "I wish to repeat that warning today, and the Governor will have my full support in any measures that he may think necessary to take to restore and maintain law and order." But the formless, yet carefully qualified sentences, and the tone of the speech, sounded the knell of good government. There was no call to the men of good-will among the African population, to loyalists all over the country, to wake up, and strangle the octopus before it strangled them. It all sounded flat and tired, without spirit or vigour, or even conviction.

Sir Evelyn Hone, small, neat and grey, was a man of the cabinet and the bureau, and it was there that he had earned his promotion in the Service.

There are few tasks more difficult, and one would think, more distasteful, than that of Governor in a Colony approaching independence. Invested with the trappings of supreme power, he must see it whittled and eroded away week by week, month by month, by those whom he very well knows are the least fitted of all to inherit it. He must face the stares of silent grief from those who have served the Government longest and most loyally, who had trusted their all to his protection and support, and he must endure, with an even sharper pang, his own feelings and conscience as they are abandoned one by one.

Many years had passed since he had served in the field, and his long tenure in the Secretariats had unfitted him now for the rush and grapple of events outside the run of regularity and routine. His mind was supple, but it lacked brute strength to face events and to master them by native force. His every instinct was for compromise, accommodation. But he was faced with men who had set themselves outside the reach of reason, themselves the prisoners of the dark elemental forces they had summoned up from below. All this, and the mental fatigue that creeps imperceptibly over those who have served long years in Africa, led him step by step down fatal courses. His habitual prudence and reserve was thought to conceal a quiet, certain strength, but now the time came and there was nothing but anxiety to do his duty by letter and by rote—*il faut en finir*—as they said in 1940.

Affairs drifted day by day until a state of chaos and disorder in parts of the country seemed but common form. The wheel swung free, and the ship yawed from side to side. Before, during the long years of peace, there had always been a precedent to follow, and reasonable men, open to persuasion on common ground. By the end it seemed easier to give way, to be content with the outward forms of deference that were preserved. Outside the windows Africa revealed itself naked, the mob howling, and ready for war. Within, the Governor must shed his imperial plumes one by one until there is nothing left but the mute reproach of those who have trusted the symbol of all that the British Government had once meant, the law, peace, and good government, and who are left with something very different. The sunset of imperial rule was without glory or any evening splendour : only the red, sullen glow of burning dwellings marked its end. Few men would have welcomed his task, which was to guide the country to peaceful independence within a strict time limit laid down in London, imposed, it would be fair to say, in the teeth of his advice.

Yet it must be recorded, of this personally amiable and upright man, that he performed it with the grey wisdom only of the rulebook. In Africa there is a higher wisdom than that. . . .

All this was in sad contrast to the unbending, almost combative personality of Sir Diarmid Conroy, Chief Justice of Northern Rhodesia, whose rectitude and at times, judicial pugnacity, kept the courts, high and low, unpolluted when all else had sunk down. Convicted murderers, guilty of dreadful crimes, guilty of burning children alive in their huts, might be freed by administrative action and erected into Party heroes: but no-one would escape the consequences of their actions in the courts themselves. They stood, they held, amid the quaking sands, by the example of one man, the last of the Chief Justices; and I, who spoke to him but once, can pay him this tribute now.

Withdrawal was inevitable: not as a result of popular pressure which was artificial and could have been contained with ease, but only because the British Government had ordained it. Yet it might have been carried through, even with a flourish and with much good feeling, as in Malaya. It might have secured good and honourable terms to the Chiefs, to every loyal servant of Government, and to the mass of the people, by the exercise of a dominant personality and by an only reasonable firmness in maintaining order.

But all these happy possibilities were cast away by a handful of men, some tired, some cynical, a few even, bent only on their own advancement. They could not, would not, halt the descent in standards, which by the end had become a simple rush towards first, appeasement, then retirement. Each sat jealously in his bureau, only emerging for yet another strategic withdrawal down the slope.

A few thought perhaps that they could serve the country best if they remained in power themselves, at whatever cost, on whatever terms. Their crime was not so much treason, as intolerable conceit. By their false finesse, by their clumsy expertise, they caused more hatred, more suffering, more death, than if they had been simple and honest, with others and with themselves. They thought that they could always control events, little realizing that by their folly they released forces that no-one, certainly not those they thought their puppets, could measure or check. With careless hands they set free the darkness of Africa! Peace to them now. They have their memories, their regrets, their sterile honours. Their own self-reproach will be more wounding than any that I am entitled to make. As De Gaulle has written: "there is no success that does not start from the truth". These men, in their weakness and cynicism, lied in their souls. They saw the truth, but they betrayed it. It followed them, and they hid their eyes from it: it embraced them, and they spurned it.

U.N.I.P. based its plan on the "strength that it attributed to human baseness". In Northern Rhodesia, that succeeded. There were indeed inequalities, there were long standing grievances, and a lack of imagination in finding out what the Africans of the country desired. The plan was founded upon their exploitation, more particularly on the natural desire of the ordinary man to better his condition, and to enjoy his share of the amenities and luxuries flourished before his eyes by the undistinguished European minority. To do this a calculated, hysterical campaign of hatred was mounted, which extended over four years.

The hands held out only in friendship were spurned, and the devotion of sixty years of effort by British Administration (by which I mean Government officers of all branches), was cast aside. For to the nationalist, or nationalist of this type, it is the liberal that is the danger. Anyone who desires to help, with any real knowledge of the Africans' customs, their background, their hopes —anyone who has friends among them—who even loves them, there is the danger, for the omnipotent Party and the Leader cannot afford to be challenged, even by a half-smile in a remote village. There, indeed, is the proper target for malignant hatred. Such dangerous men, particularly if they are in positions of power or influence, must at all costs be eliminated.

The spiritual element, necessary in all revolutions against oppression, was absent. Here was no genuine uprising of the people. It was a hollow charade, for there was nothing to strike against but devotion. So hatred took its place. Hatred the tempter, fatally easy to rouse, yet more difficult to still. In the service of hatred it is necessary to pervert every possible source of truth, to stifle every independent thought. No lie too blatant to deceive a simple people, or too vindictive to stir them to assault, arson and murder. The wells must all be poisoned. Success, too, must be made to seem inevitable, like a process of nature. But it was only inevitable to those who had no will to resist, who remained supine on the defensive without energy, or imagination, or the will to counter-attack. It would not have been difficult to surrender power, at least to men of good-will: but to surrender one's friends to this was a very different matter.

So the hate campaign mounted in intensity from the middle of

1960. As Aldous Huxley remarks : "Prolonged singing and shouting means that people breathe out more than they breathe in.
High concentration of carbon dioxide in lungs and blood, and
the increase in concentration of CO_2 lowers the efficiency of the
brain as a reducing valve and permits the entry into the conscious-
ness of experiences, visionary and hysterical, from 'out there'. If
the raw material is the propaganda of hatred, the results are
obvious." One local party leader suffered a seizure while address-
ing a U.N.I.P. meeting in Fort Jameson, and he died. He was
given a hero's funeral. Perhaps he deserved it : he had managed
to die of hatred.

Meanwhile, life must continue : and the government be carried
on. The A-Ngoni, who lived around Fort Jameson under Paramount Chief Mpezeni, were the one tribe who had seriously
resisted the advent of the Europeans. An off-shoot of Tchaka's
Zulus, they had struck up through Southern Rhodesia, through
Nyasaland, and arrived from the eastward in the middle of the
nineteenth century. From there they had raided the Bemba across
the Luangwa Valley, but had been repulsed. Though by the end
of the century they had lost the purity of their blood by inter-
marriage, they had over-run the scattered Chewa and the Tumbuka further north, and could put a force into the field. They had
resisted the first inroads of European administration from Nyasaland, attacked riflemen with assegais and shields, and lost the
son of their Paramount Chief, with numerous dead.

Since then they had somewhat self-consciously maintained
their status as a warrior-race, though it is fair to say that they
provided a large percentage of recruits for the Army and Police.
They were independent, slow to change and accept European
habits : their villages were crowded and filthy and the despair
of tidy-minded administrators from other Provinces. Their Chiefs
had great traditional prestige, but by 1960 were fast losing power
through drunkenness, incapacity, or age. They were a people
waiting for leadership, which they did not get. The young men
drifted round the villages and Indian stores, dressed in bright
clothes bought on credit, strumming ukeleles. They were too
advanced to raise their hat to the Chief when he went by : and
they sloped about, waiting, hoping, for something to happen.

These were the raw material of the political Youth Brigades, the "Jeunesse".

But in Chief Madzimawe's village, near Mtenguleni, where the Ngoni had first settled, was an echo of the past, of the peaceful years between the Wars. A spry old man sat on a log in the sun. He showed me his medals, which he kept in a cigarette tin that the Princess Royal had sent to the soldiers in Africa in 1914–15, with her profile on the lid, surrounded by the flags of the Allies. They showed that he had served from when the armed Northern Rhodesia Police were sent north in 1915, to 1945, when he had retired as a sergeant major, a total of over thirty years with the colours. He seemed, as he came to the salute, ready to serve his time again—the best of the Ngoni.

Near the Chief's village was a large tree under which I had my camp : it shaded my tent and the carriers. The air was heavy with a thunderstorm about to break, and after the evening bath I stepped outside combing my hair. I felt a sensation of being clubbed on the top of the head and under the jaw simultaneously, and found myself some seconds later lying blinking on my back, dazed and aching. I had been struck by lightning down the great tree, which I take to be a similar experience to being shot. However, I regained my feet, and took a walk while reciting some poetry, to satisfy myself that my mental and physical faculties were unimpaired. Next day, apart from some aches. I was none the worse.

Such adventures did not improve the temper, for I found the villages, all except Kamzembe, the old soldier's, lacking, and the District Messengers also. Close administration was impossible in a District comprising 200,000 people : it was impossible for instance, to know the name of almost every village Headman, as it had been in Mwinilunga. The huge population meant that only the loosest control was possible. So much depended upon the Chiefs, and the Chiefs were so poor. Even so, the basis of law and order was maintained by 45 Policemen and 30 Messengers in Fort Jameson, with smaller forces posted at Katete and Chadiza. By no means an overwhelming show of strength, as so much of the Government was by mutual consent and agreement.

But control did not go very far down the line : if the Chiefs were reluctant to take advice from the D.C., their Headmen were equally reluctant to obey them : and on the whole their people listened to neither, but rather lived as they pleased, in dirty villages, often without paths and bridges between them, which they were too idle to maintain. By that time the Ngoni seemed to have little pride in themselves, in their name as a warrior-race, or in their Chiefs. The best of them left the villages and took service with the Government, and indeed many of the second and even third generation to do this were excellent men.

By fairly long association with Europeans, and in a framework of time, method and discipline, they had become very serviceable instruments of Government, competent, willing and loyal, even though lacking in initiative. Lest this be thought patronizing, it is meant as a compliment, in contrast to the "African personality", which is simply a caricature of imaginary Western man, posturing in a toga and sandals : a verbose vacuum, an object of mingled ridicule and alarm. Heaven help Africa, if the "African personality" truly represents it. Africa can do better than that.

The Kunda Valley in Fort Jameson District was some hundred miles long by fifty broad, a definite shelf sloping down to the Luangwa River, from where the plateau descended from Nyasaland and Fort Jameson. As one went down a little pass one could feel the change in the temperature, from warmth to heat. Should one open a window, one received, instead of a cool draught, a blast of hot air. Experience soon taught that an open window had the opposite effect that it had in Europe.

Along this shelf, surrounded by game of all kinds, crouched the unfortunate Kunda tribe, a people with little self-respect and an amalgam of all those who had been pushed down into the Valley by more powerful peoples—the Bisa—the Nsenga—and some Chewa : one suspected indeed that Kunda was only the generic name for the poor fragments who lived there.

At their head was the ancient Chief Nsefu, who in his time had been a leader of his people, but was now sunk in beer and spirits. Now he no longer led, but meandered along the easiest course. He was still respected, but only so long as he did what his people wanted. Mercifully he died before the full extent of his abandonment of power became clear to him, and before he could be insulted by bands of political youths. His insignia proclaimed his descent from Mwatiamvwa long ago : the relics of a beaded head-dress hung around his neck, his magnificent ceremonial axe of exactly the same design as those of the Chiefs at Mwinilunga. This wonderful piece of work in ivory and ebony was flung into the bush by his wives when he died, and is now probably lost for ever. The one other Chief of any consequence was Jumbe, who had reigned since 1931. Stern, upright and puritanical in appearance, he had a fine command and flow of language and a sure knowledge of his people, village by village.

The African National Congress, such as existed in the Valley, had been suppressed with some rigour in 1958 : manifestations had taken place, mild in those days, and a certain measure of passive resistance. Ironically, this left the field open for U.N.I.P., particularly among the youth who had not then been involved, while the older men, who had been sympathetic, were left, high and dry.

The people in the Valley had been at odds with Government for years : they and the game disputed possession, and Government to them was represented by the Game Department. They in turn were more interested at that time in the conservation of animals than the complaints of human beings whose crops were raided. They resented too the traditional hunting rights of the Kunda, and sought to curtail them as they could. No wonder the Kunda, poor, slighted, and between the millstones of the game and Government, exhibited all the characteristics of a suppressed people, a certain servility combined with a great deal of purely passive obstruction. Almost the first action of the carriers on tour was to refuse to carry, a thing until then outside my experience. Some twenty men sat solemnly down and endeavoured to persuade me that they had been engaged to look after the camp only, not to hump loads from one place to another. I pointed out that we started in five minutes, and this was sufficient : though I was uncertain what I should have done if they had maintained their position.

The great heat of the Valley made it impossible to go round the villages in the afternoon. The people were dozing under the eaves

G*

of their thatch, and in the camp even the butter melted in its glass jar and turned to liquid fat.

At Old Kakumbi village when the Luanga was low, it curved away to the left, to leave a wide sand-bank exposed some twenty feet below where the tent was perched. Around this were the hippo, about thirty strong, most of them with only the tops of their heads and their broad rumps exposed above the surface, but every so often emerging with a huge yawn for a great wallow, a flounder, and submergence to the bottom of the river again. The young, some still touched with pink, would sport round their mothers, and come as near to a frolic as a hippo can do. Sometimes they would disturb the old bulls, who, like elderly members of a London club, would arise, thunder, and then subside.

But these splendid animals were in danger, not from the hunter but because the very efficiency of the Game Department's protection had made life too safe for them. There were too many of them, too many animals of all kinds. Hence the grazing grounds by the banks, the pastures by the river, were now exhausted. As the light fell in the evenings, as it grew a little cooler, these defenceless creatures had to march across country as far as three miles over dry, parched ground, before they found a bite to eat. It was all too much for them, and they began to falter, fail, and die.

The Game Department, supremely indifferent to the outer world, except where it threatened the boundaries of its Reserves, acted with efficiency and despatch. The authority on the conservation of wild life, Dr. Fraser Darling, was invited to report, money was found, and a new policy of thinning out the game herds decided and put into action.

As a completely new departure a number of each species was put down for controlled shooting every year; the meat was to be dried, cured and sold to the Africans at a price they could afford, for all Africans had a great hunger for game-meat. So drying and curing sheds were built, meat-hunger was to some extent assuaged, and the right and the popular policy marched happily along together.

I like to think of future generations of hippos at that bend in the Luangwa where the current flows faster and cooler over the sand in the heat of the day. May they dwell in safety, and may the grazing on the banks nearby grow green and always abundant.

Round the Valley stood the relics of abandoned European farms, tall roofless tobacco barns of red brick standing up above the long grass. They had been abandoned, surely with a sigh of relief from their owners, at the outbreak of the 1939–45 War. The soil was good, but the climate must have been intolerable.

As usual in remote places in Africa, witchcraft flourished. Men and women vanished mysteriously and their deaths were reported, "drowned in the river", "eaten by a lion", or just "coughing" or "stomach". A respectable-looking old man stood in the witness-box in Court. I was sitting as Coroner.

"Did you administer medicine to the dead man?"

"Yes."

"How did you give it to him?"

"I put it in his beer when he wasn't looking."

"What happened then?"

"He became sick: he was sick all night. He died early in the morning."

"Was the medicine put in to harm him?"

"Yes, it was put in so that he would die: and he did die."

"Why, then, did you want to kill him?"

"He had become Headman. That was not right. It was I that should have been Headman."

"Have you anything else to say?"

Witness, testily: "I have already said that I killed him. He died because I put the medicine in his beer."

There was something extremely direct about the average man in Fort Jameson District. He had said all that was necessary: what was the Coroner going on for? As usual, in this particular case, no cause of death could be established by the medical authorities so no police prosecution could take place. The most that could be done was to refer the matter to the Senior Chief, and in due course the man returned, with a case record marked: "Breach of Native Custom. Putting medicine in a man's beer. Six months' hard labour." This sentence I confirmed.

From 15th July, 1961 until the end of October that year, disturbances took place throughout the Northern Province, and sporadically in the Luapula, Copperbelt, N. Western and East Provinces—Chavuma, near Balovale, erupted as usual, and nine policemen were drowned, together with their prisoner, crossing a river after a brush there. The Chavuma people soon after erected a memorial to this man. Female missionaries' houses were burnt at Mutanda near Solwezi.

In the East about five schools were burned down at night, easy prey because of their thatched roofs, and various local disturbances took place, mainly in Lundazi District. These consisted of little more than cat-calls from unemployed schoolboys and the throwing of branches across roads. In a flash of inspiration the local political leaders got hold of a lunatic, whispered some grievance in his ear, armed him with an axe, and despatched him towards the D.C.'s house as the seat of all his troubles. His wife, who was in the kitchen, was able to summon a Messenger and have him removed before he did any damage. It was more a war of nerves, to try to convince the Government, and the outer world, that the Party enjoyed the massive and overwhelming support of the bulk of the people in the District and in the Territory. At no time, despite the Election figures, did it do so.

In Lundazi the Party's failure was complete. The mass of the people remained neutral, as they usually do. The ordinary villager was frightened by the conspirators, who were usually men of a little education, thrown out of employment through some defect of character, and they stayed quiet. But the Chiefs and their Councils, as soon as they saw that Government was behind them, reacted with vigour. With the help of the District Messengers and the Game Guards, aided by a few Police, they rounded up the malefactors within a month. One or two survived by "borderskipping" from Nyasaland and back—which by that time was friendly territory—but not for long. Perhaps the key to their defeat was the strength and robust self-reliance of the Chiefs and Native Authorities which had been built up over years, and U.N.I.P.'s failure to organize the youth. The material was all there, as was apparent later, but the District had not by then had the benefit of the attention of the U.N.I.P. high command, nor the help from their party funds, flowing in from Egypt, Ghana, Tanganyika and America. As it was, all political meetings were banned, collections for political parties forbidden, and some half-dozen troublesome characters from other parts of the country denied entry by order into the various tribal areas of Lundazi. The District was able to settle down again to a few months of peaceful progress.

However, in the Northern Province the 1961 Rebellion, for that is what it was, lasted over a far longer period. Out-stations were at one time in danger of being cut off and overwhelmed, as trees had been cut for miles along the main roads. Over fifty schools were burned, and left as blackened shells. Road blocks, such was the degree of fanatical hatred that had been worked up, were actually defended by tribesmen armed with spears and cutlasses, against troops and police, and over twenty of the most fanatical thugs were shot dead by the security forces. Slowly Government regained control, and the mass of ordinary people, simple and frightened, returned to their villages.

At the end the Northern Rhodesia Government issued an official document called the "Grey Book", giving a full factual account of the revolt. "There can be no doubt," it said, "of the responsibility of officials and members of U.N.I.P. for the disorder. Of the persons convicted in the Criminal Courts up to the end of October for offences connected with the disorders, just over 80 per cent were known to be connected with the Party. No other organization was in any way involved." Perfectly clear.

The Grey Book was well received on stations which had experienced disorder and arson. District Commissioners felt that the truth should be more widely known, as only one copy arrived at each Boma. Further copies were demanded, but none came back. Were the resources of the Government Printer under strain? Unlikely. Letter after letter followed, at respectful intervals, to remind the Ministry of Native Affairs. At length the matter could be shelved no longer. It was not considered "in the public interest" to give the Grey Book any wider field than one copy per station. The requests ceased at this significant reply.

In the Northern Province the District Commissioners who had borne the brunt put certain points to Government. U.N.I.P. must either be properly controlled and led, or its policy of sedition and terror would shortly cause the collapse of the Native Authorities as units of local government. Taxes would not be collected, development would cease, and even staff could not be paid. They collected their views together in a moderately worded memorandum, which they sent to the Provincial Commissioner.

He was an honest man, and he sacrificed his career when he supported them. Soon after he was retired, and the offending D.C.'s were transferred to other posts. In a matter of months, all their predictions came true. The Native Authorities collapsed and were kept alive only by doles from Lusaka: the Party took over control in the villages which they kept by a grip of terror. So the work of years on unpromising human material was cast away.

Later that year Mr. Macmillan asked Sir Roy Welensky whether Kaunda "was indeed responsible for the emergency last September?"

Mr. Maudling, then Colonial Secretary, answered for him. "He and his party were the instigators of everything that happened. This was an armed insurrection by U.N.I.P."

U.N.I.P.'s road to power can be traced broadly as follows:

1960   Break-away from African National Congress.
        Minority group organized on a semi-secret cell basis. Particular attention paid to youths and women.
1961   Open meetings. Attacks on established order; particularly on those friendly to Africans. Open rebellion in N. Province. Violence in Luapula, Western and N. Western Provinces. Violence suppressed, but central party organization allowed to continue.
1962   Pre-election, in October. Hate campaign continues. "Non-violence" adopted as slogan. Threats of "Master Plan", etc. Many teachers, etc., with ambition, join party.
1962   Post-election, and early 1963. Coalition U.N.I.P./A.N.C. Government. Violence continues. Remaining stubborn out-posts of anti-U.N.I.P. destroyed. Information of U.N.I.P. violence suppressed or minimized.
1963   Almost complete U.N.I.P. domination of country except

S. Province, and pockets in N.W. and Central. Also those individuals with memories going back two years, and African non-conformist religious sects. Commerce and Church and the Press hasten to make peace with the Party. Publicity build-up of Kaunda as a moderate leader begins. Collapse of centre of the Civil Service.

1964   January. Election. U.N.I.P. Government. Kaunda becomes Prime Minister. Ministry of Native Affairs abolished.

"Prison Graduates" deleted from Party cards.

"Political" prisoners released, including murderers and saboteurs.

1964   July : August. Abolition of P.A. in the field, and removal of last obstacles to one-party dictatorship in the villages.

1964   October. Kwacha !—Independence—Freedom.

So it was done.

"One cannot fight Nationalism." This might be called The Mountbatten Doctrine, as adopted by Mr. Macmillan. Lord Mountbatten's meaning was that in 1947 this country was too exhausted to resist or control it in South-East Asia, and particularly in India.

This Doctrine has since proved useful as the justification for every retreat, in good order or not, since 1945. The British Government, rattled by Mau Mau, followed by Nyasaland, overestimated the true strength of African Nationalist movements, and so equated Africa in 1960 with the India of 1945.

From this it judged that it would not be worthwhile economically to try to temper and control them. Second, as ever, it tried to justify its actions in moral terms. (Hence, the Foot family.)

To accept the Mountbatten Doctrine entire is to throw the boat-cloak of a simple sailor, with a touch of royal vanity added, over many matters that need closer scrutiny. The Doctrine takes no account of time or place, and it has been accepted far too widely, too carelessly, for its own good. Certainly it was applied to the detriment of the peoples in Africa, and now, in the face of events, it can no longer serve as an alibi, or even an excuse.

CHAPTER XI

LUNDAZI—BRIEF SUNSET

A LL this, at the beginning of 1962, seemed a long way from Lundazi District. There were at that time, 115,000 people living at peace in a long stretch of country between Dilwa Hill in the south and Manda Hill in the north, about ninety miles apart. Along this tableland, with a bulge into Nyasaland, lived some 80,000, and down in the Valley, along the Luangwa and beyond, among the game and the elephants, scratching a precarious existence, another 35,000. The plateau was the key to Lundazi, and Lundazi in turn, the key to the rich and independent Eastern Province, wealthy, peaceful, conservative. Above all, unsympathetic to U.N.I.P. and its methods of obtaining support.

Here, government by indirect rule, through Chiefs and their Councillors, had been developed in the long years of peace to its highest and most successful degree. Foremost amongst the Chiefs was Mwase Lundazi, a Territorial figure who had gathered round him a number of young, educated councillors and officers, a cabinet of technicians who developed the area along modern lines, while he saw to its good order and maintained strong traditional authority over the traditional figures, old Chiefs of proved experience and long years of service.

They were old, on the whole, but they were always there, as pillars in the changing world, and as an assurance that the changes were for their people's good. New methods of agriculture, schools, wells, drains, child-care, cattle dipping and inoculation, were all accepted, and accepted with pleasure, as bringing greater wealth and higher standards of life to the men in the village. This harmony between old and new was unique in the Territory, and was brought about largely by the efforts of the Senior Chief himself. It was a pleasure to see that system worked, and worked so well, and was the crown of many years of work by giant men of the past, Macrae, Bush. and Button, who had moulded the District and prepared it for its prosperity. For prosperous it was, though furthest away from the towns and the markets, and its spirit—or *esprit de corps*—was second to none. The petty irritations so common to Africa were absent; sloth, delay, *laissez-aller*, petty corruption. All proceeded like clockwork, houses were built, roads were made, and steadily, year by year, prosperity increased.

Behind the Chewa of Mwase Lundazi, came the Tumbuka of Senior Chief Magodi, behind, but manfully keeping pace, and far behind them the Senga of the Valley, behind maybe, but far ahead of the Kunda of Fort Jameson, in exactly the same circumstances. The District was a model for Northern Rhodesia, and as such a challenge to U.N.I.P. The pattern was clear, Congress had been suppressed there in 1953, and again in 1958, with but little effort.

The rule of the Boma, through the Chiefs, careful, prudent and progressive, had been challenged again in 1961, and the vigorous action of the then District Commissioner had vindicated it At that time the D.C. had had full support of the Government, not only from the Provincial Commissioner, but from the Governor himself.

"Restore order" was the watchword, and order had been restored, with the minimum of bitterness, and with the hearty approval of the vast majority of the people in the District. They did not want their schools burned down, or old men threatened by bands of youths armed with clubs, going about at night. They wanted peace, in which to earn money by their crops and cattle, and to give their children a better life than the hard one which, inevitably, they had had. Nor were they blind to their own advantage. A bicycle, when they had gone on foot, a shot-gun when they had had a muzzle-loader, a motor-car even, or a rifle, were not to be despised, nor a brick house in place of poles and mud. All this was going forward, slowly but with certain pace.

At the same time the position of Lundazi, a tongue of land between the Northern Province and Nyasaland, offered its opportunity. Nyasaland particularly had changed its form of government. The Chiefs had been suppressed, and District Councils, composed of Malawi Party members, set up in their place. They

ruled the rural Districts which touched on the Lundazi borders :
relatives exchanged visits and exchanged ideas. Any malcontent
from Northern Rhodesian was sure of a welcome there. Party
officials collected the taxes, and as often, kept them. The rebellion in the Northern Province had, it is true, been suppressed,
but had not the central organization, the real focus of the disturbance, been allowed to continue in being? Was it not fortified by
apparently limitless funds from mysterious sources which could
be judiciously distributed, and even earned simply by joining the
Party? Why did Lundazi slumber on, in apparently supine contentment with the reactionary colonial-imperialist régime? Surely
the moment had come to set an example, to Northern Rhodesia,
to Africa, to the World!

Lundazi Castle, built by Button during 1947 to 1952, with its
towers, battlements and turrets, symbolized in solid form the old-
fashioned atmosphere of the District, with its definite hierarchy,
and its regrettably little social mixing of the Europeans and
Africans. True, on high-days and holidays the Africans would
occasionally be invited to come down for a ceremonial drink, but
in everyday life, as of right, only the Chiefs and their entourage
would be admitted, and they came but seldom.

It was indeed pleasant to sit in the terraced garden and look
out over the still waters of the lake, to see the wild animals on the
other side nibbling the grass at the water's edge, to stretch and
to meditate. Yet it was, in 1962, not quite right to sit there so
complacently. Were we not all too symbolic? I would have liked
to see more mixed parties between the races held in what the
people, one realized afterwards, regarded as the very citadel and
symbol of European reaction and exclusiveness. Yet, from diffi-
dence perhaps, perhaps laziness, we had refrained from pushing
the matter : it was so quiet, so pleasant; and even the bathrooms,
which matched the medieval architecture in their insistence on
Gothic doorways coupled with inefficient plumbing, somehow
pleased and lulled.

To maintain that citadel, and what was far more important,
the peace and good order of the District, were thirty District
Messengers. They were indeed picked men and seemed to move
as one body. In their blue uniforms with red facings, they were a

symbol of the control exercised by District Commissioners for over fifty years. In Lundazi they had not, as in Fort Jameson and Petauke, been superseded by the Police. The Police, but for the Special Branch who were plain clothes, were 115 miles away. So beyond them there was nothing.

Their knowledge of the District was unsurpassed, and their courage unfaltering. A murder, a flood, epidemic or a famine, these were incidents in their careers, and their existence was one of hard, unrelenting work. Very seldom, unless there was an important visit of a Governor or Provincial Commissioner, were more than a half or a third on the Boma at a time. They were out, as the eyes and ears, and the arms, of the Government. Beside this picked force were the Chief's *kapasus*, or messengers, of varying quality, attached to the Chiefs' headquarters. They were useful auxiliaries with an intimate knowledge of their own areas. In quiet times they were excellent, but in stress they varied in quality, and individuals apart, were very much of the second line. A *kapasu* could retire after 15 years' service, and many did, but a Messenger served for 25 to 30 years. To cut his service, if a man was any good, was unknown : he would serve on until he had his three stripes as Head Messenger, and retire in a few years, grey-headed, a respected figure throughout the District, and spend the time that remained to him hunting elephants with the rifle he had acquired.

The Special Branch of the Northern Rhodesia Police was the third arm of the Government in the District. Its work was secret and the inspectors and constables wore plain clothes. There were only five of them and their sole function was to collect information and pass it to the Boma and to their headquarters. Since Mwini-lunga days the Branch had improved out of all recognition.

For sometimes immature European officers in charge there were now experienced African inspectors, well acquainted with the habits and language of the peoples, who could vanish among them like a stone in a pool. Little indeed escaped them, a secret meeting, a visit of a U.N.I.P. official, a plot to burn down a school, all were known. A constant flow of fresh and reliable information came in to the Government headquarters and en-sured that nothing like Mau Mau could be repeated in Northern

Rhodesia, at least not without ample and sufficient warning reaching officers both in the field and in Lusaka.

This tiny force, 30 Messengers, about 120 *kapasus*, and five Policemen in plain clothes, was sufficient to maintain order only by general consent in a District with 115,000 people, scattered over an oblong-shaped area of 100 by 200 miles. Once the general consent to obey the Government and Native Authority was undermined, and opposition could be organized to mass and operate at several places at once, it was no longer sufficient to hold the ring.

It would have to be the Police, and the Police, some 60 strong, were over 100 miles away. In their turn they had another 250,000 people or so to supervise, and the usual mass of routine crime and reports to contend with. It would be true to say that they were stretched. And so far as operating a kind of oppressive juggernaut in Lundazi District, that was clearly impossible even if one had desired. One hundred and fifteen unarmed men, even if massed together, would be hard put to it to oppress 115,000, even widely scattered.

Government, or the maintenance of the authority of the Boma, the Chiefs, and the Native Authorities, depended, first and foremost, upon general consent. And if consent was undermined in places, as it could be, Government relied on bold and judicious use of that force available to enforce law and order. Sufficient force must always be sent to ensure that it was not beaten, and at the same time enough men held in reserve in case of another outbreak elsewhere. All this time there was the routine administration of the District to be carried out, which was what the Messenger Corps was really designed for. Roads, bridges, crops, elephants, extraordinary or routine criminals, the list of commitments was endless, and fully enough to absorb the whole force.

Fortunately the Head Messenger was a man of quite outstanding ability, Yesake Gama, B.E.M., a tall Ngoni from the area of Mwase Lundazi. He was approaching his thirty years of service, vigorous, clear-headed, never ruffled even at the worst times, and always with reserves in hand. Try him as one would, he never failed. When matters were at their worst in the beginning of 1963, he never wavered for an instant: he never guessed at a time when all the world was falling about our ears, how much his calm assurance that all would yet be well, meant to me. That all was not well was no fault of his or the men that followed us without question, even in their inmost hearts.

Who then, were the men selected by the Party to break down this long-accepted fabric of order and contentment? They were as follows:

(1) a dismissed policeman of suspected mental instability;
(2) a dismissed teacher who had failed his promotion examinations;
(3) a police bugler who had left after a year;
(4) an assistant Treasury clerk who had left the Treasury under suspicion.

These, and various unemployed youths of Standard VI* education, who had failed to find employment after leaving school, had been indoctrinated by the Party propaganda machine, and maintained by them, were the instruments chosen. They were not government servants, nor teachers, who had left the public service because they disagreed with any of its policies or objectives. Far from it. They were those who had had to depart through faults of character, of conduct, or both. And government was a lenient employer—government kept everyone it could.

There were also a few women who were paid a small Party retainer and given status as secretaries and presidents of the branches of the Women's League, and who used to work themselves up to a state of frothing hysteria at public meetings. To see women behaving in this disgusting way was profoundly shocking to the more stable middle-aged members of the African community. But then, the middle-aged seldom attended U.N.I.P. meetings.

Who then did, and how did they attain such power? How did they generate enough force to put, within a year, both the plateau and the valley in Lundazi in a state of virtual revolt against an authority known, and respected, for over fifty years? And a year later, despite their outrages and excesses, gain a massive election majority there, 18,000 against 156?

* End of elementary school.

The answer is, that they appealed to the younger generation. The younger generation was profoundly bored with itself, its elders, and the Government. The war had been ended nearly twenty years, and the generation that had gone off to it were getting grey, stiff and verbose. They held the positions of authority, the cattle, and the money. On the whole, compared to the younger generation, they were uneducated. Opportunities to acquire wealth easily, quickly, were lacking; and even in Lundazi the gap between European and African standards was ostentatious.

The Europeans could go down to the Castle, drink as much as they liked, sign a bit of paper, and drive home in their cars. The sober delights of peasant farming failed entirely to appeal to many of these young men. Wealth increased slowly and uncertainly, and as a result of years of hard toil. Why indeed should not they be the masters and enjoy the fruits, now gobbled by a few Europeans and their creatures? So they sat in their villages and brooded, a dissatisfied minority at first, increasing year by year, treated in the hierarchy as of little account, as yet unorganized, but ever ready for mischief.

When the outbreaks came, and they came with unexpected suddenness and violence, it was the result of the "have-nots", the *decamisados* (shirtless ones) and the *sans cullottes* (those without trousers). Their grievances were, of course, imaginary in terms of real life, but they were real enough to them, and there was little enough that one could do to remedy them in Lundazi District. The sight of their sour, closed, embittered faces is not one easily forgotten. U.N.I.P.'s crime was the exploitation of their grievances to gain political power by means of violence to their own people. They were willing puppets, but the real guilt lies upon those who manipulated them. And it will yet rebound upon them. Violence, the creature once created, must be fed, cosseted and kept happy, once the need is over. The *Tuyewela* of the Kaonde, ever-growing, must be satisfied. How to do it? How indeed? For if the *Tuyewela* are not given enemies to devour, they turn upon their own master. So the Youth Brigades, so the *Jeunesse*.

Mr. Goodfellow, the Provincial Commissioner of the Eastern

Province, was a man of invincible optimism and resource. With his fierce moustache, his one arm—he had lost the other as a young officer in India—he looked like some battle-scarred colonel on the North-West Frontier. He was known and admired by the older Africans throughout the territory he had served for twenty-five years. That generation understood him perfectly: he would on occasion shout and drive people before him in a fury, but always he treated the Africans as man to man. He was never a cold machine, and never thought of them as units or problems, but always as human beings.

He had old-fashioned ideas. Anyone who did his best, whether as District Officer or Chief, or Messenger or ordinary gardener, labourer or villager, could be sure of his protection, his kindness, and dare one say it even now, his love. Anything that he could do for them, he would do it. But woe-betide the slacker, the idler, and the "loafer"; they were damned utterly, outside and beyond the pale, and were chased and chivied and harried until they mended their ways. It was his mission to separate the sheep from the goats, and it is fair to say, that because he had a kind heart, there were far more sheep than goats. He saw, because he was no fool, what was happening, and he tried, so far as anyone could try, to drum sense into the new political figures and to reconcile them with the old régime. For over two dreadful years, while pillar after pillar fell around him in the Eastern Province, he did his utmost to carry out the Government's policy and to make it, somehow, work. Government had no more loyal servant than he. By the force of his personality, and by the prestige of his name, he sought to maintain some sort of order amid the chaos that was becoming day by day more apparent. One by one the supports were knocked away, and still he went on, cheerful, indomitable, invulnerable.

The nationalists begged him to remain in the country, having slandered and maligned him for years: the wreckage of the Government, realizing too late what they were about to lose, did the same. But by the middle of 1964 he had done all that a man could do, and a career of twenty-five years of unceasing effort closed in silence, with hardly a farewell except from the Africans who had known him best, a few Chiefs, District Messengers, bricklayers, thatchers and labourers. They knew that he had gone, and it was as if a great hill had vanished in the night. But in 1962 he was at the helm, a sure guide and a kind master.

He knew everyone, and, as it seemed, everything, without effort : within a day he could sum up the Districts. He was our defence, not only against the kind of politician who takes tea and then advocates arson that night, but against their fellow-travellers who, amazingly enough, now appeared to be within the Government service itself.

The yellow press of the Territory now appeared upon the scene. If a youth is educated to Standard VI he is open and receptive to any ideas that may be laid before him in print. These the yellow press was well able to supply in perverted form. C. P. Scott, that revered Victorian figure, was turned upside down. "Fact is sacred, comment is free," became "Fact is fair game, and comment can follow." Now the African was brought up, first and foremost on the Bible : and on school text-books giving facts as immutable truth. And for the fundamentalist missionaries the Bible is also immutably true, not subject to gloss or critical interpretation.

It followed that all printed words were literally true, and were not subject to critical interpretation. There was—and is today—a complete failure to distinguish between fact and comment, especially when they are cunningly knitted together by skilled propagandists. A newspaper, called then the *African Mail*, was distributed with uncanny speed throughout the rural Districts of the Territory, and did much to undermine the mutual confidence between the people and the established Government. The youths could read it. Through the villages it appeared each week like manna from heaven : it formulated their grievances and their less worthy desires, in a coherent, embittered and easily digested form. In fact it was food of a much less desirable kind.

Early in 1962 the Liberal Government of Sir John Moffat, Alfred Gondwe and Harry Franklin was still in office, if not in power. They had spent their impetus, and though they enjoyed almost the monopoly of the intelligence as well as of the honesty, of the politicians that the Territory could produce, they were no longer very effective. During their years in office they had behaved with perfect propriety, they refrained from building up any sort of "spoils system" on American lines, and so they failed to build up any sort of mass following among the Africans, while the Europeans as a whole regarded them as "traitors to their class" and such-like nonsense. Studiously honest, reasonable and benevolent, they governed like gentlemen. It is fair to say that most of them fell like gentlemen also, old-fashioned, incorrupt, and doomed politically, as Asquith.

At the beginning of 1962 all seemed set fair in the District. The country was rich with cattle and maize, the mass of the population was industrious and comparatively wealthy. The most prosperous farmer in the District had just ordered and received the first tractor, amid general acclaim. Political agitation had virtually ceased and the situation was quiet enough for Senior Chief Mwase Lundazi, M.B.E., to be sent to Torquay to explore the complexities of English local government so far as they applied to Colonial Territories.

The first cattle sale was held at the Native Authority headquarters at Nthembwe, and twenty-three Grade I beasts were sold at an average price of £22 a head, no small gain to people who had been until recently subsistence cultivators. The youths, the *jeunesse*, sat scattered in the villages, as yet impotent, but waiting their moment. After the burning of the schools in the autumn of 1961 no political meetings were allowed, and no party recruitment appeared to be taking place.

The Party had gone quietly underground, where it remained, unable, apparently, to do harm. However, it was already clear that there would be another election before the end of the year, and that this position could not be maintained. Party political activity must again be permitted, but our duty must be to ensure that it remained within the law, that the people were given a choice truly free, and that the very African methods of bringing pressure to bear on political questions—beatings, burnings, and the inspiring of terror generally—were not used. In short it promised to be a prolonged, stubborn, rearguard action, with no Torres Vedras in our rear; and without even the satisfaction of a Corunna.

To prevent the collapse of the Chiefs' and Native Authorities' power, and thus the swift descent into chaos of the whole District, it was necessary to gain their consent to the relaxation of their rules, and at the same time to preserve their confidence by supporting them in the suppression of any disorder that might break out. If they had to retreat under pressure, or the appearance of pressure, from the Parties or from the population, they would break down very quickly, as already they had in the Northern Province.

The word would spread like a grass-fire : Chief So-and-So was frightened of U.N.I.P. and had had to do such-and-such : and there would be the end of his authority and the end of his use, for any practical purposes, for any function of Government. He would, in a word, be finished. There is nothing that Africans despise more, and take advantage of more quickly, than the appearance of weakness by those in authority. It must be remembered that at that time the Chiefs and their Councils were still the legal organs of government throughout the rural areas. The pure milk of Benson doctrine was still the official creed. No-one had changed it, no-one had even questioned it. Therefore the Chiefs must be supported, and at the same time disengaged so far as possible, from the political winds and waves which were so largely of our own making; that is, in the sense that the British Government and the Lusaka Government thought that they could with safety be permitted.

Chief Chikomene from the south of that District was at that time, March, 1962, acting as Senior Chief in Mwase Lundazi's place. He had served over thirty years, a sound, elderly man, completely honest, loyal, and well thought of. He was very much a caretaker, and was certainly not a man to initiate any new and bold policies. He was content to wait until the Senior Chief returned in September : meanwhile it was his function to hold the fort and to keep the machine running on the lines laid down. He was slow, by no means unintelligent, and concerned and worried about the months that lay ahead. He was a brave man, and he faced what lay before without flinching. Whatever happened, he would do his duty.

Mr. B. A. Zulu,* the U.N.I.P. representative who arrived in

* Later U.N.I.P. M.P. for Petauke. Died August 1964.

Lundazi was rather different. He was a man of education, a clerk who had arrived in politics after a varied career which included most occupations and several prison sentences. Dressed in a quiet grey suit, inoffensive tie, properly shaved and with his brief-case, he arrived in the office as a model of the new style politician. Gone were the six days growth of beard and the ridiculous Toga copied from Ghana, gone, at least for a little while, was the routine offensive manner. He was the reasonable man, ready, indeed anxious, to sell U.N.I.P. to the District, beginning with the District Commissioner. It was a "hard-sell".

The key-note to the new policy was "non-violence", and it was important to find out whether this was a mere expression, a form of words, or whether the U.N.I.P. leadership had undergone a genuine change of heart as a result of the recent failure in the Northern Province.

Perhaps the Government had made some sort of bargain with the Party, that they would refrain from suppressing it as it deserved provided that it carried on activity by proper constitutional methods only. If this was so, it was important to find this out, as Government had given no hint of its attitude. Of course, no-one held the Party responsible for the murder of Mrs. Burton* or for similar incidents, in the sense that they had been planned by the leadership in headquarters and carried out according to orders.

No, it was not that, but rather that the policy pursued and the kind of propaganda being put out, was bound to lead to similar incidents unless the party leaders took real steps to control their followers. Were they in fact the leaders, or the prisoners of the Party? There was it seemed, one test, and one test alone which would prove to unbiased people that they were both in control and acting in good faith. Would they repudiate and expel from the Party those who had been found guilty by the established courts of revolting crimes? Had the Burton murderers been expelled, or would they be?

Or the gang that had murdered two Game Guards in the Reserve near Petauke and left their bodies to be eaten. I had

* A European woman killed by four men in particularly brutal circumstances on the Copperbelt, following a Party political meeting.

helped to bury what was left of them. Was it proposed to expel their murderers, or had they done a good thing? Or nearer home, what would be the fate of various local figures convicted of burning down schools at night? Would they continue to remain good Party members? Could a Party seriously professing the principles of non-violence honestly maintain such people among their members, and often as officials? The reply was much as one had expected, with an almost weary sense of resignation.

The Party as such had not examined their cases, and therefore no measures could be taken about their expulsion.

"Would the Party examine their cases, and if so, when?"

"Well, no definite arrangements were in hand at present."

"Thank you, Mr. Zulu, I think we know where we stand."

"Thank you, Mr. Short, I think we do."

The Chewa Native Authority was due to meet within a week or ten days, and it was certain that they would lift their ban on political meetings, as advised by the Boma. Meetings would then be permitted, monthly at first, then at an increasing tempo as the Election drew nearer, provided no disorders took place.

I explained this with care to Mr. Zulu before he went off to Nthembwe to ask the Senior Chief to permit public meetings. His point was already gained. There would be no battle, but it would do no harm for him to meet the members of the Native Authority and to explain himself and his policy. If they could come to some sort of rapprochement much would be gained. If he came to repudiate violence and arson, and made a genuine effort to control the party followers, the deadlock of antagonism between the new and the old might begin to break down. One could but try.

After a day or two, however, disturbing reports began to come in from the Senior Chief's headquarters, which lay nineteen miles to the east. The youths, attracted by the presence of Zulu, had begun to mass from the outlying villages: there were stories of *kapasus* being jeered at and threatened as they went about their work, and of a series of illegal meetings being held by a subordinate party official on the outskirts of the area.

The Senior Chief was being subjected to open pressure to permit meetings. Three Messengers out of the small force available were sent to Nthembwe, and two more to scout round the outskirts and find out what was happening. The reports that they sent in were not reassuring: the rumours were perfectly true. It was time to go out myself, size up the situation, and give any support needed to the acting Senior Chief. I found him worried and nervous, though outwardly he was calm: the young Councillors were adrift in the absence of Mwase Lundazi, the older ones shook their heads dolefully and wondered what the world was coming to. The youths increased in numbers and strength up to about three hundred, and were hanging about, waiting for trouble to start.

The acting Senior Chief was not anxious to see Zulu at all. He had no education but his thirty years' experience, and this was all outside it: in his brief-case Zulu carried irrefutable arguments to get what he wanted—"oppressive federation"—"will of the people"—"full freedom of discussion", etc., which the Chief would find difficult to counter, as he started from completely different premises, held and felt by instinct, but unformulated.

Had he expounded them, they would run: "People were content, they were getting richer, there was more education, more everything, year by year. If we allow a free-for-all at this stage, there will only be trouble, perhaps complete chaos. Have the goodness to let things alone."

So Chief Chikomene, a troubled, worried old man, went off to his house at lunch-time on Saturday, still without having seen Zulu, or made any answer to his request. And after lunch, as elderly people do, he got on his bed for a nap. Now perhaps he could have a little peace, and sort the whole thing out on Monday morning.

Chief Chikomene did not sleep for long. Zulu and Tryson Nyirenda, a leader of the local youths, aged about twenty, entered his bedroom. When Chikomene woke in amazement and dismay, they began to press him to grant immediate permission for a public meeting. The old man's surprise turned to anger at being pestered at such an unsuitable time and place, and he ordered the immediate arrest of these two unwise men, who were taken into custody by a *kapasu*.

It was a serious breach of etiquette or custom to go in to a Chief's house and bedroom uninvited; this applied anywhere in the territory. In Barotseland the Litunga or Paramount Chief and the Senior indunas have their houses surrounded by palisades, and the people enter with hushed voices and clapping in a gentle, propitiary way. In the East the Chiefs were not hedged about with such ceremony, and the people prided themselves on their upright man-to-man approach. The salute to the Paramount of the Angoni, Mpezeni, was the raised right hand and a brisk *Bayete*, an echo of the old Zulus from whom they were descended. All the same, a Chief's house was his castle, and entry was very much by invitation only.

Had the Senior Chief himself been present, to enter his house uninvited would have been unthinkable: it was a large, forbidding-looking double-storeyed building of red brick with a winding staircase up to a tower top. But Chikomene had not occupied it, and lived in a more modest bungalow dwelling on one of the main roads. The pressure from behind Zulu, a new man in the area seeking to make his name as a political leader, was sufficient to make him act as he did. If he went tamely away, the youths would laugh at him: if he waited any longer his following would have begun to melt.

Yet a strong man could have waited, or returned later, for his point was already won, meetings would be permitted in a matter of days. It was not strength but weakness in the face of his followers which pushed him forward to make his gesture. If the acting Senior Chief could have seen Zulu, and told him quietly and firmly what he knew already, rather than postponing the issue for three days, and then over the week-end, trouble might have been averted. But in his turn, once he had been disturbed in his own house, he had to act as he did.

The next day, Sunday, Zulu and his fellow, Tryson Nyirenda, were brought up before a court of Native Authority assessors and fined £20 or three months hard labour in default. They were returned to custody at Nthembwe. With large numbers of youths around the headquarters the convicted men were got away at speed early on Monday morning.

As soon as what had happened had become clear, they were brought in to Lundazi. Zulu, who came from outside the District, was despatched by Land Rover, under escort, to Fort Jameson.

Before his supporters knew what had happened, he had vanished. On his way out he had been served with a restriction order by the Native Authority declaring him an undesirable person in their area, and forbidding his return.

Whether it would have been wiser to have reduced the sentence imposed upon him, to have read him a lecture, and released him, is another question. It seemed at the time essential to support the acting Senior Chief whose authority and privacy had been rudely challenged by a carpet-bagger from outside the District.

In view of Mr. Zulu's record before and since, I believe that the decision to get rid of him at once was correct : and he disappeared as a political figure in Lundazi District. At the same time it was already clear that there could be two points of view on the matter. Certainly neither Mr. Zulu nor his Party forgave or forgot.

What would the youths, the young men, do, now that their prestige had been challenged in this way, and their "leader" briskly removed from the scene? Would they stage an incident, and stand, and fight it out, or would they disperse to their villages? After some rowdiness lasting for a day, they began to trickle off home : they were no more than a collection of individuals, so far without real organization or command. As they left, to show their dissatisfaction they stripped off small branches and strewed them across the roads, and made an amateur attempt to destroy a small bridge.

To console themselves in their defeat they held a gathering at the last village near the Nyasaland border, at which there was beer, songs, political speeches, and for the first time some crude drilling by youths armed with clubs. This celebrated the release from Lundazi prison of one of the ringleaders of the 1961 disturbances, the school teacher who could not pass his examinations. The news of this gathering soon spread, and we took notice of the affair.

Very early the next morning a force of Messengers set out, and arrived in Munthaka at four-thirty, as the first people were getting up. They fanned out from Munthaka, where the meeting had been held, and told the people to stand fast and remain where they were. At that time of the morning no-one is anxious to start a revolution, and they obeyed.

Headman Munthaka was called up: he was a tall man who had once been a teacher, and long ago had left the service amid some dispute. He was by law and custom responsible for the good order and conduct of his village. Now the time had come to call him to account, not only for this occasion, but as an example to other Headmen of the District, who were tempted to wash their hands of their responsibilities. All was conducted in the correct, customary manner. We tried to emphasize that "politics" were not some new thing outside the customary frame, but if the law was disobeyed "politics" came very much within it.

"Munthaka, I greet you."

"I greet you, Bwana."

"Are the Munthaka people well?"

"They are well, Bwana."

"I have come to ask about the meeting held here on Tuesday night: was it allowed? Was the Chief asked? And where are the people who were at it, marching up and down in the middle of the village?"

"I know nothing."

"But you are the Headman, Munthaka: it is surely your duty to tell me what you know."

"Bwana, I know nothing."

"Then that is unfortunate, Headman Munthaka."

At this point the two District Messengers who had attended the meeting, disguised in plain clothes, came forward.

"Messengers, identify the men that you saw."

"That one, and that one, and that one sitting at the back."

"Headman Munthaka?"

"I know nothing."

So to the next village, and the next, and the next, repeating the question to Munthaka.

Always, "I know nothing". Some twenty youths were collected together, and driven back to the Nthembwe headquarters, accompanied by Headman Munthaka, still silent.

The sun began to rise high in the sky, and a few of the young women, seeing their young men trailing off, shouted *Kwacha* or "Freedom".

One of the youths was a boy of particular promise who had

13. Sir Gilbert Rennie.

14. Sir Arthur Benson.

managed to attain Standard VI in his village, and was about to join the Nyasaland Government service.

It turned out that he was the local "Youth Secretary" and had even built a small office of grass, covered with handwritten notices, "Freedom Now", *Kwacha—Kaunda*, etc., all perfectly illegal.

And one of the villages was a model for the District in its cleanliness, its pleasant brick houses with glass windows : but inside was only hatred. The virus had come over from Nyasaland —Malawi—where it had triumphed.

Was it equally certain to triumph here? Indeed it seemed a sad waste of time to pursue these villagers with dragonnades, even with unarmed Messengers, and it gave food for thought, what would happen if ever these same young men organized themselves for resistance. That morning they had been surprised, and obeyed. The next time would be more difficult, and the next and the next. How long could we continue to govern, once general consent had gone : and how far were we justified in continuing to do so once that point had been reached?

Certainly we could rule with guns, by force, but that had never been our way in Northern Rhodesia. Headman Munthaka's attitude had been disquieting : how deep had the rot gone? Was it a matter of a few youths in a few villages next door to Malawi country, or was it a symptom of a movement throughout the District, throughout the Territory? That was the sort of question that I asked myself in the evenings, when the press of daily affairs was over. Certainly no-one else was asking them at that time : and Government was not disposed to answer, or to admit that the question existed. A series of soothing bromides, often couched in jocose cricketing terms, was all that we received : cricketing phraseology seemed popular then, in Lusaka.

It did not seem very appropriate to us. Political events should take their "natural course", always remembering that it was the District Commissioner who was personally responsible for law and order in his District. But this was Africa. Individuals, men and their wills, could still influence the course of events, of history. We were not ants, at the mercy of machines. Besides this, we still had our duty to do.

H

At this time in Lundazi there was less time to study the habits and customs of the people in the villages than in the comparatively leisured days of Kaonde—Lunda. However, I came across many cases of interest stemming from a witchdoctor named Chikanga who lived in the north of Nyasaland. Finding out and divining causes of deaths of relatives was his speciality, and although he charged no fees he made a comfortable income from numerous presents from his clients.

He was not a political figure, though he had made his peace with the Malawi Party* and was thus untouchable in the courts under the Witchcraft Ordinance. People would come to him on foot from as far away as Dar-es-Salaam, Lusaka, or the Copperbelt, in some cases a journey of over 1,000 miles. Whole families would join the pilgrimage, and it must be admitted that some of his pronouncements made remarkable sense, enough anyway to convince the simple villagers of his virtual infallibility. He operated through an excellent intelligence system, and his subordinate doctors would chat to the clients as they sat waiting to consult the Doctor.

Whatever they found out, they passed on. Visits to him invariably caused trouble, as the furious relatives, on their return from Nyasaland, would set upon the man or woman who had been pointed out, usually an elderly and sick relative who had not felt up to the journey, and either beat them or threatened them until they had disgorged large sums in compensation. A minority of these cases reached the Boma.

The case of Chief Mulilo was an illustration of life as it was really lived, and came to notice only because of the prominent position that the family occupied. He was a Chief, if only a minor one, in the far north of the District, and cut off from the Boma by flooded rivers for about five months every year.

Mulilo III, a man of dignity and personality, had been deposed in 1948 for illegal traffic in ivory to Nyasaland. His nephew, Mulilo IV, succeeded him, and ruled uneasily in his uncle's shadow. One day, in 1960, one of his court assessors fell ill after a few drinks, and soon after, he died. No inquest was held, or

* Now, it is believed, President of the Herbal Doctors' Association of Malawi.

indeed possible. Within a matter of months, one of the ex-Chief's entourage died in a similar way.

The connection between the two events was not realized at the time, except round the villages of Mulilo. Only when another assessor fell down dead, closely followed by Chief Mulilo IV, did the authorities become concerned. Police went to the area, exhumed the bodies of all involved, and took voluminous statements from people who had been present at the numerous beer-parties which had been followed so quickly by death. Nothing of course, transpired, though the finger of suspicion pointed to one man only, ex-Chief Mulilo III. The legal experts considered the papers in Lusaka but no prosecution was possible, as no cause of death could be established. The matter rested for some months.

There was only one thing that could be done : the ex-Chief must be got out of the area, not only to preserve peace, but for his own safety. Legal processes were powerless to do anything, they were extremely complicated and appeared to have been drafted originally in the 1890's to settle land problems in Natal. This was clearly a case where the residual, unofficial powers of the Boma must be exercised. The ex-Chief was invited to the Boma and the position put to him : there was to be no prosecution, no accusation even, but he must go into exile for a period of five years. I had the impression that he was considerably relieved by this decision, and this forceful and charming man settled himself elsewhere. Peace returned : and beer could now be drunk with pleasure and without fear of the consequences. I felt, in the circumstances, that something had been achieved, by the exercise of our "inherent jurisdiction".

The "Lenshina" or Lumpa Church, was strong in Lundazi District, and particularly in the valley. In the year 1953 this simple Bemba village woman, Alice Lenshina, had fallen into a trance, she had "died", gone up to heaven and descended again, charged with certain messages to the world. These required, first and foremost, the abolition of witchcraft, and the delivering up of charms and medicines for counter-attack, of which almost every man in the village has a large store.

Alice Lenshina demanded a strict, Puritanical form of per-

sonal morality, and the abandonment of beer-drinking and tobacco. The movement, which began as an expression of
"Africanism", swept through the Northern Province, south to
the Copperbelt and east through Lundazi as far as Nyasaland.
Numerous congregations were set up, churches built of mud and
thatch in the villages and a magnificent cathedral at Sione village, the headquarters of the movement in Chinsali.

The Catholic White Fathers, with their powerful, close-knit
organization, retreated grimly before them : the Church of Scotland, with their loose framework of synods, simply crumbled and
shrank away. The secret of the movement's power was that it
was specifically African, with an African prophetess who lived
in a village, quite simply, and surrounded by her children. In
appearance she was well-rounded and pleasant, simply dressed
and perfectly friendly.

There was nothing of the Old Testament about her, except
parts of her doctrine, which had come down from older African
separatist churches. She had good, candid eyes, and her youngest
child, clean and well cared for, would be seated on her lap. When
questioned about her ascent to heaven she spoke of it with perfect simplicity : yes, she had been up there, and come down again
with the doctrines that had been given to her. It would have
seemed an unkindness to probe her, or to mock her with loaded
questions. There was no doubt that she believed in herself.

In previous years the less disciplined members of the sect had
given some trouble in Lundazi. They considered that their religion
had in some way placed them above the petty regulations that the
Chiefs would make for the better government of their areas, and
had refused to obey them.

With their two or three *kapasus* only, the valley Chiefs were
hard put to it to maintain their authority and various small
clashes had taken place. But any government would be foolish
if it alienated all the people all the time, and on arrival almost
it was necessary to make it clear that I knew the Prophetess herself, and I liked her, and that I expected good behaviour from
her disciples. The atmosphere changed in a day from distrust to
warm approval, joyful hymns were sung in the tabernacles and

there were no more petty incidents. After all, there were far more menacing clouds on the horizon.

The shameful story of the hounding and persecution of this harmless sect by U.N.I.P. in Lundazi and Chinsali Districts will now probably never be told.* The church members were not attracted by the Party: they wished to remain outside politics altogether. But they were not allowed to. Party cards were forced upon them, and when they refused, their thatched churches in the villages were burnt down, their women and children were harried, and children denied the clinics and the schools. Their crops were rooted up at night, their grain-bins burnt.

When eventually the wretched people banded together for protection behind stockaded villages they were accused of defying the Native Authority (by that time in the hands of U.N.I.P. elected members), and the Northern Rhodesian Police were used to evict them. Incidents followed, naturally, and at a clash in Chinsali in June, 1964, some forty church members were killed, and three Police. The march to freedom meant little to those people who did not desire to take out Party cards. Perhaps they would have preferred things to remain as they were. Their crime was that they looked forward to a different sort of millennium than U.N.I.P.'s: they even tried to strike back at the omnipotent Party.

The Native Authorities had duly permitted one political meeting every month in each Chief's area to prepare for the election. These made little impression at the time, and could be compared aptly to the "funeral march of a fried eel" with nonsensical speeches and sad songs.

The Party, using constitutional means, was not getting very far. So the "war of nerves" took its place. Tiny boys and girls were press-ganged into shouting *"kwacha"* at passing motor cars. On one occasion a youth, unfortunately for himself dressed in a red beret and blue shorts, strung them half-way across the road as he conducted the chorus. If only in the interests of road safety he was considered to deserve punishment, and punished he was.

* See Appendix II.

Road signs were torn down, and similar nuisances perpetrated, almost all by teen-aged youths, who by that time were beginning to organize and to enjoy the sense of power. Those who led them have been described, appropriately in the *New Statesman*, though in the context of the Margate and Clacton hooligans. "Undoubtedly much of the trouble springs from the presence among groups of youths, of people of disturbed personalities, who, by reason of their neurotic drive, become 'leaders'. The rest drift along with them out of pride, boredom or simple laziness." A rather apt description. Since that time there has been ample opportunity for the study of crowd-psychology and adolescent behaviour in the centre of England itself.

Foremost among these people was a young man called McQueen Nyirongo, the "Youth Secretary". He had been concerned in the disturbances of the previous year, but had been spirited away, through Nyasaland, then probably Dar-es-Salaam, to Ghana, where he had done a six months' course of "youth leadership".

The course certainly appeared to be run on military lines, for on his return a small camp was formed, where some twenty youths were gathered, given various ranks, put through some exercises and marched up and down with dummy rifles and clubs outside the court house of Chief Chikomene. The old Chief happened to be at home at the time. He was literally a father of his people, numbering over forty children, and he was understandably irritated. He took offence at this parade and ordered it to disperse. The youths did so, to the accompaniment of some jeers. But the "senior N.C.O.s" were soon identified and brought in, followed by the troops. All trails led back to McQueen Nyirongo, who was arrested, indignantly protesting.

He had committed several offences under the Public Order Ordinance, but prosecution under them was under Attorney General's *fiat* only, and by that time the Attorney General had given up granting his *fiat* in such cases, or it appeared, at all.

Political evolution must be allowed to take its natural course: this was little more than a harmless prank. I thought differently. I may have perverted the spirit of the law, if not the letter. The case was referred to the Senior Chief under customary law, which knew no *fiat*. McQueen was found guilty and sentenced to one year's hard labour : I heard the appeal and confirmed the sentence. Customary law could not allow the recruiting and marching of youths outside a Chief's court, without any tribal sanction, and their drilling with dummy rifles and clubs. What was this but a show of power and force independent of the Chiefs?

A little time ago and there would have been no difficulty in the matter, but times were changing. The sentence was quashed on appeal to the High Court, and McQueen released. Not, however, until he had been held out of action for over six months : legal processes in Lundazi were at times slow. What his Youth Brigades were to do within months, when they were organized on exactly similar lines, will appear.

It was the custom in Lundazi District, and this custom was mantained up to the beginning of 1963, that the women of the villages came out to greet important visitors on tour, and to follow them in procession, singing. For many years I and my predecessors had submitted patiently to a large, happy and bustling crowd, babies jumping up and down on their backs, and often smelling of a variety of scents, bought heaven knows where. It was part of the routine.

However, one of the largest villages near Mwase Lundazi's headquarters, named Vilimbala, decided to change all this. The D.C. was not to be greeted by the women any longer, but a party of youths gathered in a house at the entrance to the village, and set up a monotonous chanting of *Kwacha—Kwacha—Kwacha*. They were soon winkled out by indignant members of the Chief's court, and stood before us in a line, a miserable collection, but perhaps a symptom.

And at another place, Mudiyeghe, where the Headman had been for years the Senior Chief's own driver, the reception was icy, and the village plastered with political placards. In the middle of the crowd, with their frowning, sullen faces, sat an ex-sergeant of the Mobile Unit, Northern Rhodesia Police, with a booklet in his hand describing in detail the methods used in the Cuban revolution, with full instructions on the subject of guerrilla warfare, sabotage and the like. A seditious pamphlet hardly makes a revolution, but the attitude of the people made me think.

Here was passive resistance in action, complete lack of co-operation whenever legally possible, and insolence thinly veiled. We toured, after all, to help these people, but if this was to be their attitude, the numerous laws governing their existence could always be interpreted more strictly, and traditional sanctions applied for breaches of traditional law. Though in only a small minority of villages was it necessary to do this, their very existence was a cause of disquiet.

Could they be checked and contained until the politicians in Lusaka and London had finished their arguments? Or would they burst out into open mutiny and revolt before our masters had completed their arrangements? For it was already apparent that the reports of District and Provincial Commissioners were being disregarded in Lusaka unless they fitted in with certain pre-conceived ideas. Nothing that we wrote, seemingly, had the slightest effect upon policy: so far, however, there was only a cold neutrality that could be felt.

"The war on two fronts" had yet to begin for District Commissioners.

Normal life had, after all, to continue. In 1962 there was a serious famine in parts of Lundazi. Children, who in most African families are fed last once they have been weaned, began to pour into Lundazi Hospital, suffering from malnutrition. The authorities were cajoled into buying food at cost price and sending it to headquarters 150 miles away. Once there it was despatched by lorry to Lundazi, and on to remote Chiefs' villages. There it was sold, and as much as possible distributed to women and children.

And every pound must be accounted for to a parsimonious government which did not believe in spoon-feeding people, for fear that they would neglect to plant the next year. Here were another series of balances difficult to achieve, especially when I had visited the hospital and seen the children with their bulging stomachs, and knew that there were ten times as many in the villages.

The best that I could say at the end of it all was that nobody died directly from hunger : and yet, the infant mortality in parts of the country was 250 per 1,000. With this sort of situation to contend with it was not always easy to be patient with the antics of politicians each armed with a new brief-case of shining leather —containing what? Pyjamas? Sandwiches? Seditious literature? I never looked.

But they all come, buzzing up and down like busy bluebottles. I supposed that they wished to examine at close quarters a District that did very well without the blessings of Party government, and equally a D.C. who believed in enforcing the law with simple impartiality. How could such a thing exist in 1962, Election Year? Surely the D.C. must be a monster of oppression, a kind of jack-booted Prussian trampling up and down on the people. There must be Mobile Police—guns—armour—to enforce his direful grip? So they came, a sad distraction, month after month, spouting stale rhetoric about India and Ghana, and sewing discontent, distrust and hatred behind them whenever they could.

With their new suits, their seemingly easy acquaintance with important people at the centre of affairs in Lusaka, and above all with their lavish promises of plenty when they attained power, they seemed to many to be the messengers of a new and a more hopeful world :* the Sugar-Candy Mountain of George Orwell's *Animal Farm.* It proved not so sweet in Lundazi.

The south-western part of the District was cut off for months in the year by the Lundazi River which flowed through a large lake at the Boma and then fell down in a raging torrent towards the Valley. Even the children could not get to school except by a perilous foot bridge cobbled together with bark-rope : and vehicles would stick in the middle of the torrent with their engines flooded, their passengers wading out discomforted.

Here was the opportunity to do some good, and a practical demonstration that the days when the Boma had built the Castle with its towers and pinnacles, were not yet over. In short, an act of power and of benevolence. Might one even say, an example to our visitors? In four months the bridge had been thrown over

* There is an interesting parallel here with the myth of "The White Ship" in New Guinea and the Pacific Islands.

H*

the narrowest part of the river, its slim concrete piers founded upon solid rock, its big boxes at the sides filled with rammed earth, its beams, girders that had once served as railway lines, and crowned with sawn planks instead of crude tree-trunks. The waters, which rushed along at great speed, and could rise 10 feet an hour in the rains, were pushed by the boxes into the middle of the river, when they met as little resistance as possible from the narrow piers. It was a work of art, as well as of use, and it stands today as a memorial, solid, enduring, of what could be done, and what was done, when all men worked together in goodwill.

When His Excellency the Governor, the Queen's representative, visited an out-station, all routine work was put aside in the District. Now was the moment when the Chiefs and the people gathered to show their loyalty and devotion, when the good men were rewarded, and evil men, if any, were chastized.

The Governor chose the Nyika Plateau for the first two days of his visit, to relax from affairs, to fish, to view the game and to stay at a tiny rest house far from any villages. There, among the high moors and streams described by Van Der Post in *Venture into the Interior*, there if anywhere, he could relax. A slight, amiable figure, he would sit by the fire in the evenings and chat carefully about our work.

The party came down by car, and then by aeroplane to Lundazi where an investiture of one faithful old Chief, and a retired Head Messenger who had distinguished himself, was held after lunch. All went perfectly, and His Excellency moved about greeting the Chiefs, the European and African officers and their wives. The three senior Chiefs were brought into the office, and Mwase Lundazi, just returned from England, presented a leopard skin. They had all been under as much pressure as the party politicians could muster for over eighteen months, and they had stood firm. They were faithful, and they stood by the Government that they believed in, as they had done all their lives. If one had faltered, the other two could not have stood. Here was the moment that they had been waiting for—that word of praise, of comfort and reassurance. All would yet be well: Government would exert its power, they would be protected and vindicated. Or perhaps, all had come to an end? There would be great changes: the time had come to make terms with the politicians, or at least refrain from further irritating men, who whatever their record, would be in power within two years.

He would speak of these things: he must speak. But he did not. No word came, beyond customary civilities. The Chiefs filed out in a dejected silence. For it was good breeding and self-discipline that had kept the Chiefs silent, hardly, at that stage, indifference. When we bowed our good-byes the next morning by the carcase of an elephant being cut up in the Luangwa Valley, when we had exchanged our last salutes, we knew then that we were alone.

Nothing remained but to surrender to U.N.I.P. at discretion and to stand by as onlookers at a reign of terror and revenge, or to hold on as long as possible, but now without hope of relief. That being the position there was in fact no choice. One course alone remained—Defiance! Defiance, not of our own Government which was fast abandoning its responsibilities, but of a one-party dictatorship maintained by hatred, force and fraud over the people. That, at least, could be resisted to the end.

Chapter XII

THEN THE DARK

AFTER His Excellency's visit to Lundazi, the election remained.

Over nine hundred people were registered, each completing a lengthy form. The purely administrative side was prepared as never before, with ballot-boxes, seals, rolls and other impedimenta arriving in great profusion. Still, in some areas habits died hard. The Headmen in at least three refused to register themselves, believing as they said, that it was "something to do with Federation".

There was now no time to coax and cajole them, and when some of them found it would be possible to vote for U.N.I.P. as a party they came in at great speed. By then, unfortunately, the registers had closed and it was too late.

African National Congress never started in Lundazi : such local figures as appeared were quickly silenced by intimidation, and visits from the party leaders were fleeting and embarrassed. To such a state had the inept leadership of Harry Nkumbula reduced them in the Eastern Province, without organization, without ideas, without funds.

The Liberals drifted into the election certain of defeat, but with the secret, shameful hope of being allowed into a coalition with U.N.I.P. if they won. This disgraceful secret leaked out through the mass of amiable liberal principles which that party addressed to the voters, and the voters turned from it in contempt.

The veteran Sir John Moffat* had been at the centre of affairs for so long that he could hardly tolerate the thought of exclusion. But U.N.I.P. did not need a Grey Eminence, and his defeat in the Luangwa common roll constituency was one of the most crushing of the election. Harry Franklin, who honourably re-

* In 1971 the descendant of Livingstone returned to Scotland.

fused to abandon principle for the sake of office, fought almost alone in the south of the territory, and he suffered a similar fate. After the election he retired from politics, which he and others had made respectable.

Elections in Northern Rhodesia are sufficiently tedious. The dusty polling stations, the working apparatus of democracy, are thoroughly drab. The patient explanations to those who have little idea of what it is about, the long hours of waiting interrupted by single voters or by busy-bodies. But, the duller the better: at least for a quarter of an hour the voter is free from pressure and intimidation. Much play is always made of the absence of incidents on polling day.

"The Model Election", say the newspapers, forgetting the streams of assaults that precede and follow it. In the same way it is possible for tottering government to ignore the cumulative effect of a series of inflammatory political meetings in a quiet rural district, and to live on capital for month after month.

Mr. Wesley Pillsbury Nyirenda (U.N.I.P.) was returned as the member for Lundazi and the Northern section of Fort Jameson: there had been a heavy poll, and I had noticed that few of the Lundazi voters would meet my eye as they placed their papers in the box. They shrank away, as it were, with the knowledge that they were doing wrong, that from whatever motive, greed, fear, or simple malice, they were sinning against the light. They made a miserable sight as they passed by, some with a feeble attempt at jocular confidence, most with an embarrassed shuffle, and averted eye.

It was a relief to get away from such people to tour Chief Chikomene's country in the south, one of the worst affected areas in the 1961 troubles, but swung back to loyalty to the Government and peaceful development by the steadfast attitude of the old Chief. He was back among his family now, and the patriarch was still able to cover twenty miles a day on his bicycle through the villages. He kept up the worship of the ancestral gods who had a miniature thatched hut of their own under a tree near his village, and were represented by little sticks clad in tiny grass skirts. They still received their offerings of meal and beer from the older members of the family. Nor did he despise more modern inventions, and had recently bought a fine .404 rifle.

An incident on tour brought home the malice which party politics had put into the hearts of some of the people. A young man slouched with his wife at the entrance to a village, failed to greet the Chief or to take any notice of his presence : he was told to wait until we had seen the people when an assessor would have given him a lecture on good manners and let him go. Instead, while we talked to the people, he took flight, and as he left, placed a lighted ember from the fire under one of the sticks holding up a grain-bin.

No doubt his object was that the bin would catch fire, and the confusion assist his escape. He escaped only to be caught a month later, and brought back with his wife. He received a well-merited sentence of two months hard labour, but his wife was set free. A wife should stick to her husband, the Chief said, and he was right. But she proved in fact to be married to someone else, while he was a tax-defaulter who had been turned out of his village in Fort Jameson. Such people formed the keenest Party members.

But it was good to find that the political virus had begun to die out : villages which had been silent and hostile at the beginning of the year were now friendly and full of laughter about the past, and some of the notorious malcontents were going off to live elsewhere. The people were as though they had been relieved of a burden of guilt and hatred.

A period of reconstruction began after a year of futile excitement. Tax for the year was collected, 100 per cent of the estimate, and ambitious plans were laid for the next, a new piped water-scheme, several schools to replace pole and thatch, a dispensary for the sick, staff houses and minor improvements everywhere, over and above the existing services.

All this was gall and wormwood to the Party, in contrast to the other Provinces where they dominated, where the Native Authorities led a hand to mouth existence, with no development and kept alive only by doles and subsidies from the central Government.

The existence of Lundazi District, happy, prosperous, contented, with the Party in being but kept under control by the Chiefs and District Commissioner, constituted a challenge that

U.N.I.P. could not afford to ignore. We had done more that year than some of our superiors had guessed, or believed possible. We had fought Party aggression on its own ground, village by village and Chief by Chief, and had broken its force. Now it was for our superiors, after their long, cryptic silence, to take command again, to issue orders and objectives, even to retreat in good order if need be, after a "soldiers' battle" that had lasted not a day, but a year.

How they turned victory to defeat in Lundazi District will now be told.

The first object of U.N.I.P. was to break the stubborn determination of the Boma that order must be kept. It would have been impossible, even if we had wanted to, to exercise any sort of oppression over the people with 30 unarmed District Messengers. But it was possible to insist that public meetings were held in an orderly fashion, and that gangs of youths, calling themselves Zambia Police, were unable to roam the country and institute a reign of terror. Taxes too must be paid, and the orders made by the Native Authorities, such as the compulsory dipping of cattle, must be obeyed. Otherwise, and the reasoning was simple enough, the cattle would die of disease.

Soon after the coalition government was formed between U.N.I.P. and the African National Congress, and Kaunda became Minister of Local Government and Social Welfare, a press campaign began about Lundazi District. Terrible happenings—beatings—mass arrests—the whole armoury of sensation was brought out. People in Lundazi who read the *African Mail* looked around them to see all this going on. It must be true, the papers said so : but where? Who had been arrested? No-one that they knew. And there seemed much the same number of prisoners, forty-five or so out of a hundred and fifteen thousand.

No newpaper reporter, naturally, ever troubled himself to visit the disturbed area, seething with discontent : they relied entirely on sensational telegrams sent by local Party officials, the best of which were passed on by Special Branch. It must have been discouraging when nothing happened, and the long expected rioting failed to materialize.

There was clearly a situation in Lundazi District. The Press had said so. If it did not exist it would be necessary to invent it : even help, perhaps, to create it. High Party functionaries joined in the game. Wesley Nyirenda assumed an air of morose concern. He would pay secret, flying visits and leave without discussing at the Boma the numerous complaints that he must have heard from all quarters. Instead, much more effectively, he would exercise his privilege of raising them in Lusaka, and long, plaintive letters would arrive requesting immediate reply, and entailing much needless research into cases often nearly a year old.

The guiding principle was clear, if one disseminated a parcel of lies big enough and often enough, sooner or later a part of them might be believed : after all "there must be something in it". In fact there was nothing in it, no mass arrests, no intimidation, no "situation". People went about their lawful occasions without fear. It was in other parts of the territory that the intimidation existed : but it was the intimidation of the Party. There it was that the people dreaded the knock on the door at night, and the sudden bludgeoning assault on the highway.

Life was made no easier at this time by a circular from the Attorney General stating that there were to be no prosecutions for the wearing of political uniforms unless authorized by his Department. From long experience of the Attorney General's Department that meant that no prosecutions at all could take place. That a man wearing a paper hat or a Party shirt in Lusaka, with ample police available, was different from a gang of youths in Lundazi not only uniformed but armed with clubs and batons, was not appreciated. The reasonable man, "the man on the Clapham omnibus", did not reach very far into rural Districts of Africa. If a man was allowed to wear a political uniform, the Party reasoned, then he could carry a weapon and use it as necessary to enforce his own particular version of the law. So, of course, it turned out. As this circular was marked "Not for publication" I assumed that it would be some time before Party officials as far afield as Lundazi became aware of it : in fact it reached them with uncanny speed.

"Kaunda was coming", said the *African Mail*. Kaunda was coming to Lundazi to see the situation for himself. He would settle it. Kaunda was always coming : he was by now part of the war of nerves. But he never came. I began to hope that he was a paper tiger, as much a figment of the imagination as the "situation" itself. Besides he was now a Minister and presumably he would be given plenty of work to do, that is if our superiors knew their business. At any rate, as a Minister and member of the Executive Council, he would be bound, by certain sworn oaths and constitutional rules, to behave himself in a proper and responsible manner.

However, the ground must be prepared. Besides U.N.I.P.'s Land Rover with its load of unemployed youths aboard, must be kept busy cruising hither and thither on Party business; tension must be created by public meetings proclaiming that the Party was now in power. These were duly held, at Magodi, the Tumbuka headquarters, and at Chikwa, early in December, 1962. Despite careful, and I thought friendly, talks with local Party officials, a system of full-scale anarchy was proclaimed at crowded meetings. U.N.I.P. was now in power—*Kwacha! Ngwee!*—and all who opposed it would see what would happen to them.

"No-one need pay tax any more—all game could be shot whether in Reserves or not—marriage certificates—all rules— were now at an end. Freedom had come at last : and the white dog Short would now see what would happen. So would Chief Magodi, who had opposed the Party."

This was, of course, a direct challenge to authority, and if it had passed unanswered, all authority would have broken down. The same melancholy course would have been followed as in the Northern Province, where the Chiefs and Boma dragged out existence as á despised appendix while the Party held power by terror and corruption. Our duty was to make the transition in an orderly and peaceful fashion, not to become idle spectators at a revolution. And until Government decided otherwise the Chiefs and Native Authorities, as at present constituted, were the lawful organs of local government in the District, and they would be supported.

Quite apart from the law of sedition, which required the Attorney General's *fiat*, given very seldom in recent times, there was ample material for a prosecution in the speeches that had been made. Those who had made them were therefore arrested, brought to trial in the Chief's court which had jurisdiction, and given, in the circumstances, light sentences.

Nothing over two months hard labour was awarded, a lesson it was hoped, and regarded by the people as the natural reaction of a Government which intended to retain control. But was this enough? How to bring home to the people that the folly, and the malice of the local Party leaders was being justly and swiftly punished, that the old sanctions for good behaviour still applied, and that the reign of anarchy was not yet inaugurated?

For months the area round Chief Magodi's capital had been simmering, helped by the release from prison of those convicted in 1961 of arson and other crimes, by the touring Land Rover and the distribution of Party funds. It must be shown who ruled : Her Majesty's Government in which U.N.I.P. members were included in their proper constitutional framework, or the young local party officials. Unless the situation was made physically clear to the people on the ground, at village level, there would continue to be a doubt as a result of these two meetings.

So it was decided to make things clear. To Magodi we went just before Christmas, four Messengers, and the two Party officials under arrest. On arrival at the camp, twenty-three miles north of the Boma, "serious trouble" was reported to the north, and the Chief and his *kapasus* had gone off to deal with it. Leaving a Messenger to guard the officials in camp, we followed. It was like old Chief Magodi to have "marched to the sound of the guns" without waiting for help. He was always stout-hearted and always straightforward. As it turned out, all was well : three young party members had been creating a disturbance and had been over-powered without great difficulty by the three *kapasus*. They sat together in a gloomy huddle under guard, while the Chief, in the middle of his people, was enjoying a well-earned cup of beer after his exercise, all joking and laughing together.

The next day some seventy of the nearby Headmen were called together, and the exercise in political counter-attack began. For too long the Party had held the initiative in exploiting every grievance, real and imaginary, in spreading lies and racial hatred. Now there would be an account and a reckoning. The Party officials were produced before the Headmen, sitting on the ground, not ranting from a platform, and silent with shame. Point by point their lies were exposed.

"Taxes there would be, marriage certificates, game licences—all still held. Magodi would remain, here he was, on a chair beside me, if any doubted. A new Government had come, with members of each of the African parties as responsible Ministers. If changes came they would be decided by responsible people, and not by irresponsible youths. Let those who listened now know that it was the Government that ruled, and would continue to rule. Foolish young men who tried to mislead people would be punished: two of them were sitting close at hand. Here was the result of their folly: let there be no more of it. Let Lundazi keep its good name for abiding by the laws, for peace and progress."

Some thoughtful looking men made their way homewards that day. They had been told so often that the Party was invincible: and now a doubt must have entered their minds. This proceeding was, of course, a mortal affront to the Party.

Christmas was quiet, and the first part of January. Press attacks did not depress me, as I did not read the papers concerned. For one thing, I was too busy, and for another, as Balfour said, it was hardly worth grubbing through a rubbish dump in the hope of coming upon a cigar-end. Afterwards, I was surprised at their virulence.

U.N.I.P. kept very quiet, touring round and round, but no longer coming to the Boma. The rains fell, and dampened political enthusiasm for a little while.

At a conference in Fort Jameson early in January, the Provincial Commissioner was unshakably optimistic. True, there was still some restlessness around Magodi, but on the whole all was quiet. If Lundazi could survive the political circus that was soon to tour the Eastern Province, then we might look forward to a good harvest and a happy year.

At that time we did not know the storm that had been prepared, or how carefully the powder-kegs had been laid. We should have known, for it was the task of Special Branch, Northern Rhodesia Police, to send out such information. This organization was unrivalled at the collection of information within the District, and reporting to the D.C. and headquarters. But an attack on a District from the centre of power was new to them, and nothing came but a telegram announcing their days of arrival and departure from the Ministry of Native Affairs. The telegram came in late at a party at the P.C.s great house, with its pillared portico and wide verandah, once the Residency of North-Eastern Rhodesia. A somewhat light-hearted attitude prevailed, but a word to the Officer Commanding the Police ensured that an Inspector and four constables would leave for Lundazi the next morning.

So the party arrived in Lundazi. Kaunda, Skinner,* a black-haired Dublin-Irish lawyer who could never forget the injuries to his country and whose shouts of *Kwacha* from Party platforms had disconcerted the African villagers, Wesley P. Nyirenda,† and Haydn Banda,‡ a "hatchet-man" in the Party who had served a sentence for sedition. He had a wall-eye, and a manner of un-pleasing rudeness, until challenged, when all at once he became an apparently quiet and amiable individual.

They had chosen their moment well: the District Officer, Mr. Milligan, who knew the District like the palm of his hand after three years, was to go on leave the next day. All the District Officers, Banyard, Mapoma, Ling, were new: all however, were stout-hearted. The Party elected to stay at Lundazi Castle, sym-bolic, it was supposed, of taking the Bastille by storm. The best rooms were thrown open to them. Mr. Milligan's farewell took place that same night, and there was dancing on the ramparts. We all hoped that our visitors were sound sleepers.

They were off early enough the next morning for a political meeting at Ntembwe, the headquarters of Senior Chief Mwase Lundazi. Just over a thousand people gathered, and the meeting took place without incident; despite some minor breaches of the law there was nothing to make anyone of normal courage fear a breach of the peace.

The Party neglected to call upon the Senior Chief, who was at his house nearby, and curiously enough had been at school with Kaunda. This was not remarkable, as a few weeks before

* Attorney General, at Independence.
† Speaker, at Independence.
‡ Minister of Independence.

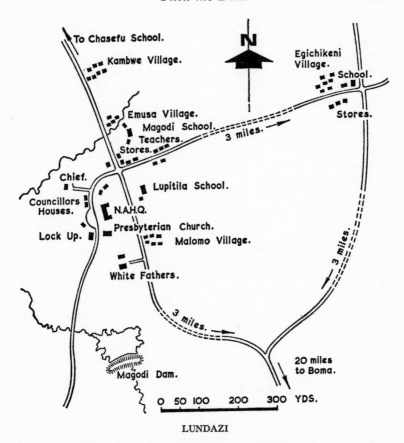

LUNDAZI

Mwase Lundazi had been subjected to a U.N.I.P. demonstration at Lusaka, when he had come out of a meeting of the House of Chiefs. A band of young Party thugs and hooligans, recruited from the ranks of the unemployed, had jeered, threatened and hooted at him as he came out of the Secretariat.

The police on duty—by whose orders?—had stood inactive during this disgraceful demonstration. The Senior Chief strode through with sublime unconcern, and went on to the town, where he was greeted by his people. Shortly afterwards he received a letter of fulsome apology signed by Kaunda, beginning "Your Royal Highness".

This soapy flattery was rightly ignored. Nor did the Minister make the usual call, prescribed by etiquette, at the Boma. I would have welcomed the Minister's ideas on the development of Local Government and Social Welfare in Lundazi District, not to mention his views on how peace and good order might be combined with political advance. They were not forthcoming, and instead the people were treated to a series of direct personal attacks on Government servants, beginning with the District Commissioner. The time had indeed arrived when such attacks were a tribute.

The next day, Sunday, was a more serious occasion. A grey damp morning with heavy rain, was succeeded by a bright afternoon. U.N.I.P. weather indeed. Numerous formed bodies of Party members marched in in procession, bearing banners and beating drums, and often wearing a crude type of uniform. All this was in breach of the law, but was unremarked by the Party leaders present. The officer-in-charge of police did not wish to provoke a breach of the peace by any action, and as Kaunda was there in person it was unlikely that any rioting would take place. At the same time the aggressive attitude of the people, the open flouting of the law, and the virulent tone of the speeches made, which were reported to me, were sufficient to cause most serious concern. So long as Kaunda was present open violence on the spot would be avoided. If he were not present, then anything might happen. In that sense certainly, Kaunda was the symbol of non-violence.

But Kaunda would not be present the next day. When he woke up that morning he found that he had been stricken by a severe attack of "Conjunctivitis" (or "pink-eye") which must have caused him considerable discomfort. He asked the Nursing Sister to call upon him. She found him in bed, surrounded by anxious attendants. She gave him the appropriate remedy, and he was well enough to speak at the meeting held at 2 o'clock.

After it had ended however, he found it necessary to return at once to Lusaka, accompanied by Wesley Nyirenda and Skinner. If there were to be trouble they were better out of the way, especially Skinner, who was the Party lawyer and who defended many Party members before the courts.

Their departure left Haydn Banda and the local Party officials in possession of the field. There was no guarantee of peace now, quite the reverse. Their very presence could be an incitement to disorder. Chief Magodi had been "pointed out" at U.N.I.P. meetings as one of the two foremost Chiefs in the territory who would not co-operate with the Party, and it was he who would be the first to suffer. He himself was quite unafraid, but we owed it to him to protect him and his staff.

At six o'clock in the evening, seeing the U.N.I.P. Land Rover weave up the Magodi road, loaded with singing, drunken Party youths beating a drum as they went, I decided that the meeting next morning should be cancelled, that it must be if the certainty of a serious incident was to be avoided. There was no-one to turn to for advice, and the P.C. would have replied that I must act upon my own responsibility as the man on the spot.

At such times the weight of responsibility is great. One is quite alone. So, in keeping my own counsel, I went to bed. It had been a tiring two days, and if my feeling was the same in the clear light of morning, I should act accordingly. Easy to see now that I should have spoken to the P.C. on the wireless, and asked at least for advice and additional Police. The forces available, an Inspector, three constables, eight Messengers and the *kapasus*, good men as they were, were quite inadequate to cope with the virulence and determination of the people the next day. Only the show of a strong force at the start of the proceedings is, as was afterwards proved, sufficient to prevent a riot getting under way in such circumstances.

The next morning I found that my feeling of the night before had now become firm conviction. It was impossible in my judgement to allow the meeting to take place without the risk of a breach of the peace. It must, therefore, be cancelled. Just after eight o'clock the force set out for Magodi, to find, as we passed, people already on the road. Arriving, greeting the Chief and explaining the situation took not many moments, and parties fanned out along three of the four roads leading to the Chief's capital to tell the people to go home. They would not do so. They would not believe that Kaunda had returned to Lusaka—they would not recognize that their meeting had been cancelled, under the powers held by the District Commissioner under the Public Order Ordinance.

The long months of undermining authority had done their work, and the stage had been reached when the people, when massed together in what they thought sufficient numbers, would accept no authority but that of the Party. So far had we come. The first back was the Police Inspector, reporting determined resistance to the south near Kanyanga Mission, then Mr. Banyard the D.O., from a large party on the road from Chasefu School. Other groups were gathering on the road to the south-west past Magodi Dam, though for the present they hung back.

It was necessary to deal first with the Kanyanga group, who were approaching in force with batons, flags flying and drums beating. They meant business. We approached them in a line: they stood. We told them the news, and they turned. But one or two, "natural leaders" stood and shouted like madmen. After a brisk scuffle they were arrested by the Police, whereupon the women began to scream. It is quite impossible to control women in these situations without the use of considerable force, which is distasteful. However, they incited their men to stand. On such occasions one must be prepared to "mix it" if necessary, and forming a line of Messengers and Police across the road we forced them slowly back.

By now, however, it became apparent from the roar like a football crowd in the distance, and by the boom and rattle of numerous drums, that the other parties had closed in on Magodi to our rear. It was necessary to return to the centre, or to be cut off. We therefore left the Kanyanga group at the entrance to the Mission, stationary but still formed.

It was apparent on our return that the worst had happened. Two very large parties, those from Chasefu and Egichikeni, had united at Magodi and were awaiting us in a large and hostile body. The third, from Magodi Dam, had greatly increased and was waiting to join them. Mr. Banyard was therefore sent back to the Boma to bring up every available Messenger and to send a wireless message to Fort Jameson. Meanwhile the third group, and the fourth group, that had by now come in from Kanyanga, had joined the first two, and all was prepared.

We took our stand across a narrow road which led to the meeting place in front of the Chief's headquarters, myself and the imperturbable Head Messenger Yesake Gama in the front, with the Police in close support. These occasions are always trying, but experience had dulled the nerves, and once affairs had started they would continue on whatever course was predestined for them.

The roaring and drumming grew louder and louder, and the younger and more impatient spirits urged the crowd forward. On they came, a dense mass about seven hundred strong. Now was the moment. We stepped forward a few paces into the middle of them, told them that the meeting was cancelled, and that they must go home. It was like reciting the lines of a play, for one knew already what the answer would be.

No crowd, carried forward to that stage, and drummed on from behind, is going to go home meekly and without a row. Nor were they: they refused, and stepping back to Mr. Wright, I requested him to clear the ground. In he went, followed by his three constables and a few Messengers, and the crowd swayed, broke and ran. He could not pursue far because his force would be scattered and lost: so the crowd reformed behind houses, then came on again. Again it was charged, and broken, leaving a few vigorous stone-throwers on the flanks; one man, who had been prominent at Kanyanga and whom I had pushed gently backwards over a small fir-tree (planted by the good Fathers), was especially accurate.

"Remember that man," I remarked to the Head *kapasu* standing beside me, and he did.

When the second charge was over it seemed that they would disperse. But we had no luck that day, the U.N.I.P. Land Rover was heard approaching, and in a trice they had re-formed again, from behind walls, trees and buildings, out of the long grass, as aggressive as ever. It was necessary to push through this mob to get at Haydn Banda who was in the Land Rover with the other officials at the centre of it. As I went through them, I felt their hatred. It was, after all, a simple choice: the meeting had been cancelled, the crowd repeatedly refused to disperse.

Either Haydn Banda gave his assistance in dispersing them,

or the maximum force would have to be used. That would, of course, have meant the use of firearms by the Police: and if Banda had refused to help to disperse the crowd I am bound to say that I would have had no compunction in ordering their use, whatever the official consequences. As it was, Haydn Banda saw the writing on the wall, and getting on the bonnet of his Land Rover, drew the crowd after him. That was a wise and sensible action, for which he should receive full credit. And so, after a great deal of shouting and protest, the crowd dissolved. Something had been achieved at least—there had been no bloodshed that day. But we had been on the brink many times. There had been, it is true, many breaches of the law, and a mass defiance of lawful authority, though only a few arrests. All, except the two men from the Kanyanga Mission fight, were released at the end of the day. We came home that evening, clearing tree-trunks cut across the roads by the people.

Why, having shown such unexpected good sense on Monday, did Haydn Banda tell his party followers to come back to Magodi on Thursday, when a meeting then would have no semblance of legality, and could only lead to the trouble that he had helped to avoid? It was an open secret that he had done so, and the next two days were spent in visiting as many villages as possible to tell them not to come out, and in dispersing various small groups of youths. Could it be that Party headquarters wanted to be ready for another riot in three days time, so that "pressure" could also be mounted in Lusaka?

In Africa one hopes for the best, but it is prudent to expect the worst: and it is fair to say that at this time the worst usually happened. I had hoped that repeated warnings to as many villages as possible would have had some effect. No permit to hold a public meeting had even been requested, so that the whole proceedings would be illegal from the start, and a simple act of defiance of lawful authority. Warnings had no effect whatsoever, and back the people came.

This time, however, Party officials took care to be absent. But it was beyond the bounds of possibility that four large parties of people should again assemble, again armed, at four different points, all several miles apart, completely spontaneously and just because they felt like it one fine morning. Today, however, was to be "The Day of Dupes" and proper preparations had been made for their reception. The Police were there. As a force they were lacking in "qualifications".

But they had far more : they had tenacity, courage and loyalty. There were, on this occasion, the Police Officer Commanding Eastern Division, Superintendent Taylor—one of those splendid men whose very presence is worth a Company, some fifteen Police and fifteen Messengers, an organized force perfectly sufficient to deal with any opposition likely to be found. The situation was clear : any unauthorized assembly would be warned, and if it refused to disperse instantly, would be charged and scattered. By just after eight o'clock the force had reached Magodi, and all was prepared. The Land Rovers moved off towards Chasefu, and soon came across a group of about 70 coming down the road. The vehicles stopped, the Police formed up, and once again Yesake Gama and myself went forward with the usual demand. The group had broken in two on both sides of the road.

"Bwelani Tsopano Kumidzi—pitani" :—"Go back to your villages, disperse now."

Again, *"Iai Sitidzabwela"*—"No, we won't go."

And a shout from behind from the Police who had seen the crowd closing in behind us, led by a man who appeared to be a lunatic and suffering from severe leprosy. Next moment the Police had charged, and the crowd had vanished, running as hard as they could for Kefa village.

We followed closely as the Police and Messengers ran forward, gathering up most of the leaders. It was over in five minutes : Rodwell Nyirenda, the brother of Wesley P. Nyirenda, M.L.C.,* was dragged out of his house having plunged his fingers into a bowl of porridge as he shut the door, to give the impression that he was peacefully at his breakfast. It did not avail him.

While the Police and Messengers searched the village and regrouped, the familiar roaring and drumming was heard coming from the east. A far more formidable group, this time some 300 strong, was marching down the Egichikeni road with its banners. When we halted and formed a line across the road, they halted

* Member of Legislative Council.

also. Bearded figures danced like dervishes in front of them, shouting insults, while others tried the range with stones and knobkerries.

It was necessary to get close to be able to charge effectively, but as we edged forward so they edged imperceptibly back and the distance between remained the same. We began to edge backwards ourselves, to pretend to give way a little and lure them on. But they would not advance without the utmost caution and we made no progress. Meanwhile they appeared to be in animated debate whether to charge themselves : had we exercised a little patience they might have done so, and been much more severely handled than they were.

But we could not afford to waste time; there were two more roads to be accounted for, and the first group might return. We decided to move back in the Land Rover out of sight, turn round, which could not be heard above the noise and din going on, return at speed, and charge home. It succeded almost too well. As the Land Rover went forward the crowd wavered, swayed, and broke, with the Police in hot pursuit.

They fanned out after the crowd into the tall maize fields and soon prisoners began to come in. One man, covered with blood, had tried to cut the throat of the Police sub-Inspector, African, with a sickle. There were shouts and confusion, quickly swallowed up into the bush.

It was the end of the group from Egichikeni as a formation : they left numerous weapons, batons, drums and a flag behind. That particular group of villages had always been particularly virulent against Senior Chief Magodi, and had a pretender of their own always ready. Egichikeni had been the home of the previous Magodi, deposed and exiled over fifteen years before for converting the Native Authority funds to his own use. His people had not forgotten : they still wanted him back, or if not him, their pretender, who was nearer related to him than the present holder. The deposed Chief lurked over the border nearby in Nyasaland.

Although we did not know it, there was to be no further opposition worth the name that day. Turning back into Magodi the south-western group had begun to muster early : at the head of it some youths in cowboy hats had been immobilized by being told simply to sit down. On this occasion they obeyed instructions, and later did valuable work for the security forces reconstructing a bridge and removing tree-trunks that they had previously cut down from across the road.

The main body had formed somewhat behind them and scattered before they were charged: by this point the Police were becoming disinclined to waste time. We followed, and a woman, entangled in her long skirt, fell flat, at full length on top of a small ant-hill. There we were together, as she looked up with frightened eyes. I could not help smiling at a sight so incongruous: she could hardly move. She smiled back. I put out a hand. It was all over, and off she went home.

Another group fled across Magodi Dam as soon as it sighted us: they had cut across from Kanyanga on some obscure strategic plan. We came up with them again grouped uncertainly outside their own village, and again they scattered. Some poisoned arrows were picked up, but it was clear that no-one would stand again that day. So we returned to Magodi.

Once there the officer commanding Police and myself considered the future. He had, after all, the whole of the Eastern Province to cover, with a population of 500,000 people. He could not afford to keep more than a section in Lundazi for more than two or three days, but it was clear that the area must be policed, and a strong force should remain to prevent further outbreaks of violence.

Reinforcements must be called in from outside the Province, and that meant a platoon of the Mobile Unit, a highly trained force totalling in all thirteen platoons of forty men in each, specially kept for dealing with riots and disturbed areas. It was highly unlikely that there would be any riots to deal with in Lundazi for a while, but their presence in camp, marching, and demonstrating various techniques, would, we thought, have the effect of quietening the area for many months to come.

It would also, as it turned out, have been of the greatest value in the whole Eastern Province. However the telegram turned out to be a tactical error at that particular point, for instead of the Mobile Unit it brought Kaunda, Bean, acting Minister of Native

Affairs, as well as Day, Deputy Commissioner of Police, and Wesley Nyirenda, by aeroplane the next day. It did not have the desired effect, but the exact, precise opposite.

At this time it was decided to harry the Egichikeni group who would have fallen back on their parent village and the stores round it. This could be done by driving back towards the Boma and up into the rear: sure enough this succeeded, and about fifty were found still hanging about. They were not expecting us by that particular road, and a number were arrested. After this the force drove back to Magodi, surrounded Kefa village in silence, and at the blast of a whistle closed in suddenly. We found innocent looking villagers at their evening cooking pots, exchanged a joke or two, and bade them good night.

We drove back in the evening along the road to the Boma. All was peaceful and quiet, Magodi had been settled for a long time. They would not come back in arms again: the bubble had been burst.

The Chief and Native Authority could tidy up the loose ends, and a friendly tour of the villages would re-establish the good, cheerful relations between the Boma and the people that had existed so long. There was no malice in them, but only in a few unemployables and youths inflated with propaganda and looking for a cause. The mass of the people came along to see if the Government, the régime that they regarded with cheerful animosity, was really finished at last, as they had all been told.

We had good cause to be content, and remarkably few people had been hurt, only one seriously, the man who had attempted to cut the sub-Inspector's throat. Not a shot had been fired. A Messenger was sighted coming up the road: in his hand he had a telegram. "Kaunda and Bean, with Day and W. Nyirenda, will arrive at yours at 0900 hours tomorrow, possibly accompanied by Provincer." Provincer—Goodfellow—was the only consolation out of the lot of them. We hoped, we prayed even, that he would come. If he did not, the proceedings would turn into a court of inquiry on our conduct, and not on the causes of the riots. But sufficient for the day was the evil thereof, and it was time for a rest.

The discussions took up the whole of next day. Mr. Bean's technique was to treat the whole matter with jocular cheerfulness, a small incident to be ironed out between sensible men. We took our cue from the Minister, always regarded as the head of our service under the Governor and Chief Secretary. We were calm, factual and we refrained, in the interests of the surprising harmony which seemed to prevail, in bringing up the cumulative and exciting effects of Mr. Kaunda's visits, and the policy of open subversion pursued by his Party.

Kaunda's own contribution was minimal. He appeared embarrassed and not easily able to follow the proceedings in English : he had a few minor complaints about a woman who had got a black eye, a bicycle that had been damaged, and a few U.N.I.P. youths who had been kept waiting at the Boma, while the riots were proceeding in the north. Bean never left his elbow the whole day, except when he spoke to his own Party officials, ostensibly to tell them to control their followers and themselves. Here, one hoped for the best, but one could only judge by results.

Kaunda, a man of medium height, with hair brushed straight up and touched with grey, appeared tired and embarrassed. He had prominent eyes which were sometimes turned upon an opponent and opened full, in the manner of Gladstone : but Gladstone's fire was absent, and they hardly intimidated those who were not intimidated already. There was no magnetism, but only, it seemed, the anxious features of an actor unsure of the audience. Before he went into politics he had been a primary school teacher at a Mission, and retained a somewhat didactic manner of speech. To me he appeared a man of limited intelligence and capacity, who was hardly of the same calibre as Lawrence Chola Katilungu, or of many an African chief.

My impression was that he was the prisoner of his own Party, but open to fleeting, very fleeting, advice from European officials, who had somehow, got on terms with him. Before lunch Kaunda walked out a little round the Boma. The Northern Rhodesian Police were now supposed to salute Ministers : but suddenly the Police had no hats, they had all left them somewhere, anywhere. A young Inspector caught unawares in his head-dress vanished behind a notice board and studied the horizon. Never had the District Messengers' salutes to the formidabe P.C. been so resounding. Without ignoring the other members of the delegation it appeared that they did not see them.

After lunch at Lundazi Castle we resumed. Now Mr. Bean, Goodfellow, myself, sat alone. The "pressures" on Kaunda were very great. The rights and wrongs of the riots were a matter of opinion : but it would be better if I went on leave. It was felt that I had been somewhat rigid in the handling of the District : it was time now for a more flexible policy. So that was that : I had been relieved.

Loyal old Goodfellow burst out : "I don't want you to think that you go under censure—not that at all." That was sufficient consolation, for the moment.

So now the first objective of U.N.I.P. had been achieved. They had removed a will determined to keep order and avert a Party dictatorship. Next, they would turn their attention to the Chiefs and the Native Authorities : where they would not bend, they must be broken. There was no doubt in my mind that the visits of the Party leaders were in execution of a carefully thought-out plan with the local Party officials, to reduce Lundazi, the key to the Eastern Province, to complete Party control.

First, work up a state of tension by a press campaign and inflammatory public meetings. Second, the Party leaders appear to crown the excitement. Kaunda then withdraws with his eye-trouble, leaving Banda in control. Banda finds the meeting cancelled, and tells the people to come back in force in three days. He then leaves for Lusaka to tell Kaunda that there will be a riot on that day. At the same time Nyirenda tells Kaunda he will resign if the D.C. is not removed. Kaunda is "under pressure". The riot duly takes place. It is essential that he flies up to the seat of the trouble. He will bring the Party to order, but the D.C. must be removed. Admirable, plausible, and in the circumstances of that time, practically foolproof.

Within one day, on Saturday, the *African Mail* dated Friday appeared.

"D.C. Lundazi Removed. Kaunda Settles Problem."

It was remarkable how quickly the news of the change at Lundazi reached the Press, who, perhaps were waiting for it. I

15. Sir Evelyn Hone.

16. The New Africa : Dr. Kaunda addresses a meeting with Mr. Lewis Changufu, M.P.

now felt moved to protest : if this continued my successor would
be left naked. Some sort of correction was therefore issued.

What more could I do until our departure in six weeks time?
It was necessary to re-establish good relations with the people of
the troubled areas. They had been beaten from the field : now I
must heal the wound to their pride. Things were as they had
always been, the Boma was there to help, we were their friends.
So once again with Yesaki, Senior Chief Magodi and a *kapasu*,
we visited all the villages that had risen. The youths sat somewhat silent and ashamed, the old Headmen and the mature men
who had worked or been in the war greeted us with delight. At
one place, on a high ridge, where Chief Magodi led his little
grandchild along by the hand, we might have been back twenty
years ago. The peace of the Government, that people had been
used to so long, had come back to the land. The men in the
villages prayed that it might last. "Peace in our time"—the
prayer of Africa!

Mere cleverness, subtlety without principle, is an amoebic
creature without a backbone. Defeat had been snatched from the
jaws of victory. Lundazi might have escaped disgrace and disaster
if our Government had kept its nerve when the winds began to
blow. But now government had made a habit of flexibility when
it should have stood adamant, and the results were soon there for
all to see.

These petty skirmishes, for this is all they were, were the
heralds and the outriders of the storm. Now was a time of disgrace and humiliation all over the country, for a service which
had been built in better times by better men. D.C.s were forced
to close their eyes at unjust dismissals of faithful servants, at
peculation and corruption, at Party terrorism, the denials of
everything they, and those who had brought them up, had stood
for, and for many years. In Lundazi a Party "prophet" appeared
in remote Chikwa,* preaching the usual doctrine of anarchy. A
group of District Messengers despatched to restore order and
arrest him was compelled to retreat in confusion and disgrace
before overwhelming force. It is true that the party suffered from

* Chief Chikwa, who caved in before this, was later killed by Lenshina
followers in August, 1964, murdered in his hut as he slept.

I

defective leadership, but the Messengers had never before retired in Lundazi, let alone ignominiously. No expedition from the Boma was permitted, and the whole Chief's area was sealed off, and left for several weeks, to work out its own destiny. A legalized anarchy reigned supreme within the "Chikwa Box", but happily it did not spread. We posted "stops" to see that it did not. It was a forerunner of the "No-Go" areas.

Meanwhile the unfortunate D.C. who had succeeded to this legacy saw the District go from disaster to disaster, to the very edge of chaos. Independent Party Youth Soviets sprang up like mushrooms in the night. Everyone went armed, especially to political meetings, to assert their power. The new African District Officer, James Mapoma, a man of peace whose only wish was to help his people, was set upon by one of these armed gangs and beaten senseless, together with two District Messengers. Two others made their escape. The dipping of cattle, which had for years protected the herds against East Coast fever, was forbidden by the Party Youth, doubtless as a protest against imperialism, and ceased. The disease began again, and spread, but no cattle in Lundazi are dipped to this day. No tax was collected, so no development took place. Salaries were paid out of shrinking capital reserves.

In an attempt to arrest the fomentors of the disturbances near Nthembwe the Officer Commanding Police was clubbed from behind with an axe-handle and seriously injured. Finally the whole area around the capital burst into flame. Parties of youths, hundreds strong, from all quarters, converged upon it, singing, beating drums, dancing and screaming in an hysterical state. Senior Chief Mwase Lundazi was forewarned, and alone in his great gloomy tower of a house, his nerve went for a moment, and he fled into Nyasaland by car, taking his rifle with him. There he was disarmed by the Malawi Youth Brigade, and pushed on, a humiliated refugee. He had been under an intolerable strain for months, and the constant changes and trimming of the Central Government proved for a moment too much for him. He felt that the rock on which his house was built, had changed to sand in the night.

If it is true that nevertheless, he should have prepared to die where he stood, he can be forgiven for his sudden flight. He was a man of good courage, and I believe he fled then so that he could serve his people again. The Party Youth converged upon and met at Nthembwe, to be confronted by seven Police and an Inspector left there on detachment. They held out in the court building all day while the waves swept round them, burning and destroying the other buildings, which were thatched. They ran out of tear-gas. Youths rushed up baring their chests, screaming to be shot. In the end the Police had to open fire with buck-shot, but in the legs. A platoon of the Mobile Unit which was at Lundazi was held up the whole day by masses of trees cut down across the roads, and only reached Nthembwe that evening. The youths dispersed, and an uneasy calm, like the aftermath of a debauch, returned to the area, once one of the richest and most peaceful in the territory.

News of these untoward events had, of course, reached Lusaka. Flexibility had apparently failed, and if Kaunda had appealed for peace and order, then his appeal had been disregarded. High ranking officials and police hurried back to Fort Jameson. Through a window now could be seen Mr. Bean, his face drawn with anxiety at the collapse of his policy. The unfortunate Minister flew over the scene of his last visit, through the smoke of villages now burning. He did not land.

Then to Lusaka, where further reinforcements were hurried up to remedy a situation which had begun to look all too like the Congo. Mass arrests, two platoons of Mobile Unit Police, a permanent Police force with a Police station, halted the downward slide, for the moment. But what a contrast, this overwhelming force of uniformed and armed might, to six months ago! Then, just a little support for the un-armed District Messengers would have sufficed, representing as they did, the achievement and prestige of the Boma over the years. Break this, and real force was required to take its place.

But the Party had achieved its objective, and its victory over its own people. In a little while it was supreme, and the remnants of Government acted on its sufferance. "Elected councillors" were forced upon the Chiefs, tax ceased to be collected: there was no revenue, and there were no more rules. The Millennium had arrived, but the cattle died, and there was no money. Central Government kept the once proud, independent and progressive Native Authority going on doles. It was a sad end.

It might have been very different. Local councillors might have been elected under proper and orderly conditions, even members of the Party, but in such a way as to integrate them into the system which had worked so well, and not as revolutionaries, determined above all to tear down what had been built. As it was, the development of the District and the improvement of the standard of living of the people was set back five years at least by the events of 1962.

Fatal appeasement had contrived to bring one of the happiest Districts in the territory to its ruin, a District once renowned for the friendliness of its people and its ready co-operation and acceptance of new ideas. Truly a triumph for the Party, but a field sewn with dragon's teeth, teeth of the sharpest and most sinister kind, for what had been done once could so easily be done again.

The District Messengers went on to the end. They never failed, they never faltered. Not only together, surrounded by armed mobs, but often alone, surrounded by the hostility of their own relatives, and in remote villages far from any possible help, they continued to do their duty.

They, and many others were betrayed by a Government determined not to win, by generals who had already surrendered but who feared or forgot to tell their own troops. As they took off their uniforms what must they have felt? Left defenceless in the hands of men whose plans they had thwarted again and again, whom they had tackled and arrested without fear, they could expect at best a precarious toleration once the last barriers were down. They, the most loyal of the Government's servants, were betrayed from the rear. That is a shameful story.

Early in 1964 the Ministry of Native Affairs, held in nerveless hands, ran down towards its end. "Objectivity" was the current watchword: an objectivity of the kind that prompted Marshal Petain to say, "We must surrender", and to end at Vichy with Laval.

The long personal conversation between the District Officers and the Africans was about to end forever, its place taken by an incessant nationalist blare at mass meetings and on the wireless. At last, on 22nd January, the Ministry of Native Affairs was swept away when the new Cabinet took office, a wholly U.N.I.P. Government. They enjoyed the smiles and support of the British Government, the Mines, the Church, the "Establishment", the well-educated, and the press.

Only the people knew. The full story of the beatings, burnings and killings in the years 1962–63 will never be published, and now will never be known, as so much of the evidence has been destroyed. Few of the cases were even reported. Sufficient to cite the slow decapitation of the old man near Petauke in public before a crowd of people, for refusing to buy a U.N.I.P. card, the Fort Jameson burnings, and the beating to death of Macdonald Lushinga shortly afterwards.

It is literally true to say, as did His Excellency the Governor, that there were no incidents of any kind on the days of the Election. However, except under the direct eye of the Police, the people lived under a reign of terror for months before and months after. We would laugh at Welensky's tales of the intimidation of Africans who supported Federation : they did not exist. But from 1961 it ceased to be a laughing matter, it was with the people in the villages night and day, and especially by night. Behind the soothing assurances of Government that law and order would be maintained, lay the almost complete failure to do so in some areas, and the suppression of all information that could be suppressed. This false, or anti-history, has of course been carefully recorded, step by step, by George Orwell. It was sad that it could happen in what was still a British Protectorate.

To take one Province, the Eastern. On 2 January, 1964 thirty-six houses were destroyed in five villages by a party of U.N.I.P. supporters near Fort Jameson, and two small children shut in a house and burnt to death. On the 30th of that month two Lenshina Church followers were killed in Magodi's area of Lundazi. On 24 March Macdonald Lushinga, the Provincial Secretary of A.N.C., and one of the few energetic men they had, was caught on the high-road ten miles from Fort Jameson and beaten to death with knobkerries. The point is not that prosecutions and convictions for murder* did not take place, but that a few years previously such crimes would never have occurred. True enough, only a few days after the new Cabinet had taken office, the honorific title of "Prison Graduate" was removed from U.N.I.P. party cards. Respectability was now the watchword, but it was a little late. Fires had been lit, not easy to put out.

That rare jewel, a royal epigram, "Nationalism is the cloak of dictators",† sums up the position. And its toys are dictatorship's ornaments—the flattery of a servile press—new stamps and coins bearing the features of the leader—new flags—a "national dress", and as much money as necessary. In the midst of all this glitter the leaders stand, ostensibly so modest, so retiring, but in fact relishing it all.

Behind this façade lies the reality—blood, rubbish and confusion—swollen conceit and legalized brutality, with little or no idea of the true problems of the country, disease, malnutrition, disorder and tribal divisions still standing large and menacing as ever. That is the tragedy.

Power had been given to men whose only qualification had been the organization of confusion, and whose merit had been measured by what they had broken down, never by what they had built up. The Bible says: "Wherefore by their fruits ye shall know them." Behind the elaborately organized celebrations of independence and "nationhood" looms the shadow of a new Dark Age, ushered in to the sounds of rejoicing. For it is in Africa now that the lights are going out, one by one.

Every official organ was at pains to pretend that the grant of independence in 1964 was the result of simple and inevitable processes which could not have been halted even if the British Government had wished. Nothing could be further from the truth. The engine of U.N.I.P. could have been broken up from within at any time between 1960 and the end of 1962, possibly even after that. It could have been contained, as it was contained in Lundazi District, by the slightest exercise of determina-

---

* The new Government reprieved the murderers, and soon afterwards released them.

† Prince Philip to Dr. Banda.

tion and will-power on the part of the higher officials in Northern Rhodesia and London. After all, they had only to support their own officers in the field.

It could have been so different. Federation expired without a sigh at the end of 1963. It needed but seven, ten years at the most, before a stable, purely African Government was ready to take power, and all would have served under it with the greatest promptitude and good-will, and possibly with an even greater zeal than before. The African graduates were emerging from the student stage and beginning to hold their own as they should. From their upper ranks should have been drawn the Ministers. But no; all was to be broken up at the very moment when the work was ready to be crowned, to satisfy a collection of mal-contents financed from abroad, with a talent only for mob-oratory. Instead of reason there came hysteria, for mutual respect between the races, envy and hatred, for charity between them, greed, and suspicion of every move. An ill legacy indeed, and an unworthy one after over sixty years.

What does it matter, it may be asked, this chronicle of events in a dark corner of an obscure colony, now independent, now "Zambia"—and none of our concern? What does it matter if, with a gesture of carelessness and langour, we shrugged off re-sponsibilities a few years before it was right, before even, it suited our own interest to do so?

It matters, I suggest, only because there once existed standards of duty, fairness and honesty, which guided our work and which were, unfortunately, far higher than those which obtained during the last years of British rule in Africa. Nor will African historians of the future fail to reproach us for not completing and crowning our work. A few more years would have been enough to end with honour and without bitterness. There would have been no "victors", no "defeated" in a struggle always within the ultimate control of the British Government, but only friends, as we had always been and should always have remained.

It was left to a Frenchman, a White Father, a missionary who had devoted his life to the people, to say what discipline forbade. "I do not know how you say it, but in France we call it *Honneur*. Your Government has lost it : it has betrayed the people. But it was not your fault!

True France, which had given chivalry to Europe, and to Africa, had at least understood.

The long ranks of the betrayed reproach us. I see them now. All those who had trusted us, "uneducated" men mostly, all who tried to do their duty until the end, and after it. The loyal Chiefs, their Councillors, the Police, the District Messengers, the great mass of the ordinary people in ordinary villages, what can we say to them now? And how much more is their reproach addressed to those responsible for their betrayal— that is the burden that they must always bear, however it may be glossed over. Writing as I do, in the shadow of the defeat of all that was built up, and of all our hopes, I pray only that the country may find worthy men to rule it.

To those who believed in us until too late for their own advantage, even safety, I say that there is still hope. The good old causes are never lost for ever—justice for corruption, honesty for political half-truth, duty for inflated conceit, and respect between men, for racial hatred. Let them remain, as our legacy. Even let them rise again, as our country's memorial, and as the true foundation on which Africa may build, no matter what flag shall fly over it.

Chapter XIII

RETURN FROM ZAMBIA

WHERE was the Colonial Office, amid the faceless crowds and the traffic? It must be somewhere, with its "sound men" in dark suits, who sat quietly in London and knew all the answers: calm, competent men, above all men who were in control of events. There would be a bust of Joseph Chamberlain in the lobby and a portrait of that fierce bantam, Lugard of Nigeria, on the staircase. As one entered one would pass Margery Perham going out, the one link left, it seemed, between realities in Africa and the verbal fantasies of London and New York. The background, the nerve-centre, would still be there, solid, rather Victorian, but in command.

I was guided to a sky-scraper, with a writhing statue in an anonymous courtyard. No fountains played there, nor would ever play. The place seemed under permanent repair. There was a small box of an office, lit by strip lighting, with one or two functional and uncomfortable chairs. There I waited.

What should I say to the man? That law, order and government was collapsing around us in Northern Rhodesia? That it was wrong to betray our friends? That, moral issues apart, it was not even expedient? That there would be a blood-bath in Africa, if not today, then within a matter of years? Surely all this was still some concern of ours?

The door opened, and Mr. Merrifit came in, all smiles, all affability.

What his position was I never discovered, but I believe he was an Assistant Secretary. He wore a light suit and elastic sided shoes. He was informed, "civilized"—the vogue in the days of Kennedy and MacMillan's "stylish" government.

I said my piece. A nervous titter. . . .

"Oh, well, you see, we're pulling out of Africa," and he was gone, in a flurry of smiles and apologies about another appointment.

It would not be long before one joined the faceless crowd, no longer unpopular, no longer the object of political frenzy, no longer anything.

"Blessed are the peace makers." "Blessed are they who hunger and thirst after righteousness. . . ." There is a certain stimulus in unpopularity, and a good deal of temptation to glory in it. What would one find in England? Kindness, somewhat impersonal; charity, a little chilled. A remote interest in Africa; in the curious habits of people they saw as savages, despite their polite amazement, their civil assent; Africa, a big place where they once had an uncle.

But then I realized that I was indeed a rich man, and wealthy beyond the dreams of avarice. Not so in terms of money, certainly, but rich for ever in my friends. There is the magic stone of Africa, and it is reward enough.

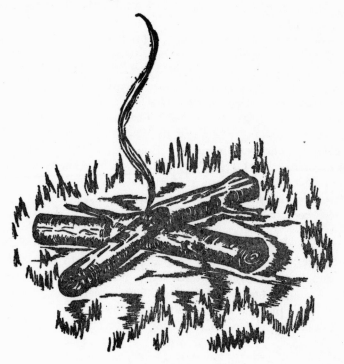

THE LINE OF THE MWATIAMWA

I.   Mwaku. XVIth Century.

II.   Yala Mwaku, his son.

III.   Konde, his son.

         Had two sons, Chinguli and Chinyama, who were cut out of the succession.

         Chinguli founded the kingdom of Imbangala in what is now Angola, and which remained in relations with the Lunda until near the end of the XIXth Century.

         Chinyama travelled south-west, and a group detaching themselves from him founded the Chokwe people. The succession from Kande passed to his daughter, Luezi.

IV.   Luezi f. married Chibanda Ilunga.

V.   Luezi handed the insignia of chieftainship to her husband, Chibanda Ilunga.

         Having no child, Luezi gave her husband a second wife, Kamonga Luaza.

VI.   Lusenge Nawezi, child of Chibanda and Kamonga Luaza, succeeds.

         First part of XVIIth Century.

         Lusenge Nawezi invests Luezi as queen-mother, and she lives to a great age.

         Died in an ambush.

         Luezi, still living, invests Lusenge Nawezi's son Yavo Nawezi as Chief.

VII.   Yavo Nawezi. Called "Mwatiamvwa" or "Mwata Yavo". He founded the Lunda Empire. His brothers' descendants held the Chieftainships of Kanongesha Shinde, and Kazembe in N. Rhodesia and Musokantanda in the Congo.

         He dies in an expedition in the Congo.

VIII.   Muteba, his son. Died of illness.

         End of XVIIth Century.

263

IX.	Mulaji, brother of Mulēba.
X.	Mbala, brother of Mulēba and Mulaji.
XI.	Musaka, brother of the three above.
	End of XVIIIth Century.
	Placed governors in the outlying Provinces. Killed in an expedition against the Kasai.
XII.	Yavo Ya Mbanyi.
XIII.	Chikombe Yavo. Beginning of XIXth Centeury.
	Obliged to resign after a reign of two months.
XIV.	Naweji Ya Ditende : died about 1852.
	Disposed of the pretenders to the throne and made war.
	Beat off an invasion of Chokwe.
XV.	Mulaji A Mmbala, died in 1857.
XVI.	Chakasekene Naweji.
	Killed by a palace revolution for his cruelty.
XVII.	Muteba Chikombe, died in 1873.
	Made war.
	The Portuguese introduce tobacco and the potato.
XVIII.	Mbala.
	Resigned the Chieftaincy and retired as a consequence of internal troubles.
XIX.	Mbumba.
	Killed Mbala. Employed the Chokwe with muzzle-loading guns.
XX.	Chimbundu. Succeeded 1883.
	Killed by a conspiracy of notables, or courtiers.
XXI.	Kangapu. Succeeded in 1884.
	Killed by his successor,
XXII.	Mudiba.
	The great invasion of the Chokwe. Mudiba was killed by them.
XXIII.	Mukaza.
	The invasion continues : Mukaza deposed for lack of energy.
XXIV.	Mbala Chilembe.
	Succeeded in 1887. Killed the same year, at Mushiri's orders.
XXV.	Mushiri.
	The Lunda fled before the Chokwe invasion and the Chokwe possessed the Lunda country for ten years,

between 1888 and 1899. Mushiri and his brother Kawele re-conquered the country, and pursued the Chokwe, who had neglected to fortify their villages.

XXVI.   Muteba.
          Killed Mushiri and Kawele, 1909 (?) and reigns until 1920.

XXVII.   Kaumba, 1923–1951.

XXVIII.   Mbaka. A peaceful and dignified man brought up by American missionaries.
          1951–61. Father of Lueji of Chavuma, and father-in-law of President Tshombe. Visited America during the Congo troubles and returned.

The following military titles are of interest as they are still borne by village Headmen of the Lunda and Kaonde today.

Kalala—Commander of the advance guard : also tribute collector.
Swana Mulopwe—Commander of the flank guards.
Inakapumba—Commander of the rear guards.

OFFICE BEARERS IN THE HIERARCHY :

Lunda

Chifwankene—Second in Command, officiates at coronation.
Kambanji—war leader.
Kabwita—auditor and factotum.
Katamu—servant, and bearer.
Mumbailunga—regent.

Kaonde

Mumbelunga—regent.
Mwanaute—heir apparent.
Mulopwe—flank guard.
Mutonyi—assessor.

(It is of interest that Mulopwe is also an honorific title of Senior Chief Mwase Lundazi of the Chewa.)

It would be of great interest to learn the titles of the court officials of Mwatiamvwa. Unfortunately these are not available. M.

Vehulpan, administrator and authority on the Lunda, gives the following symbols of the Mwatiamvwa chieftaincy :

(1) Kazekele—amulet.
(2) Ngoma Ya ukamba—gong.
(3) Leopard skin.
(4) Lumbembu—double bell.
(5) Munange Niombe—drum.

APPENDIX II

THE LENSHINA OUTBREAK
OF JULY 1964

It was ironic that the "Independence" Constitution should grant the right of every lawful inhabitant of Northern Rhodesia to reside where he wished. The members of the "Lumpa" Sect, followers of Alice Lenshina, exercised this right with results to themselves that will be described.

So far back as May 1963 local U.N.I.P. leaders in the Chinsali and Lundazi Districts, finding it intolerable that Lenshina followers would take no part in politics and refused to buy Party cards, had begun to persecute them.

It started by burning their thatched churches in the night, but as it gathered momentum these unfortunate people were denied access to clinics and schools, assaulted, and from time to time murdered. There is no question but that the central U.N.I.P. leadership knew of this situation, and whatever efforts they may have made, they failed to stop it. Certainly there is no record of any denunciation by leading members of U.N.I.P. of what was known to be going on.

Lenshina supporters did the only thing possible under the circumstances. Leaving their own villages they banded together in settlements for protection, and surrounded them with stockades as security. Their relations with the Police were good, as they spent much time protecting them from attack. Indeed, hearing of an attack planned on Christmas Eve, the Police at Lundazi went to the nearest settlement and ate their Christmas dinner in the middle of them. It is important to remember this background of over a year of incessant and vicious persecution of these people by local U.N.I.P., and that it was despair that drove them finally to armed resistance and outrage.

Kaunda made the disbanding of the Lenshina settlements a personal issue : it was intolerable that in his home District, Chinsali, there should be any organized body that would have nothing to do

267

with him, or indeed any political party. It wounded his *amour propre*. U.N.I.P. officials were sent round with the Police Mobile Unit, which succeeded in identifying the Police with the Party in the eyes of the Lenshina people. And at that time the order was simply that they should return to their old villages, which would have meant anything from very severe persecution, to death.

Late in July 1964 the order to disband the settlements was finally given by the U.N.I.P. Government : and three Police, two European and one African, were killed in ambush by Lenshina followers in Chinsali. The police replied by taking the settlement by storm, killing some forty people. A few days later Sione settlement, the centre of the movement, was taken by the combined Army and Police, with casualties of seventy Lenshina killed.

There the women and children had taken refuge in the great church, the size of a cathedral. It was said that in the heat of battle a soldier burst in, and before he could be stopped, fired two magazines of Bren-automatic into their midst. The church was blown up and razed to the ground.

The idea behind the operation was the display of irresistible force by the new nationalist Government, and to administer a sharp lesson to members of a religious sect who had defied the orders of the Prime Minister. Once a few had been shot, it was argued, and the settlements burned, they would return to their old villages, and cease to be the irritant of even a non-political opposition.

It had the opposite effect to what was intended. The Government miscalculated first the fanatical despair with which the Lenshina followers would fight : and second, the killing capacity of modern automatic weapons.

The belief that bullets will turn to water, shared by the Lenshina, is a common feature of African risings and can be traced back as far as the Maji-Maji (Water) Rebellion in Tanganyika, 1906, through the Chilembwe Rising in Nyasaland in 1915, the affair at Bullhoek in 1923, to the Lenshina Rising, and to the "Mulel-istes" in the Congo, who opposed Colonel Hoare on the road to Stanley-ville.

Two days after the fall of Sione the Lenshina followers to the east of the Luangwa at Lundazi, struck back. They over-ran the Boma in the middle of the night, killing all they could, numerous villagers and one Chief who had become identified with U.N.I.P., Chikwa. Troops were flown in to restore the situation, and a day later the nearest Lenshina settlement was taken, with heavy

Lenshina losses. By this time the number of dead had risen to over 300.

At a political rally in Lusaka the Prime Minister denounced Alice Lenshina as the cause of the rising and demanded that she be brought in "dead or alive" to answer criminal charges. What charges were never specified, nor, if she were brought in dead, how she was to answer them. Waving a black handkerchief at a political rally he proclaimed a week of national mourning. "I will be a savage", he said.

Meanwhile the Lenshina people took to the "bush" and there was deadlock. Supporters of the sect had been outlawed and driven to despair. There was every inducement to remain at large and do as much damage as they could before they were killed, none to return to normal life. What sort of reception could they hope for?

Too much blood had been spilled on both sides, too many women and children killed. To insist on unconditional surrender, backed by troops, meant only extermination. The number of deaths rose to 400. Never in the history of Northern Rhodesia under Colonial rule had there been such a holocaust. Day after day the slaughter continued.

It was at Mpaishuko settlement between Chama and Kambombo in Lundazi that the most bestial episode took place. Men from the Lenshina settlement had run wild, killing as they went. The local Party, now backed by the people, organized themselves and broke into the stockade. The next day hardened journalists were disgusted at what they saw : for before they died all had been tortured, and the women and girls staked out on the ground and raped by members of the Youth Brigade.

The plentiful publicity that this received in the English press, aided by an excellent article in *The Spectator*—"Zambia's Holy War"*—caused more humane counsels to prevail. Government became frightened at the number of dead : and at the attitude of the Police.

Alice Lenshina† and her family were induced to give themselves up on promise of safe-conduct, and the remaining settlements invited to surrender, which many did. They were not to be sent back to their villages to certain death, but to "Re-Habilitation Camps" for the present. What of their future, no-one knows.

The Prime Minister refused a judicial inquiry. It was well-known,

* By Harry Franklin.
† Still so far as is known in detention in 1972.

he said, what the causes of the outbreak were. It was indeed, but not, I believe, in the sense that he meant it. Because these people would not join U.N.I.P. their lives were made impossible in their own villages, and they banded together for safety, for survival, in settlements of their own. District Officers volunteered to approach them under a flag of truce.

That they were hunted and blasted out by the armed forces, unwittingly involved in doing the work of the Party, is one of the most shameful episodes in the history of British Colonial administration, even in its last moments of decay.

By the 20th August the official figure of the dead was 557: double that figure would have been more accurate, according to reports from the Districts. What, it may be asked, do numbers matter at this stage?

The point has been made. But for those who served there, each one is an individual, and not so long ago our responsibility. Malata Mvula, the old Head Messenger decorated by the Governor on his visit: harmless old retired Samuel Kumwenda, Simon Tembo, who had taught our children and one of the stoutest of the younger generation, Gideon Mtonga—all friends, and all gone.

Now, the danger is that unless there is an amnesty granted for all crimes but murder, those that have fled into the bush or the Congo may never emerge. They may band together to form a secret society, possibly devoted to ritual murder with certain peculiar mutilations. That indeed would be a sad, final legacy, and the final comment upon the abandonment of our responsibilities.

APPENDIX III

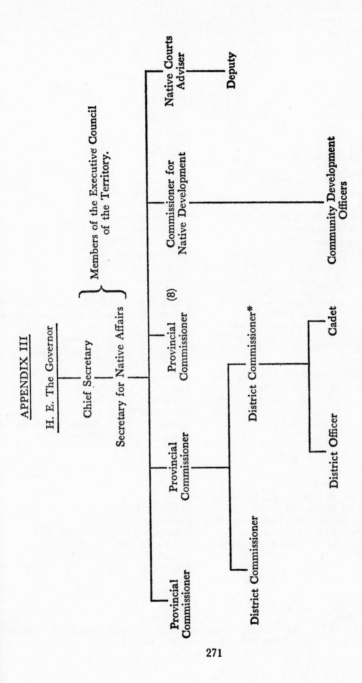

H. E. The Governor

Chief Secretary

Secretary for Native Affairs

Members of the Executive Council
of the Territory.

Provincial Commissioner

Provincial Commissioner

Provincial Commissioner (8)

Commissioner for Native Development

Native Courts Adviser

District Commissioner

District Commissioner

District Commissioner*

Deputy

Community Development Officers

District Officer

Cadet

* 5 to 10 per Province depending upon the number of stations.

271

INDEX

A

African Affairs Board, 84, 85, 180
Africa Bureau, 131
African Mail, 212, 235, 236, 252
African Mineworkers Trade Union, 110, 111, 116, 117, 121
Afrikaners (Dutch South Africans), 68; Government, 180
African National Congress, 115, 147, 155, 158, 162–3, 171, 197, 232
Amboteka (religious sub-sect), 95
Americans, 123
Angola, 58, 66, 132, 151, 152, 176
Apostles, fire-walkers, 167
Arabs, slave-raiders, 23, 93
Archbishop of Canterbury, 103
Archbishop of Northern Rhodesia, 189
Ascot, 33
Attorney-General, N. Rhodesia, 1962. Responsible for granting fiat for prosecution of political offences, 226; does not prosecute, 236; does not grant fiat, 237

B

Balfour, Arthur J., 239
Balovale, District, 59, 65, 92, 142
Bancroft, Boma, 108, 109
Banda, Haydn D. (politician), 240, 245–6, 252
Banda, Dr., President of Malawi, 258
Banking-system, African, 182–3
Banyard, C., District Officer, 240, 244
Barotseland, 18, 24, 26, 32, 39, 86, 90, 218
Bean, C.M.G., M.B.E., Minister of Native Affairs, 249–50, 252, 255

Beer, 44, 45, 149, 173
Belgians, 140, 167, 168
Bellis, 27, 134
Bemba Tribe, 131; system of cultivation, 165
Benson, Sir Arthur, G.C.M.G., 26, 81, 82, 129, 132, 137, 142, 155, 164, 181, 184, 186, 214
Bentley, John, O.B.E., District Commissioner, 118
Bisa Tribe, 196
Blackwell, Q.C., 124
Bledisloe, Lord, 80
Bourbons, 60
British South Africa Company, 134
Brookes, Raymond, early prospector, 105
Bruce Miller, administrator, 135
Bunche, Dr. (U.N. Official), 188
Burton, Mrs., murdered, 215
Busanga Swamp, 28, 34
Bush, C.M.G., O.B.E., Secretary of Native Affairs, 74, 205
Butterflies, 42
Button, M.B.E., District Commissioner, 205; builds castle, 206

C

Catholics, Roman, 30, 224
Caesarian operation, 50
Ceremony of greeting Chiefs, 173
Chadiza, Sub-Boma, 195
Chamberlain, Joseph, 261
Chaminuka, Headman, 62
Chaplin, Charlie, 53
Chavuma, 142, 143, 200
Chewa, Tribe, 194, 196; native authority, 216
Chibanza, Simon (Chronicler of Ba-Kaonde), 23

272

Index